SHORT
HISTORIES

Short Histories are authoritative and elegantly written introductory texts which offer fresh perspectives on the way history is taught and understood in the 21st century. Designed to have strong appeal to university students and their teachers, as well as to general readers and history enthusiasts, *Short Histories* comprise novel attempts to bring informed interpretation, as well as factual reportage, to historical debates. Addressing key subjects and topics in the fields of history, the history of ideas, religion, classical studies, politics, philosophy and Middle East studies, these texts move beyond the bland, neutral 'introductions' that so often serve as the primary undergraduate teaching tool. While always providing students and generalists with the core facts that they need to get to grips with, *Short Histories* go further. They offer new insights into how a topic has been understood in the past, and what different social and cultural factors might have been at work. They bring original perspectives to bear on current interpretations. They raise questions and – with extensive bibliographies – point the reader to further study, even as they suggest answers. Each text addresses a variety of subjects in a greater degree of depth than is often found in comparable series, yet at the same time in a concise and compact handbook form. *Short Histories* aim to be 'introductions with an edge'. In combining questioning and searching analysis with informed historical writing, they bring history up-to-date for an increasingly complex and globalised digital age.

For more information about titles and authors in the series, please visit: https://www.bloomsbury.com/series/short-histories/

A Short History of . . .

the American Civil War	Paul Anderson, Clemson University, USA
the American Revolutionary War	Stephen Conway, University College London, UK
Ancient Greece	P J Rhodes, Emeritus, Durham University, UK
the Anglo-Saxons	Henrietta Leyser, University of Oxford, UK
Babylon	Karen Radner, University of Munich, Germany
the Byzantine Empire: Revised Edition	Dionysios Stathakopoulos, University of Cyprus, Cyprus
Christian Spirituality	Edward Howells, University of Roehampton, UK
Communism	Kevin Morgan, University of Manchester, UK
the Crimean War	Trudi Tate, University of Cambridge, UK
English Renaissance Drama	Helen Hackett, University College London, UK
the English Revolution and the Civil Wars	David J Appleby, Nottingham University, UK
the Etruscans	Corinna Riva, University of Erfurt, Germany
Florence and the Florentine Republic	Brian J Maxson, East Tennessee State University, USA
the Hundred Years War	Michael Prestwich, Emeritus, Durham University, UK
Judaism and the Jewish People	Steven Jacobs, The University of Alabama, USA
Medieval Christianity	G R Evans, Emertius, University of Cambridge, UK
the Minoans	John Bennet, British School of Athens, Greece
the Mongols	George Lane, University of London, UK

the Mughal Empire Michael H Fisher, Emeritus, Oberlin College, USA

Muslim Spain Amira K Bennison, University of Cambridge, UK

New Kingdom of Egypt Robert Morkot, Independent Scholar

the New Testament Halvor Moxnes, University of Oslo, Norway

the Normans Leonie V Hicks, Canterbury Christ Church University, UK

the Ottoman Empire Baki Tezcan, University of California, Davis, USA

the Phoenicians: Revised Edition Mark Woolmer, Independent Scholar

the Reformation Helen L Parish, University of Reading, UK

the Renaissance in Northern Europe Malcolm Vale, Emeritus, University of Oxford, UK

Revolutionary Cuba Antoni Kapcia, Emeritus, University of Nottingham, UK

the Russian Revolution: Revised Edition Geoffrey Swain, Emeritus, University of Glasgow, UK

the Spanish Civil War: Revised Edition Julián Casanova, Central European University, Hungary

the Spanish Empire Felipe Fernández-Armesto, University of Notre Dame, France, and José Juan López-Portillo, University of Oxford, UK

Transatlantic Slavery Kenneth Morgan, Brunel University, UK

the Tudors Richard Rex, University of Cambridge, UK

Venice and the Venetian Empire Maria Fusaro, University of Exeter, UK

the Wars of the Roses David Grummitt, University of Kent, UK

the Weimar Republic Colin Storer, University of Warwick, UK

A SHORT HISTORY OF THE TUDORS

Richard Rex

BLOOMSBURY ACADEMIC
LONDON • NEW YORK • OXFORD • NEW DELHI • SYDNEY

BLOOMSBURY ACADEMIC
Bloomsbury Publishing Plc
50 Bedford Square, London, WC1B 3DP, UK
1385 Broadway, New York, NY 10018, USA
29 Earlsfort Terrace, Dublin 2, Ireland

BLOOMSBURY, BLOOMSBURY ACADEMIC and the Diana logo are trademarks of
Bloomsbury Publishing Plc

First published in Great Britain 2024

A catalogue record for this book is available from the British Library.

A catalog record for this book is available from the Library of Congress.

ISBN: HB: 978-1-3501-7045-2
PB: 978-1-3501-7042-1
ePDF: 978-1-3501-7044-5
eBook: 978-1-3501-7043-8

Series: Short Histories

Typeset by RefineCatch Limited, Bungay, Suffolk
Printed and bound in India

To find out more about our authors and books visit www.bloomsbury.com
and sign up for our newsletters.

To Maximus Rex ('... good name')

Contents

List of Figures   x

Introduction   1

1   Establishing the Tudor Regime, 1485–1515   7
2   From Reform to Reformation, 1515–1534   35
3   Reformations, 1535–1553   63
4   Reformations Reversed, 1553–1568   93
5   The Elizabethan Exclusion Crisis, 1568–1587   123
6   The War with Spain and the Succession,
    1587–1603   153

Conclusion   181
Notes   185
Further Reading   201
Index   209

Figures

1.1 Portrait of Lady Margaret Beaufort from the Hall in
St John's College, Cambridge. Courtesy of Alamy Images.   12

1.2 Henry VII and Elizabeth of York monument, Westminster
Abbey, London, England. Courtesy of Alamy Images.   19

2.1 The Winchester Round Table in the Great Hall. Courtesy
of Alamy Images.   39

2.2 The Wriothesley Garter Book – Henry VIII in Parliament.
Courtesy of Alamy Images.   59

3.1 Jervaulx Abbey, North Yorkshire, 2014. Courtesy of
Alamy Images.   66

3.2 Painting depicting Edward VI of England (1537–1553),
with his advisors. Sixteenth century. Courtesy of
Alamy Images.   84

4.1 Medal seal of Philip II of Spain and Mary I of England.
Courtesy of Alamy Images.   100

4.2 View of Hampton Court Palace from the south, with the
river in the foreground, 1558. Courtesy of Alamy Images.   120

5.1 Thomas Cartwright c. 1535 to 1603. Courtesy of
Alamy Images.   132

5.2 Elizabeth I, Queen of England, depicted with a sieve in her
left hand. Courtesy of Alamy Images.   138

6.1 The execution of Mary Queen of Scots. Courtesy of
Alamy Images.   154

6.2 Queen Elizabeth I's tomb and monument by Maximilian
Colt, 1603, Westminster Abbey, London, England. Courtesy
of Alamy Images.   180

INTRODUCTION

Was there any such thing as 'the Tudors'? Not according to C. S. L. Davies, who once pointed out, quite rightly, that the five Tudor monarchs never themselves used the name, which was mostly applied to them only by such rivals or foes of Henry VII and his descendants as wished to cast doubt on their legitimacy by denigrating their Welsh ancestry.[1] Thus when Henry was just a rootless adventurer dreaming of a crown, Richard III dismissively labelled him 'Henry Tydder', traitor. The word 'dynasty', likewise, is hardly found in English prior to 1580, and not in connection with England's own ruling house or houses.[2] The chronicles penned in sixteenth-century England do not refer to their sovereigns as 'Tudors'.

Yet 'the Tudors' are not hissed off the stage of history quite so easily. Of course the Tudor monarchs did not finish their signature with their family name, any more than King Charles does today, instead using the customarily understated abbreviation 'R' (for 'Rex' or 'Regina', as appropriate) to indicate their sublime status: 'Henry R', 'Elizabeth R', etc. And from the start of Henry VII's reign, royalist publicists emphasised the reconciliation of the internecine conflicts between York and Lancaster that had been achieved in the Lancastrian Henry's marriage to Elizabeth of York and even more in the children of their union. Loyal subjects echoed and amplified these messages. The dominant note in the public representation of Henry VII's reign was neither the legitimacy of his Lancastrian claim nor the invalidity of that of the Yorkists, but the pragmatic notion that by his marriage he had brought together the warring houses. The sense that a distinct era was marked by his accession was clear enough, and was voiced in the chronicle published by the London citizen Edward Hall halfway through the century, *The Union of the Two Noble and Illustrate Famelies of Lancastre and Yorke.* Even though Hall started with Henry IV, the climax of his tale was his long and loving account of the reign of Henry VIII, the 'flower and very heir of both the said lineages'.[3] By the time Mary had seized the throne, the statute that conferred upon her the traditional grant of 'tunnage and poundage' (customs duties chargeable on imported goods) picked out by name only her 'noble grandfather', her 'most dearest father', and her 'most entirely beloved brother' among the royal progenitors who had been granted this same favour.[4] The sense of a house of Tudor was very clear in the parliamentary mind.

Fear of the dreadful horrors of civil war was earnestly inculcated by a regime which never stopped claiming credit for bringing an end to the struggle between Lancaster and York. That message was first preached in 1486, and still had enormous resonance and traction when it was canonised over a hundred years later in the history plays of Shakespeare. The combination of the red rose and the white in royal iconography was the most potent visual symbol of this new political identity. Those who lived under those five monarchs may not have needed a family name for them, but they recognised in Henry VII and his descendants a distinctive political reality. We do need a name for them, and the name of Tudor, the family name borne by Henry VII's father, has long met that need.

It is almost inevitable in writing the history of a personal monarchy to proceed reign by reign, and with the Tudors that temptation is particularly strong. Henry VII really did achieve something remarkably like 'bringing medieval England to an end', although of course nothing is ever as simple as that simplistic phrase. But Henry VIII could not have done much the same thing for the medieval English Church had his father not so mightily humbled the nobility. The Protestant Reformation that was introduced under his son, Edward VI, would likewise have been impossible had Henry VIII not so mightily humbled the Church. The change in religion changed England's relationship with Europe. Never again would an English monarch cross the Channel in an attempt to vindicate the ancestral claim to the throne of France.

Mary I had to seize power in 1553 rather as her grandfather had done in 1485, though from a vastly stronger position. That she was able to do so is an indication of how far English politics had changed. Henry VII had taken the throne during the lifetime of his mother, Lady Margaret Beaufort, through whom he derived his claim. In 1485 it was unimaginable that a woman might ascend the throne. In 1553 there was no alternative: the succession was disputed between two women, and the next best claimants were half a dozen more women, the only other living descendants of Henry VII. What brought Mary to the throne in practice was the new English politics in the service of the old English religion. The English gentry, on whom royal power now depended, rallied to her and not to her rival, Lady Jane Grey, whom the machinations of a Court clique had sought to advance in order to safeguard Edward's Protestant Reformation. Mary I, notoriously, reversed the religious changes introduced by her brother and her father. The ease with which she did this revealed how little, but also how much, the Reformation had achieved. The Reformation had commandeered the bodies and in particular the lips of the English people, but it had not won their hearts or their souls. The gentry welcomed back the Catholic Mass, but they would not give back the lands that they had acquired from the Catholic Church. Recognition of their new lands was the price for their recognition of the old faith. At a deeper level, twenty years of religious change had shaken the foundations of the ancient religion in more senses than one.

The accession of Elizabeth I was as smooth as Mary's had been turbulent, and revived the Protestant Reformation almost, but not quite, as easily as Mary had reversed it. Yet it also brought the process of Reformation to a premature halt. The relentless momentum of change under Edward VI was never recovered, and for all the rhetoric of divine providence and even miracle with which Protestants greeted Elizabeth, the veil was now ripped from the temple. Religious change was too obviously the work of human hands, and too often of grasping or vengeful hands at that. The impact of Elizabeth's personal option for Protestantism had wide repercussions: in Scotland, where the Reformation was enthusiastically welcomed; in Ireland, where it was fiercely rejected; and in Europe, where it broke the old link with the Burgundian–Spanish axis against France and left England at times friendless. It led finally to all-out war with Spain, the nearest thing the sixteenth century had to a global superpower.

The apparently natural logic of dividing the Tudor era into its five reigns is so compelling that it can make us forget that all divisions of time and period are artificial. The narrative offered in this book is therefore deliberately cut somewhat differently, not in an attempt to erase the boundaries between the reigns, but in order to remind the reader that other moments could be just as important. The first chapter therefore ends not with the death of Henry VII, which did not change anything much, but with the rise of Henry VIII's first great minister, Cardinal Wolsey. Wolsey clambered to power through managing the logistics of his sovereign's first invasion of France, and it was that return to a traditionally aggressive 'foreign policy' which showed that England had emerged from the deep political insecurities of the later fifteenth century. The second chapter ends not with Wolsey's fall but at the 'Break with Rome', the rejection of papal authority which was necessitated by

Henry's determination to divorce his first wife, Catherine of Aragon. That rupture, which might have been thought at the time a mere expedient, and probably a temporary one at that, led unexpectedly to a period of profound religious change, the 'English Reformation'. The third chapter pursues the story of that Reformation not only through the reign of Henry VIII but through that of his son, Edward VI, during which the English Reformation became unmistakably Protestant.

The succession of Mary I in 1553 brought the juggernaut of the English Reformation to such a juddering halt that even in this narrative it must remain a critical dividing line, a line made still bolder by the fact that the unprecedented accession of a woman to the English throne hints at a deeper story of political change. In that context, continuing the chapter to cover the first phase of the reign of Elizabeth I makes sense because the prolonged absence of adult male kingship consolidated that change, contributing to the emergence of the 'State', that more abstract political reality that has been central to political life and thought since the later sixteenth century. Ending the fourth chapter in 1568 helps to emphasise how uncertain things still seemed at that moment to those who were living it. Elizabeth had resuscitated the English Reformation, but its long-term survival was still by no means secure.

The fifth chapter opens with the unexpected arrival in England of Mary Stewart, Queen of Scots, because it dropped a millstone into the pond of English politics, provoking a Catholic rebellion which might have led to civil war and which certainly led to the excommunication of Elizabeth by Pope Pius V. Paradoxically, it was Mary, whose very existence as a potential Catholic heir threatened the religious and political security and stability of Elizabeth's Protestant England, who dominated English politics from 1568 to 1587. The final chapter therefore begins with her execution, which solved that particular problem but thereby precipitated the Armada campaign of Philip II of Spain. It thus embroiled England in a protracted and expensive war for survival that would be ended only with Elizabeth's death and that would exacerbate the sufferings of her subjects through a decade of natural disasters.

Philip II's war against England aimed at the overthrow of Elizabeth, her replacement by a Spanish princess, and the consequent restoration of the Catholic faith. Elizabeth herself had no children, and never took so much as a single step to settle the open question of who should inherit her throne. From one perspective, therefore, Tudor England ended exactly where it had started, amid uncertainty and anxiety over the royal succession. England itself, though, was a very different kingdom in 1603 from the one it had been in 1485, not least in that it had developed the capacity to resolve the succession without necessarily resorting to civil war and bloodshed. So the transfer of Elizabeth's crown to James VI of Scotland was in the end smooth and peaceable.

However, to portray a century of a nation's past in just 75,000 words means leaving out much more than can be put in. To attempt within that limit to cover – to follow merely alphabetical order – agriculture, architecture, the arts, class, demography, economics, the family and gender, literature, politics, religion, towns and trade, would confine the analysis to generalisations of the most superficial kind and preclude any serious level of understanding. In this presentation of the Tudor century, the author has opted for a traditional focus on politics and religion for which his own expertise best fits him. There are many other angles from which to approach the topic, and a new generation of historians has been opening them up aplenty. The suggestions for further reading at the end of this volume draw the reader's attention to just some of the most innovative among them. Yet the option for focusing on religion and politics is not simply a matter of necessity deriving from the author's strengths or limitations. There is a real case for seeing the political and religious experiences of Tudor England as the most fundamental aspects of its history.

First and foremost, this is because Tudor England was a traditional society and, like most such societies, was culturally shaped by what we would call its religion (at the start of the century, 'religion' meant a Catholic religious order; by the end, it meant, as it still does, a distinct system of metaphysical belief, public morality and communal worship). Its politics, even, was fundamentally religious: kings ruled 'by the grace of God', as it said on the coins; the law was rooted in the law of nature, which was divine law, the law God had laid down for the world he had created. It is difficult for a nation that has ceased to think of itself as a Christian country to imagine what that was like. That is one reason it is all the more important to emphasise the point now. Although Christianity has long since ceased to dominate English or British politics, until relatively recently it required little if any imagination to appreciate the importance of religion in Tudor England. Now it is easiest to attain understanding through an analogy. Religion was to Tudor politics and culture what economics is to modern politics and culture: it was that within terms of which all else was weighed and measured, that to which all else was ultimately referred. God then was what 'the market' is now – or should that be the other way round? Christianity held the place of capitalism. And the differences between Catholicism and Protestantism, though perhaps miniscule from the perspective of outsiders today, mattered to people as much then as the differences between 'free market economics' and 'socialism' matter to people now. Maybe concern for the environment now threatens that hegemony of 'the market' and 'economics'. If so, a cultural upheaval on a scale akin to that of 'the Reformation' or even to that of 'secularisation' might soon be seen. But such crude analogies must not be pressed too far.

The justification for the approach taken in this volume, then, which is not the only possible approach to Tudor history, is that knowing about and understanding the great change in the national religion and constitution that was accomplished under the Tudors puts the modern reader in a position to grasp the enormous significance of the political and cultural changes that accompanied it or followed from it, while also setting the scene against which the other stories of Tudor England were played out. If this account of Tudor England can give readers some sense of how and why England had changed under the Tudors, then it will be of some value. If it encourages them to explore the deeper reaches of Tudor history behind what historians and dramatists then and now have so often put centre stage, all the better.

1

ESTABLISHING THE TUDOR REGIME, 1485–1515

On 27 August 1485, Henry VII entered the city of London at the head of his victorious forces and made his way to St Paul's Cathedral. There, inside the north door, he made a thanks offering to the 'Rood of Paul's', a wonder-working image of the crucified Christ that was much venerated by Londoners. His offering comprised the three banners under which his troops had triumphed over the followers of Richard III at Bosworth Field five days earlier. One was St George, for England; the second was a red dragon on a green and white background – the dragon for Wales and its background the family colours of his father's line, the Tudors; and the third was the Dun Cow (the dark or black cow), the emblem of his hereditary title as Earl of Richmond.[1] Such thanksgiving for victory was a conventional enough gesture, yet in Henry's case it betokened a piety as true as it was deep. Throughout his reign, he saw an intimate connection between the spiritual and temporal welfare of his two bodies – his own royal person and the 'body politic' of his kingdom. This did not make him a saint. The fate of his cousin, Henry VI, murdered in the Tower in 1471, was a painful reminder that saintly men do not often make effective kings. Traits of grim ruthlessness and a chilling calculation of material interest cohabited with Henry VII's piety, inducing occasional paroxysms of guilt.

In the dour political reality of late fifteenth-century England, Henry VII had won the throne by conquest. But in the realm of medieval ideas, monarchy was all about justice, and it was important that he be seen as a legitimate king. His tortuous path to legitimation ended with a papal 'bull' (or edict) from Pope Innocent VIII which recognised his claim to the throne and put the whole weight of the Church behind it:

His Holiness confirmeth, establisheth, and approveth the right and title to the Crown of England of the said our sovereign lord Henry the Seventh . . . as well by reason of his nighest and undoubted title of succession as by the right of his most noble victory and by election of the Lords spiritual and temporal and other nobles of his realm and by the act, ordinance, and authority of parliament made by the three estates of this land.[2]

This brief summary of Henry's claim reflects the logic of events: his appeal to hereditary right ('undoubted title of succession'), his defeat of Richard at Bosworth ('victory'), his coronation ('election'), and his recognition by Parliament. His coronation was indeed celebrated not long afterwards, with all the customary ceremonies, on Sunday 30 October. The sacred oil associated with St Thomas Becket was brought from Canterbury as usual for the anointing. There soon followed the opening of his first Parliament, on Monday 7 November. The nobility of England, largely conspicuous by their absence from Bosworth Field, were almost all present in person for the coronation, and stayed in London for Parliament. Its first substantive business was a bill moved on the king's behalf in the Commons, to recognise that Henry was and remained the lawful King of England. This at once received the endorsement of the Lords and the royal assent.[3] Henry elaborated on this assent with an address setting out his claim to the throne in much the same terms as in the later papal bull. This unprecedented statute reveals just how vulnerable he felt. It was not quite as crude as when Henry IV walked into Parliament and coolly announced that he was now king because Richard II had 'resigned' the day before. But the act of attainder which declared that those who had fought against him at Bosworth had committed treason the day before the battle was somewhat tendentious.[4] And the *potpourri* of reasons Henry VII threw together in vindication of his claim was manifest testimony to his insecurity. His use of statute to clarify royal authority and the succession set an unwitting precedent for the Tudor era which in the long term would undermine the mystique which can alone sustain hereditary monarchy.

What did more than anything else to anchor Henry's position was his marriage to Elizabeth, the daughter of the Yorkist Edward IV. Even before his invasion in 1485, Henry had been negotiating with discontented Yorkists about this dynastic union. The wedding took place on 18 January 1486, as soon as the pope's representative in England had issued the dispensation that was needed because their shared descent from Edward III put them within the very broad range of cousins between whom the medieval canon law of the Catholic Church forbade marriage. The birth of their first child, Arthur, on 19 September that year, portended divine blessing upon the Tudor project. But Henry also sought the blessing of his vicar upon earth, and petitioned the pope, Innocent VIII, for confirmation both of his marriage and of his claim to the throne.

A summary of the papal bull authorising his marriage and endorsing his claim to the throne was translated and printed as a flysheet, becoming the first public statement of the theme for the new dynasty:

> [After] the long and grievous variance, dissensions, and debates . . . between the House of the Duchy of Lancaster . . . and the House of the Duchy of York . . . willing all such divisions in time following to be put apart . . . [the pope] . . . approveth, confirmeth, and establisheth the matrimony and conjunction made between our sovereign Lord King Henry the Seventh of the House of Lancaster . . . and the noble Princess Elizabeth of the House of York . . .[5]

It was the first and for many years the only printed proclamation of the reign.[6] This union of Lancaster and York was for Henry and his four successors the supreme achievement of their house. By uniting the rival lines in one house of indisputably legitimate blood, they proclaimed, this marriage ended decades of internecine strife. It made a claim upon the gratitude as well as the loyalty of their subjects. The theme would be restated frequently, almost endlessly, over the ensuing century, and was still going strong in Shakespeare's history plays in the 1590s. It took visual as well as literary form, in the two roses, red and white, badges of Lancaster and York, depicted entwining, or superimposed, white on red, in what we call the 'Tudor rose'. Poems and plays, pictures, windows and sculptures took up these tropes and kept the people in mind of the Tudor myth. Print, of course, could multiply images as well as text, and before long some of Henry's 'official' publications were appearing with ornate title pages decorated with the royal arms and livery badges (roses and portcullises).

The crudely printed version of Pope Innocent VIII's bull was the first time an English king used print to communicate a political message to his subjects. It inaugurated a long tradition, one which grew significantly through the following century. William Caxton (d. 1492) might therefore be regarded as one of the most significant figures in Tudor history. When he brought the first press to Westminster in 1475, he unwittingly inaugurated a new era in English politics. Printing from movable type had incalculable consequences for the political, religious and social life of Europe. Although the new industry developed slowly at first, in Tudor England the steadily increasing output of text on paper accompanied and facilitated far-reaching changes in the government of both the kingdom and the Church by building new capacity for the authorities in both institutions to communicate their wishes and their instructions to intermediate authorities and thus to the people at large.

The governmental use of print had actually begun under Richard III (1483–85), when for the first time new acts were printed after a meeting of Parliament (STC 9347). His regime doubtless saw this as a suitable way of advertising Richard's legitimacy as king. But it was Henry VII who reaped lasting benefit from the new technology as, starting in a small way, print was put to the service of the Crown. Royal commands were more widely disseminated than ever before. A shift in the language of government from French to English had commenced back in the reign of Edward III, in the context of the increasingly nationalistic conflict now known as the 'Hundred Years' War', and the wider dissemination of official texts accelerated this. The statutes of Richard III had still been framed and printed in Law French, the peculiar Norman French argot that was the language of record for England's common lawyers. Henry VII's statutes were framed in English, and the first edition of any statutes of England in the English language was a collection of the statutes of his first three Parliaments, printed by Caxton in 1491. By 1504, Henry saw enough potential in print to create the office of 'king's printer'. Although the first holder of this office, William Faques, produced relatively little, his successor, Richard Pynson, appointed in 1506, held the office until his death in 1529 and was to make a lot of money working for Henry and his son.

The invention of printing was itself made feasible by important innovations in the production of paper, and paper likewise left its mark on government and social life in the Tudor era. Writing had always been, among other things, a technology of power. Through financial and then judicial records, it enabled rulers to exert control and extract resources more effectively. It was not for nothing that, in 1381, the peasants who rose across southern England in rebellion against secular or ecclesiastical overlords often set about burning their written records, the tools and symbols of their oppression. Until the reign of Edward IV, the majority of England's public records took the form of rolls composed of sheets of parchment stitched together. Making such documents was laborious and expensive. From Henry VIII onwards, the bulk of the public archives are documents written on paper, though the more durable medium of parchment was still used for especially important records, such as the parliament rolls (the authoritative record of acts of Parliament) and the patent rolls (registered copies of the 'letters patent' by which kings made grants of land and office). The reign of Henry VII saw the beginning of that shift from parchment to paper, a change which not only increased the quantity of records made and kept but also broadened the scope of what was recorded. The scale of English public record-keeping underwent continual increase from this time. More paper meant more record-keeping, and more record-keeping meant improved accountability and control (as well as more raw material for later historians).

The early years of Henry VII were troubled. While it is tempting in retrospect to see the Battle of Bosworth as the end of the 'Wars of the Roses', it did not seem so final at the time. Descended as he was via his mother, Margaret (Figure 1.1), from John Beaufort, Marquis of Dorset and Somerset, the illegitimate son of John of Gaunt, he had but a flimsy claim to represent the Lancastrian royal line. The fact that his mother, through whom he derived that claim, was still alive when he took the throne is especially worthy of note. There was a view in fifteenth-century England that a woman could transmit a claim to the throne. It was the entire basis of the Yorkist case against the House of Lancaster. But no one thought a woman could claim the throne in her own right.[7] That said, Henry VII preferred to emphasise his connections with his uncle, Henry VI, who supposedly foretold his eventual succession, and more tenuously still with Henry V, whose widow, Catherine of Valois, was his paternal grandmother.

Henry's bid for the throne in 1485 had been a gamble. He might have been killed at Bosworth just as easily as Richard. If his success, rather against the odds, taught any lesson, it was what might be achieved with a little bit of luck by anyone with a vague claim to the throne and a small army. Within a year, that lesson had been taken to heart. There were half-cock Yorkist risings in the north and the Midlands, fomented by Francis Lovell (Viscount Lovell), one of Richard's former henchmen. Henry was engaged at the time in a perambulation of his realm which took him broadly up the Great North Road to York, and then south-west across the Midlands to the Severn Valley, so he was well placed to quell these stirs. But probably not even he was surprised when a putative Yorkist claimant burst onto the scene in Ireland towards the end of 1486. History knows this figure as Lambert Simnel, but he was presented to the public

Lady Margaret Beaufort

Henry VII's somewhat tenuous claim to the English throne was derived from his mother, Margaret Beaufort, great-granddaughter of John of Gaunt. One of the most striking changes in the English polity under the Tudors was that while it was inconceivable that Margaret claim the throne of England in her own right in the later fifteenth century, by the middle of the sixteenth century female succession was recognised as a reality.

as Edward, Earl of Warwick, the nephew of Edward IV. The real Earl of Warwick had been in the Tower since 1485, but that did not discourage the powerful Fitzgerald interest in Ireland from taking up the pretender. This family, whose head was the Earl of Kildare, was the leading house among the English ruling elite in Ireland. The Fitzgeralds had long been Yorkists, and were prompt to endorse this implausible claimant for their own ends. Reinforced by John de la Pole, Earl of Lincoln, who brought a couple of thousand mercenaries to Dublin from the Netherlands (at the expense of Margaret, Duchess of Burgundy, Edward IV's sister), the would-be Edward VI crossed the Irish Sea in early summer 1487. The rival armies met at Stoke (now East Stoke), a few miles down the Fosse Way south-west of Newark, on the south bank of the Trent. Henry's troops inflicted a crushing defeat on the Yorkist forces, who ended up cornered in a loop of the river and were cut to pieces without hope of retreat.

After Stoke, Henry set off on a tour of the northern parts of his kingdom that was more a reconnaissance in force than a mere royal progress. As Duke of Gloucester, ruling the north from the Neville fastness of Middleham Castle in Wensleydale, Richard III had established close personal and political ties with the magnates and gentry of the region even before he seized the throne. Henry needed to make Tudor rule a reality there.[8] This would take time, and was a delicate task. The Earl of Northumberland, Henry Percy, required particularly careful handling. He had brought a sizeable force to Bosworth Field in 1485, but had refrained from committing it to battle on either side. His armed neutrality had been a response to Richard III's failure to grant him the lieutenancy of the north after he had become king. That error cost Richard his throne. After some hesitation, Henry VII gave the earl the regional position Richard had denied him, and was repaid with loyal service. York was strongly Ricardian and Yorkist in its sympathies, and when Henry reached it during his first royal tour, in April 1486, Earl Percy turned out with a handy retinue to help overawe the citizens. He raised a substantial force to keep the north in order during the campaign of 1487. Even after this, though, the north was twitchy under Tudor rule. The collection of a royal tax in spring 1489 provoked resistance in North Yorkshire. Percy sallied forth with his men to face down this disobedience, but when he tried to disperse a crowd at South Kilvington, just north of Thirsk, the rioters mobbed and killed him while his retainers held back and looked on, both groups still resenting his betrayal of Richard.

Percy's son was only 11 years old, and was taken south to be brought up at the Court, so another solution was required for the problem of the north. It proved to be a most surprising choice: Thomas Howard, who had fought against Henry at Bosworth. His father, the Duke of Norfolk, had died there, and Thomas, whom Richard had made Earl of Surrey in his own right, had been attainted of treason, deprived of his lands, and consigned to the Tower. Yet after the lynching of Northumberland, Henry reinstated Howard to his earldom and despatched him to take charge in the north. It was unusual to give authority on the borders to someone with almost no lands or connections in the region, but perhaps this reduced local jealousies. In any case, the region remained quiet through the 1490s, and Surrey himself built up effective working relationships with the northern elites.

The kingdom that Henry took over in August 1485 existed in a social order predicated upon the ownership and exploitation of land. A military landed elite exercised 'lordship' from their dwellings, mostly manor houses built of brick or stone, but in the cases of the great lords, castles, such as Skipton (seat of the Cliffords) or Castle Bolton (seat of the Scropes). The peers and a few other great magnates might lord it even over other landowners, by means of a retinue of clients and followers. Knights and gentlemen in turn, whose substance might range from broad estates scattered over several counties to one or two nearby manors, dominated local society. This elite did not work its own land: it was a rentier class, living off the sweat of tenants and labourers. The social price it paid for its leisured lifestyle was reckoned in military service. The 'right to bear arms' was the defining characteristic of the gentleman, a right restricted to the elite. The elite was trained in the use of arms and armour, in combat on horseback or on foot. This superior armament and training gave a relatively small class the capacity to rule over far larger numbers of people. Even a handful of well-armed and well-trained mounted men could quell a troublesome crowd that was equipped with little more than agricultural implements. That was the equation upon which a fragile social order rested.

The two major variations in this pattern were the Church and the towns. The Church, in the sense of the institutions and personnel of the clergy, was also closely related to the land. The greater clergy, namely the bishops and other dignitaries attached to cathedrals or grander churches (known as colleges), were substantial landowners by virtue of their ecclesiastical positions, but their consecrated status exempted them from military service. Their estates, though, would still furnish fighting men to the Crown, led by stewards selected from the gentry. But the bulk of the land held by the Church was in the hands of the monasteries.

The religious houses of England had over many centuries acquired vast endowments, amounting to as much as a quarter of the productive land of the realm. In a world in which land was the currency of power, this made the Church a mighty institution – or set of institutions.

The towns stood one step away from the predominantly agrarian economy. Their wealth was based on trade in goods and services rather than on primary production. The wealthiest and most successful townsmen aspired to raise their families into the ranks of the landed elite, and were able to do so through marriage or purchase. Wealthier townsmen might well attain the status of gentry, though the first-generation gentleman would always remain something of an upstart in the eyes of those whose 'blood' was 'noble'. Their children and descendants, however, were rapidly and easily assimilated into the ranks of what was, for its time, the relatively open elite of English society. The towns themselves were usually distinguished from the surrounding countryside or hinterland by a level of self-government. In the 'boroughs' (that is, towns constituted by royal charter), this autonomy, which freed them from the jurisdiction of secular or ecclesiastical lords, was formally recognised as accountable only to the king and his courts. But even in towns such as Reading or St Albans, which still recognised the jurisdiction of a feudal overlord (in these cases, the local abbot), governance structures based on voluntary religious associations (called 'guilds') managed the day-to-day running of affairs. By 1500, the towns of England had a crucial part to play in the local economy: they were the hubs of economic life for their districts. The royal boroughs were all represented in Parliament – that was one of the benefits of borough status – as were some seigneurial towns, though generally the electorates were restricted to the urban elite. Their MPs sat in the House of Commons alongside those for the counties or shires, local knights or gentlemen selected by an electorate consisting mostly of their social equals.

The model by which most English people then understood the society in which they lived was still envisaged in terms of the three 'estates' or 'orders' originally imagined in eleventh-century Europe: clergy, nobility, commons; in Latin *oratores*, *bellatores*, *aratores* (those who pray, those who fight, those who plough).[9] By 1500 the model was no longer working very well, but it still had some purchase. Thus the papal bull confirming Henry's title spoke of Parliament as 'the three estates of the realm'. But the towns had long been an anomaly in this model, and the English Parliament comprised only two houses, the Lords and the Commons. The presence of the bishops and a couple of dozen great abbots in the

Lords was a gesture to the representation of the first estate, but those prelates were present as landowners, not as representatives of the clergy. The clergy of England, as the first estate, were represented in a separate body, Convocation, which always met at the same time as Parliament, but apart (having effectively withdrawn from Parliament in the fourteenth century).[10] The men of the Commons were for the most part anything but common, though they were 'commoners' (that is, neither royal nor of the peerage). The majority of them were gentlemen, many of them knights. The lowliest members of the Commons in social terms were the representatives of the towns. But many towns were already electing local gentlemen to represent them, a tendency which became more marked through the Tudor era, while actual burgher members were usually wealthy men in their own right. The ploughmen were represented only notionally. In theory, Parliament represented the kingdom: in practice, it represented the elites.

The first estate, that of the clergy, held enormous and unmistakable political power. Two of the greatest offices under the Crown – Lord Chancellor and Lord Privy Seal – were almost always held by a clergyman, usually a bishop. The clergy were, broadly, exempt from the direct taxes voted by Parliaments, and instead voted taxes to the king in their own Convocations. By 1500 that was a dubious privilege, as they usually paid more in taxes than their lay counterparts. The Tudor century was to see the virtual political eclipse of the clergy, collateral damage of what we call 'the Reformation'. But the reign of Henry VII gave no hint of this. His closest political adviser was the former Yorkist John Morton, who had fled Richard III's regime to join Henry in exile in 1484. After his victory, Henry appointed him Lord Chancellor and Archbishop of Canterbury, a dignity also held by his other two Chancellors, Henry Deane and William Warham. That Warham's successor, Cardinal Wolsey (1515–29) had to be content with the archbishopric of York did nothing to change the underlying pattern. Although Henry's reign can be seen in some ways as consolidating royal influence within the Church of England, this was more symbiosis than predation. Church and Crown benefited from mutual support, as they had done for centuries. There is a sense in which an alliance between Crown and Church helped kings to manage their often unruly barons. As long as a king supported the traditional 'liberties of the church' stipulated in Magna Carta and affirmed by every monarch in his coronation oath, then the Church, in the appointment of whose bishops and principal abbots the king had a predominant influence, was a reliable buttress of royal authority.

Henry was personally devout, and took care throughout his reign to defend the interests of the Church. He was a particular patron of the movement for strict observance within the Franciscan friars, and Virginia Henderson has argued compellingly for seeing this well-known and well-documented commitment on his part as motivated by genuine devotion, and not as the merely political and hypocritical outward show that it has seemed to many historians.[11] He founded several houses of Observant Franciscans during his reign, in particular those of Greenwich and Richmond, both of them immediately adjoining the royal residences there. Indeed, he began work on the Greenwich project within weeks of taking the throne. Evidently, moreover, he saw heavenly intervention at work in his own life. In July 1487, after defeating his challengers at Stoke, he informed the pope with some relish of the awful fate of a felon who was among the many criminals who took refuge in the sanctuary at Westminster Abbey. Hearing a false rumour of Henry's defeat in that battle, the luckless John Swit roundly denounced the futility of the papal excommunications of his enemies that the king had secured from Rome, saying (the king reported):

'So much for ecclesiastical censures and papal sanctions! Surely you can see that these interdicts are utterly worthless. Before our very eyes we have seen those who sought them overthrown, and their curses brought down on their own heads.' No sooner had he said this than he fell down dead, with his whole face and body rapidly turning blacker than pitch, giving off such a foul stench that no one could even draw near. That, Most Holy Father, is exactly what happened; nor would I have brought it to your attention had I not known it for certain.[12]

In thanksgiving for his victory at Stoke, Henry sent his battle standard as a votive offering to the shrine of Our Lady at Walsingham, one of the greatest shrines in England, a sure sign that he had made a vow to do so in the event of success, for he had taken a detour to pay a visit there on his way to meet his challengers.[13] He was equally devoted to the cult of St Thomas of Canterbury, where he went several times on pilgrimage, and to which he donated a votive image of himself in his will. Moreover, he seems to have felt a profound association between royalty and sanctity. This is evident in the plethora of royal saints with which he surrounded images of himself and his close family in the great stained-glass window planned for (and probably installed in) the chapel he built at the Greenwich Observant Franciscans.[14]

On one visit to Canterbury, in May 1498, Henry intervened personally at the execution of a priest, a 'Lollard', who was to be burned to death for heresy, and persuaded him to recant – despite the fact that the sentence could no longer be nullified.[15] 'Lollardy' was a pejorative term for a loosely defined set of dissident religious beliefs and practices which had been inspired by the teachings of John Wycliffe, an Oxford theologian, towards the end of the fourteenth century, and which troubled the bishops intermittently until the 1520s. There was a small and scattered network of Lollards on the Kentish Weald, which the unfortunate priest had perhaps served, and similar groups were found in a few other regions, such as the Norfolk Broads, the Chiltern Hills, the Forest of Dean, Coventry, and London itself. The reigns of Henry VII and his son were notable for the renewed vigour and determination with which the Church authorities acted to suppress Lollardy, and this was evidently with firm royal support. There were numerous burnings of recalcitrant heretics and a larger number of recantations. Since the reign of Henry V the Crown had given strong support to action against Lollardy, and Henry VII's personal zeal in this cause was probably one aspect of his concern to demonstrate his monarchical legitimacy.

The king's personal generosity towards the Church was most evident in the spectacular Lady Chapel that he built at the east end of Westminster Abbey, next door to the royal palace of Westminster. He planned this chapel as a dynastic mausoleum. He was to be buried there, alongside his wife (Figure 1.2). He also intended it to become the shrine of a new English saint, his Lancastrian predecessor Henry VI, whose canonisation he was promoting.[16] 'Good King Henry', popularly regarded as a martyr on account of his murder at the hands of the Yorkists, enjoyed the fastest growing cult in late medieval England. His body was at this time enshrined at Windsor Castle, in the Chapel Royal of St George. That this imposing royal castle was the destination of England's most popular pilgrimage in 1500 says a great deal about the cultural affinity between royalty and religion in Tudor England, and may go some way to explaining the success of the Reformation there. Miracles were widely credited to the royal saint, and Henry VII himself figured in one of them. According to his publicists, when the young Henry Tudor had been presented to his royal cousin at Court as a boy, the king had foretold – or prophesied – that the boy would one day become his successor and wear the crown. So Henry VII planned to bring the royal saint from Windsor to Westminster. It certainly did the king nothing but good to be associated with this cult, and his plans for Westminster would have harnessed it even more

Tomb of Henry VII and Elizabeth of York
The king's executors commissioned this remarkable Renaissance monument from
the Florentine sculptor Pietro Torrigiano, who is best known for having broken
Michelangelo's nose. It still stands in the Lady Chapel that Henry VII himself had
built at the east end of Westminster Abbey as a dynastic memorial.

closely to the Tudor chariot. Henry's relationship with the first estate,
then, was very traditional. He was on excellent terms with the papacy,
with which he established what amounted to continuous diplomatic
relations.[17] It was perhaps partly because his general relationship with
the Church was so warm that Henry was also able to consolidate some
elements of royal control over the clergy, especially the hierarchy, for
example through limiting 'benefit of clergy' (the extent to which clergy
could escape the rigours of royal jurisdiction for the relative mildness of

the ecclesiastical courts) or holding bishops more accountable for the security of the prisons in which they confined clerical criminals.[18] The tightened control Henry exerted over the clergy and the unprecedented levels of taxation he exacted from them were seemingly acceptable to his bishops as the price for a political and social alignment that bolstered the position of the Church in English culture and society.

What really changed in England in the first decades of Tudor rule was the relationship between the Crown and the second estate – that military landed elite comprising the nobility and gentry. Change was driven by Henry VII's enduring suspicion of the magnates, the most powerful peers and knights. One contemporary analysis of the woes that beset England during what are now known as 'the Wars of the Roses' traced them to the problem of 'overmighty subjects'. Some modern historians have countered this by suggesting that the real problem was 'undermighty kings' (to be precise, the long reigning Henry VI, whose mental illness rendered him incapable of effective rule). But the impact between 1450 and 1485 of, successively, two Dukes of York, the Earl of Warwick (the 'Kingmaker'), the Duke of Gloucester (aka Richard III), and the Duke of Buckingham, together with the contributions of such other powerful families as the Percys (Earls of Northumberland) and the Herberts, lends credibility to the contemporary analysis.[19] Both Henry VII and Henry VIII seem to have shared this view.

Under Henry VII there was no Duke of York until he vested the title in his younger son. The surviving Earl of Warwick was brought up in the Tower of London, until he was executed on spurious charges of treason in 1498. There was no Duke of Gloucester. The young Duke of Buckingham was made a ward of Lady Margaret Beaufort, the King's Mother (the phrase was virtually her official title), and although treated with every honour throughout the reign, was on more than one occasion put under significant financial restraint. This is not to say that Henry VII set about some purge of the nobility. There was no attempt to extinguish noble power as such. Many noble lines had died out through natural wastage, death in battle or execution for treason. Very few of their titles were restored or reassigned, and hardly any new peerages were given out. Henry made his uncle Jasper the Duke of Bedford, but Jasper had and was probably expected to have no heirs (he married only late in life). The king's reluctance to ennoble even his closest supporters was a remarkable departure from medieval custom. And he mostly held on to whatever noble estates fell into the Crown's hands for any reason. The threat posed by Scotland compelled Henry to delegate military capacity to someone in the north, but his anxiety about this is perfectly captured by the fact that, as we have seen, after the lynching of the Earl of Northumberland, he entrusted that task to a magnate from the south. And even Surrey's years of loyal service could not redeem the duchy of Norfolk from the king. There was no similar threat from Wales to require Henry to establish a powerful regional magnate in the Welsh Marches. Even in Ireland he shied away from traditional practice, especially after the early support for the pretenders shown by the powerful Fitzgeralds. Instead, he preferred to rule through English emissaries such as Edward Poynings. The fruit of this general suspicion of noble power was first that the English peerage declined in numbers through his reign, from 55 to 42, and second that a series of laws further eroded the traditional power of the magnates, imposing restrictions on 'retaining' and seeking to subject the practice to royal control through licensing. The vigorous implementation of selected laws, old and new, enabled the king to achieve still more control over the nobles by exacting fines for misbehaviour and bonds for good behaviour. By the end of his reign, the ancient nobility of England was well on the way to being thoroughly domesticated, and Henry VIII kept the leash tight.

The bulk of the second estate consisted of the gentry, not the peerage. The diminishing numbers and role of the peers under Henry VII made it inevitable that greater reliance would be placed on the gentry in local and indeed central government. At the centre, this was evident in the 'new men' to whom he turned for advice and for the implementation of his will. Laymen of mostly gentry background, often with some training in the law, these men looked to him alone for power, influence and reward. They did not displace the great officers of the Crown, still often clergymen, but they showed that the path to the top of politics did not have to go through the Church.[20] The foundation of English local government was the commission of the peace, the panel of local lords, clergymen, gentlemen and officeholders that was appointed to preserve law and order in each county. Justices of the Peace (JPs), as the commissioners were called, had substantial powers and responsibilities within their counties, and were expected to act individually or collectively to repress disorder, arrest malefactors and try such crimes as were not serious enough to merit the attention of the king's professional judges in the assizes that sat periodically in the main county towns. As the informal dominance of the peerage declined, the role of JPs grew in importance. Henry VII's Parliaments passed over 20 statutes which further defined or strengthened the scope of these commissions, and there was a steady growth in their size throughout not only his reign but the entire Tudor era. Detailed research has shown that the shift from informal magnate rule to a greater reliance on JPs was no panacea.[21] Disorder and lawbreaking could increase in the transitional period. England was not everywhere better governed in 1500 than in 1485. But by 1600 the system was functioning smoothly: governance was more consistent and general levels of peace and order were higher.

What was true of England, however, was not true of Wales. Despite Henry's Welsh ancestry, he did nothing to improve the position of Wales and its people under the English Crown. The conquest of Wales had been completed under Henry IV, and the title Prince of Wales had long been customary for the heir apparent to the English throne. But no more than Ireland or Calais was Wales 'part' of England. Some areas had been anglicised, but Welsh remained the predominant language, and no attempt was made to impose the language or laws of England on the Welsh. English people were seen by the Welsh as conquerors, and Welsh people were seen by the English as foreigners, and as such faced severe discrimination under English law. Crime and disorder were rife in the 'Welsh Marches', the English shires bordering Wales and still sometimes prey to Welsh raiding. English towns there such as Ludlow and Shrewsbury still guarded their walls against this persistent threat. The 'Marcher Lords', peers or knights with substantial lands in the region, often enjoyed a freedom of action and everyday power beyond that of their equals elsewhere, so that they could meet force with force. Not much was to change in Wales and the Marches until the 1530s.

Henry VII did not have much direct contact with the third estate, those who worked the land and those who crafted and traded, or simply served. He was not a king who even put himself much on view for his subjects. But times were on the whole good for ordinary people in the later fifteenth century. The long demographic recovery from the Black Death of the fourteenth century was still under way, and while epidemics were a recurrent reality, they were not on that calamitous scale. Even the civil wars between Lancaster and York did little to inhibit growing prosperity: the belligerents dealt in set-piece battles, not in sacking towns or scorching the earth. The king's peace was mostly kept under Henry, thanks to the gentry who served as JPs. His reign provided some level of stability and certainty – though the latter could only be relative in any era before that of modern medicine, because death was then so much closer to everyone, from beggars to kings. The most noticeable impact of any king upon his humbler subjects was likely to be negative: the levying of taxation to finance war. Henry VII did remarkably little of this, which was perhaps the best thing he ever did for his subjects.

Fiscal policy under Henry focused not upon taxation but upon the exploitation of the ordinary revenues of the Crown and of the various fees and fines the Crown could levy upon landowners or others because of the 'prerogatives' it enjoyed under the old Norman 'feudal' system that still haunted the land law of England. England was no longer, in practice, a kingdom in which feudal military service to the king was the true basis of most landownership. But there were many relics of that feudalism still in use, most notably wardship – the custom by which a child who inherited estates held in theory from the Crown was made a 'ward' of an adult landowner who became their 'guardian'. The guardian enjoyed the free disposal of the entire income of their ward's lands until the child reached maturity, and along the way had a very good chance of inducing the ward to marry into their own family. Accident and disease ensured a regular supply of plum wardships. It was the Crown's prerogative to assign these to guardians (for a fee), and the business-like management of wards proved a major source of royal income from the time of Henry VII until that of the early Stuarts. It was worth about £9,000 a year to Henry by the end of his reign. The Crown likewise reaped the profits of justice: fines for breaches of law were simply part of the king's income. Henry VII employed a team of smart lawyers to search out breaches of all kinds of laws, including many that were obsolete, and thus to maximise the cash flow from fines for bad behaviour and bonds for good behaviour. His most notorious agents in this task were Richard Empson and Edmund Dudley, whose ruthless acquisitiveness went well beyond the bounds of the strictly legal. According to Dudley's later confessions, the fines exacted were often groundless and extreme. One Sir John Pennington was fined over £130 for leaving the kingdom without the king's permission – yet Dudley had seen the king shake his hand when he took his leave. A wealthy London haberdasher was fined £500 on the basis of a rumour picked up from a prostitute.[22]

Parliaments were reasonably frequent in Henry's early years, though this mostly arose from the recurring need to attaint new tranches of rebels for rebellion or treason. Parliament was the forum for the traditional gift exchange by which the king redressed the grievances of his subjects through enacting new laws at their request, while those subjects reciprocated by voting him taxation. It still functioned effectively, and in 1492 Henry felt secure enough to consider emulating his royal predecessors by invading France. It is hard to take his plan seriously, as he crossed the Channel too late in the year, with too few men, to have been pursuing any genuine military goal. It seems likely that the point of the exercise was its actual outcome, namely, to bring the French to the negotiating table and induce them to resume paying the annual protection money first extorted from them by a similar raid of Edward IV's in 1475. Heavy French military commitments in Italy in the 1490s left them all too willing to buy Henry off. Whether Henry's nobles thought well of such a mercenary rather than military intervention is doubtful. But his people were doubtless grateful.

The French campaign did not lend Henry the aura of military glory that might have won him more love and respect from his more eminent subjects, and thus rendered him more secure. Indeed, he remained transparently insecure throughout the 1490s. London witnessed a grim series of executions for treason, totalling at least 40, through a decade whose politics were overshadowed by the bizarre career of Perkin Warbeck, a textile trader and male model turned political adventurer.[23] It seems that while he was on a sales trip to Dublin in 1492, Yorkist diehards saw in him some resemblance to the late King Edward IV – a claim borne out by a surviving sketch of his appearance – and persuaded themselves and others that he was in fact Richard, Duke of York, Edward's second son. Thus began an odyssey around the courts of Europe, as his backers successively sought countenance for his claims from France, the Netherlands, the Empire, and Scotland. While his role was chiefly as a puppet with which to threaten Henry, he gained credibility when the Yorkist matriarch Margaret of Burgundy accepted him as her nephew. It is a sign of the real vulnerability of Henry VII throughout the 1490s that this shallow pretence could cause him such trouble. Plotting focused on Warbeck was almost continuous, and included an abortive invasion plan in 1493; a planned rising in 1494–95 that involved one of Henry's hitherto most trusted henchmen, Sir William Stanley; an attempted invasion of Kent by 'Richard' in 1495 (resulting in about 50 executions for treason across Kent and East Anglia), followed by an attempted rising in Ireland in which he took part; and finally an invasion from Scotland in 1496 – which, in the event, was easily repelled.

The Scottish invasion provoked the greatest crisis of the reign, when in early 1497 Henry persuaded Parliament to vote him taxes for a punitive expedition against the Scots. Discontent over this levy in the far south-west erupted into rebellion, and a substantial force marched on London under the leadership of a local baron, Lord Audley. Until this moment, Audley had been a loyal servant of the regime. He had fought for Henry at Stoke, crossed with him to France, and served in Somerset as a JP. However, he did have family ties to Edward IV, and the likeliest explanation of his *volte face* is that the excitement whipped up by Perkin Warbeck in the previous couple of years had rekindled his Yorkist sympathies. Hence perhaps also the decision of the rebels to head round London to Kent before assaulting the capital. Kent had tended to support the house of York through the recent wars. The army that Henry had gathered to punish the Scots was summoned south to deal with the rebels instead, defeating them on Blackheath in July. Warbeck himself tried to seize the moment by landing in Cornwall, but he arrived in September, far too late, and was unsuccessful in his bid to capture Exeter. By early October he was in Henry's hands and he remained in custody in the royal household until, after briefly escaping in summer 1498, he was confined to the Tower. Either because he plotted with the Tower's longest serving inmate, the Earl of Warwick, or because Henry was simply tired of the whole business, Warwick, Warbeck and other prisoners connected with him were tried and executed for treason in autumn 1499. After these executions, the Yorkist threat to Henry dwindled. There were still potential Yorkist claimants at large, most notably Edmund, Richard and William de la Pole, the last surviving nephews of Edward IV. Edmund and Richard fled the country in 1501, more unnerved than overawed by the execution of Warwick in 1499. From 1502 William de la Pole was imprisoned by the king, who manoeuvred and negotiated tirelessly for the return of Edmund and Richard from their various refuges in Europe. Edmund eventually fell into Henry's hands in 1506, while Richard lived on as 'Blanche Rose' or 'White Rose' to become a thorn in the side of Henry VIII.

The remaining ten years of Henry's reign were marked chiefly by a continuation of the ruthless fiscal policy pursued through the 1490s, but also by a series of personal losses. The king's high hopes for his eldest son, Arthur, blossomed in the marriage arranged for him with Catherine of Aragon, a daughter of the 'Catholic Kings', Ferdinand and Isabella of Spain, whose conquest of Granada and acquisition of territories in the 'New World' across the Atlantic had made them the most prestigious monarchs in Europe. Catherine married Arthur at St Paul's Cathedral in November 1501, and the couple were sent to set up their household at Ludlow Castle in the Welsh Borders, where Arthur was to learn the trade of kingship through presiding as Prince of Wales over the Council of the Marches. But within six months Arthur was dead. Henry's wife and their newborn daughter died the following year, and the king himself almost died in 1504. He was never the same again. Until this time he had carefully audited the account books of his treasurer, famously signing off on every page. Now he was a spent force, making his last years a tribute to unambitious government. The king's daughter Margaret was sent northwards to marry James IV of Scotland in 1503, with a view to improving relations between the neighbouring kingdoms. After Arthur's death, Catherine was swiftly betrothed to his brother Henry, perhaps largely to ensure that her generous dowry did not have to be repaid. But the king was thereafter in no rush at all to solemnise the marriage, and a four-year engagement ensued. No wars were fought, though Henry paid lip service to the medieval dream of a crusade. His people reaped the dividend of peace. Parliament met just the once, in 1504, to vote a grant in recognition of the late Prince Arthur's marriage. The continuing fiscal feudalism was doubtless resented by its wealthy targets, but there is no indication that elite discontent was at threatening levels. In any case, the massive treasure that Henry had amassed by the time he died on 21 April 1509 was insurance against any conceivable military challenge. His edifying deathbed penitence was backed up by a plethora of devotional bequests in his will, which famously ordered 10,000 Masses to be said for his soul, and made handsome donations to a dozen or more religious houses as well as a massive contribution towards the completion of King's College Chapel in Cambridge. Henry VII died as he had lived, devout and anxious.

It was nearly a century since the last unproblematic succession of a new king in England, so it is not surprising that no one quite knew what to do when Henry died. The news of his death was kept quiet for a couple of days before Henry VIII was proclaimed king on the evening of St George's Day (23 April). Next morning, the two most influential and most widely hated of the late king's henchmen, Empson and Dudley, were arrested for treason. The legalistic extortions of the previous regime were thus repudiated, and the accession of the robust young Henry seemed, even more than usual, to herald a new dawn. Thomas More greeted the event with celebratory Latin odes. In May, William Blount, Lord Mountjoy, who had once studied at Paris under the great scholar Erasmus, wrote his old tutor a letter extolling England under its new king as a land flowing with milk and honey, one that offered rich pickings for men of learning.[24] Erasmus was in England by the end of the summer, and made his home there for the next four years. The young king, it must be said, did not show undue interest in his kingdom's eminent visitor.

Henry VIII was much more interested in the prospect of marriage, and immediately kicked new life into the negotiations to conclude his marriage with Catherine of Aragon, so long deferred by his father's stalling. The wedding took place on 11 June in the church of the Observant Franciscans at Greenwich, a religious house founded by Henry VII which was in effect part of the palace complex there. Unlike his father, Henry VIII was keen to have a queen by his side for his coronation, which took place on the feast of St John the Baptist, 24 June. In the city of London, fountains were made to run with wine to lubricate the celebrations. There was even, for the first time ever, a commemorative pamphlet, printed with a fine woodcut frontispiece depicting Henry and Catherine seated beneath, respectively, the Tudor rose and the pomegranate of Aragon. The author, the minor courtier Stephen Hawes, was careful to emphasise that 'when the red rose took the white in marriage', the resulting unification of lineage had left Henry VIII the undoubted King of England. The horribly deteriorated state of the woodcut in some surviving copies indicates that it was reprinted until the block wore out, and thus that it sold in huge quantities.[25]

Henry VIII's accession was part vindication and part repudiation of his father's rule. The abrupt dismissal of Empson and Dudley announced a new departure in relations with the nobility. The Court of the young king drew peers and knights in droves to its festivities and tournaments. It was not apparent to any of them that these old forms of war were passing away and that 'tilting' (jousting on horseback) was now merely a game. It remained popular throughout the Tudor era, and tournaments attracted huge and partisan crowds. Even under Elizabeth, tilts celebrating the day of her accession continued into the 1590s, fading away only amid the mounting costs of an interminable war. Henry VIII continued his father's good relations with the first estate, and improved relations with the second and third. Bonds and recognisances imposed under his father were made subject to a sort of judicial review, and new bonds were used chiefly for genuine reasons of maintaining order or guaranteeing good behaviour, not as a fiscal expedient or a tool of intimidation.

Henry aspired to a better relationship with his nobles than his father had enjoyed, and was far more lavish with peerages and favours and grants of land. Thus Buckingham's brother was made Earl of Wiltshire in his own right in January 1510, and the Earl of Northumberland was released from a fine set at £10,000 and a recognisance set at £5,000. One level down, Henry was extravagantly generous for the next few years to the lively young men he gathered around him as knights or esquires 'of the Body'. Sir Thomas Knyvett, appointed a Knight of the Bath at Henry's coronation, was made Master of the Horse early in 1510. In September 1512 Sir Thomas Boleyn was granted a handsome package of lands that had once been Francis Lovell's. Charles Brandon's rise from Esquire of the Body at the start of the reign was startling, culminating in his being made Duke of Suffolk on 1 February 1514. Henry Guildford, Master of the Revels, had a central role in the fun and games that fill the pages of the chronicle of Henry's early years that was later compiled by Edward Hall. Henry and his friends loved dressing up and dancing, feasting and jousting, and Guildford did his best to turn the king's Court into the kind of thing they read about in Arthurian legends. All that was lacking to crown his joys was a son and heir. His marriage to Catherine was not as fruitful as that of his father to Elizabeth of York. New Year's Day 1511 brought a baby boy, named Henry. But a few weeks of joy soon turned to grief as the child sickened and died. Catherine's other early pregnancies ended prematurely.

Henry VIII's reign began in a spirit of reform. The Parliament that met in January 1510 gladly voted the king 'tonnage and poundage' (customs duties) for life and voiced its reforming hopes in statutes against perjury and extravagant clothing. An act against malfeasance by royal officials served to distance the regime from the excesses of Empson and Dudley. But the call for reform was even more insistent in spiritual and ecclesiastical affairs, echoing developments in Europe, where print had amplified reformist voices such as that of Girolamo Savonarola, the charismatic Florentine preacher of the 1490s. In England, the tone was set by John Colet, the Dean of St Paul's and friend of Erasmus who preached the keynote sermon at the Convocation that accompanied the first Parliament of the reign. His ringing indictment of contemporary priestly misbehaviour, while exaggerated, as calls for reform usually are, was nonetheless a serious demand for action. The connection between spiritual and temporal reform was made clear by another reformist preacher, Stephen Baron, the Provincial of the Observant Franciscan friars, whom Henry appointed his personal confessor. In this capacity Baron penned a brief treatise for the young king, *On Monarchical Rule*. It is a deeply conventional and rather pedestrian piece of moralising, underpinned by the notion that divine providence will assure personally virtuous monarchs of the security and welfare of their kingdoms.[26] Kingly virtue includes not only personal behaviour of a truly Christian kind but also public concern for the good of the Church and the orthodoxy of his subjects. Henry certainly took this aspect of the royal role to heart.

A fresh surge of action against Lollardy, especially in Kent, London, the Chilterns, and Coventry, which saw dozens recant and several burned alive, was undertaken with his full approval and backing.

From the moment Henry ascended the throne, shrewd commentators predicted a return to war with France. His decision to engage his kingdom once more in this project offers an early insight into his characteristic blend of self-interest and self-righteousness. The dream, as ever, was to vindicate the empty boast of the royal title, 'King of England and France', whose reality had for half a century been reduced to the enclave of Calais. Like Henry V a hundred years before, he simply wanted to reclaim what he believed was his by right. However, the aging King of France, Louis XII, whose own vainglorious ambitions were directed towards Italy, had become frustrated by papal opposition to his policies there, and had encouraged a faction of cardinals to attempt the overthrow of Pope Julius II by convening a would-be General Council of the Church in 1511. This 'silly little council' (*conciliabulum*) served only to goad the pope into excommunicating the king, which invested the alliance of his enemies with the moral status of a crusade. Henry leapt upon this excuse to clothe his adventure in the robes of holy war, and aligned himself with the emerging Holy League against France, which included King Ferdinand of Aragon and the Emperor Maximilian.

The first English campaign in this war was to be fought in ancient Plantagenet territory, to reconquer Aquitaine with the aid of King Ferdinand. An expeditionary force landed on the north coast of Spain in June 1512, to join a Spanish force with a view to invading France via Bayonne. But the wily Ferdinand was playing his own game, using the English troops as a threatening distraction while he set about annexing those portions of the kingdom of Navarre that lay to the south of the Pyrenees. After months of demoralising idleness, during which it became obvious that Ferdinand had no intention whatsoever of helping them invade France, the English returned home. Henry continued to prosecute the war with naval actions and coastal raids against Brittany, and despite Ferdinand's treachery, he pursued his own alliance with Julius II's 'Holy League'. The papal bull against Louis was formally promulgated in England by Wolsey in September 1512, and was at once put into print by Richard Pynson to make sure it reached the widest possible audience.[27] And an embassy was despatched to negotiate the terms of England's participation in the Holy League in the opening months of 1513.

These early years of Henry's reign saw the rapid rise of his first great minister, Thomas Wolsey, which showed that the Church was still a pathway to power for men of humble origins. Originally brought to Court by Richard Fox, Bishop of Winchester, towards the end of Henry VII's reign, Wolsey caught the new king's eye by assiduous attendance and an almost unscrupulous readiness to do his will. He was soon rewarded with the deanery of Hereford, and in the new reign he was appointed King's Almoner in November 1509. This made him one of the king's most intimate spiritual advisers, and a vital intermediary for those seeking grants of land or office from the king. By summer 1512 Wolsey was the king's most trusted councillor. When news arrived of the death of Sir Thomas Knyvett, a boon companion of the king's, in a naval engagement off Brest in August, Wolsey wrote to his old patron, Bishop Fox, telling him to keep the bad news quiet for a while, and assuring him that at Court (which was then at Farnham in Hampshire, on its way back to Windsor after Henry had inspected the fleet at Portsmouth) only 'the king and I' were as yet privy to the information.[28] This may be the first occurrence of what was to become his catchphrase. In the long list of charges lodged against him when he fell from grace in 1529, it was quoted against him, to insinuate that he regarded himself as the king's equal. But this was pure malice. The point of the phrase was to emphasise how close he was to the king, and it was a reminder to Wolsey and his readers and hearers not simply of how powerful he was, but also of how completely his power depended upon the royal will and pleasure. But these years seal Wolsey's emergence as chief minister in a political world with far more information circulating than ever before. It was the sheer volume of information that made it imperative for early modern kings to have chief ministers.

Preparations for war got under way in earnest in 1512. Parliament met twice that year, in February and again in November. The Parliament of early 1512 voted three 'fifteenths and tenths' to support the king's ambitions, two to be levied at once, and the third in autumn. The Parliament of autumn 1512 voted him a tax on a new basis, called a 'subsidy'. Assessed, like the 'fifteenth and tenth', on income from land, it was calculated on fresh valuations undertaken by county commissions. Its yield, some £160,000, was prodigious. Perhaps it was the fading memory of war that made Parliament so acquiescent in Henry's militaristic venture, or perhaps it was a genuine enthusiasm for reviving the good old days of Agincourt with the added incentive of fighting in a papal holy war. Either way, these parliamentary grants were at a level not seen since the fourteenth century, if then. The 'subsidy' would be the bedrock of direct taxation under the Tudors, and its yield held up remarkably well through Henry's reign, even though its real value and eventually its cash yield would be eroded respectively by inflation and corruption during the reigns of his children.

Henry crossed to Calais in June 1513, with a substantial force, certainly well over 20,000, including most of the able-bodied members of the English peerage. The young king was as much playing at war as fighting one, but it remained a serious business despite the luxurious accommodation and commissariat of the king and his nobles. The campaign took him further from England than he would ever go again, when he took time away from the front in September for a summit meeting with the Emperor Maximilian at Lille. An exhilarating cavalry engagement, the 'Battle of the Spurs', drove off a relieving force and delivered Thérouanne into Henry's hands in August, after which a powerful siege train brought down the walls of Tournai and induced it to surrender in September. Not since the 1420s had English arms gained ground in France. Such gains were far harder to achieve in an age of rapid technological advance in both artillery and fortification.

At much the same time, though, James IV of Scotland was crossing the Tweed with an army of about the same magnitude as Henry's, However, he was held up for a week besieging Norham Castle, which enabled Catherine of Aragon, who had been appointed Regent in Henry's absence, to gather an army adequate to the threat. Field command was entrusted to the Earl of Surrey, who had been left behind by Henry VIII against precisely this contingency. As Henry VII's lieutenant in the north through the 1490s, Surrey had earned the respect of the often fractious northern barons and gentry, and he was the perfect choice to lead them in battle. Having seen an English king go down in an all or nothing bid for victory at Bosworth, Surrey now saw a Scottish king fall in the same fashion, at Flodden Field, just a few miles south of the Tweed. A dozen Scottish earls fell with James that day, among more than 10,000 of their countrymen. Scottish losses outnumbered English at least ten to one. Flodden was a military disaster of colossal proportions. It ensured that England need not fear invasion from the north for at least a generation, and removed a significant constraint on Henry's decision-making.

Henry VIII thus ended 1513 on a high, with famous victories over England's two old enemies, and new acquisitions across the Channel. However, there was no clear strategy to follow through, and in 1514 the strategic context shifted dramatically. Pope Julius II had died in February 1513, and the new pope, Leo X, elected in March 1513, was far less militant than his aptly named predecessor. King Ferdinand, having secured Spanish Navarre, was now keen to seek an alliance with Louis XII in order to strengthen his dynastic position in Italy. And the Emperor likewise was pursuing a separate peace with France. So when Louis XII suddenly found himself a widower in January 1514, Henry had no hesitation in offering his seventeen-year-old sister, Mary, as a suitable bride for a man three times her age. England and France were once more at peace. If the peace was short-lived, the marriage was more so. Mary only came to Louis in October, and he died on New Year's Day 1515, giving rise to ribald speculation as to the cause of death.

The developments of 1513–15 set the pattern for the next 15 years, seeing the emergence of the triumvirate who would dominate politics under the king: Thomas Wolsey, and the Dukes of Norfolk and Suffolk. Wolsey rode to power by organising Henry's invasion of France, and his reward was first to be made Bishop of Lincoln, in February 1514, and then, later that year, Archbishop of York. Thomas Howard's victory at Flodden earned him promotion to his father's former title, as Duke of Norfolk, while his eldest son was made Earl of Surrey in his own right as he had once been. And Henry's boon companion Charles Brandon, who had been prominent in the Tournai campaign, was rather more surprisingly made Duke of Suffolk at the same time, perhaps as some sort of counterbalance. Suffolk then pulled off an unlikely coup by marrying the king's widowed sister, Mary, in Paris when he went to fetch her back to England after Louis XII's death. The older Henry would have had his head for that. But the young Henry was more forgiving, at least of friends.

London was incensed in December 1514 when a wealthy London merchant was found hanged in the 'Lollards' Tower', the ecclesiastical prison of the Bishop of London. The merchant, Richard Hunne, had been engaged for years in litigation with various London clerics over his refusal to hand over the 'mortuary' gift customarily paid to the parish priest after a burial – in this case, the burial of Hunne's infant son in March 1511. Hunne had been excommunicated in 1512, had countered with a charge of *praemunire* against his clerical foes in the Court of King's Bench in 1513, and was arrested on charges of heresy in October 1514. His death was interpreted by his foes as suicide, but to his friends and supporters it was evident that he had been murdered, and his case excited the sympathy of many Londoners. Two days after the discovery of his body, a coroner's jury concluded, on the basis of their inspection of the body and of their consideration of circumstantial testimony from a number of witnesses, that Hunne had been murdered by the chancellor of the diocese of London, Dr William Horsey, with the assistance of Charles Joseph, the 'summoner' of the London ecclesiastical court. The Bishop of London immediately sought Wolsey's intervention against what he saw as a malicious slander against his chancellor, requesting that Wolsey get the king to establish an impartial investigation.

From that time until this, controversy has persisted over whether Hunne's death was murder or suicide, with the division usually following partisan lines – Catholics, such as Thomas More, arguing for suicide and Protestants, such as John Foxe, for murder, though the most recent reconsideration, by G. W. Bernard, as thorough as it is impartial, tends to agree with More.[29] In 1515 the division was a matter of anticlericalism rather than doctrine. Hunne almost certainly was a Lollard, as his accusers maintained, but that was not why Londoners sympathised with him. They saw a substantial fellow citizen being harried and done to death by avaricious and merciless clergymen. The debate over his fate was scarcely finished when a full-scale confrontation broke out over the limits of ecclesiastical and royal jurisdiction, with the Abbot of Kidderminster insisting on the traditional legal privileges of the clergy, while a Franciscan theologian then in favour as a Court preacher, Dr Henry Standish (Warden of the London Greyfriars), insisted that the clergy were subject to royal authority in temporal matters. For this temerity Standish found himself summoned to appear before Convocation that autumn on a heresy charge, and the matter was only resolved at a Great Council that autumn, convened by the king in person at Baynards Castle in London, by which time Wolsey had received his cardinal's hat.[30] The solution was a fudge. Horsey was to remain under house arrest with Warham until the Hunne furore had subsided. Convocation dismissed the case against Standish. And the question of clerical immunity from temporal jurisdiction was laid quietly to rest. It would return to the public forum in the early 1530s. In retrospect, the political controversy provoked by the Hunne case may be a sign of growing instability in the 'medieval compromise', in the distinctive balance or tension between the spiritual and temporal power that, in different ways, had marked Western European society for half a millennium. No one at the time, however, could have dreamt that within twenty years that balance would be completely tipped over by the determination of Henry VIII to have his own way in a matrimonial dispute.

2

FROM REFORM TO
REFORMATION, 1515–1534

On Thursday 15 November 1515, a papal envoy on his way to London along the road from Canterbury was met at Blackheath by a welcoming party that included the Bishop of Lincoln and the Earl of Essex. The principal purpose of his mission was to confer upon Thomas Wolsey the rank and honour of a cardinal of the Roman Church, symbolised by the conferral of the red hat, the traditional mark of that dignity. According to a later story, the envoy was made to wait on landing in England until Wolsey had sent him a new suit of clothes of expensive silk, so that he would cut a more impressive figure. From Blackheath he was escorted along what is now the Old Kent Road to the city of London, where he was greeted in Cheapside by the Mayor and Aldermen. Continuing through the city, its streets lined by citizens resplendent in the liveries of their trade guilds, the procession wound its way to Westminster Abbey, where it was met by the Abbot of Westminster, flanked by the abbots of some of England's leading monasteries (including St Albans, Bury St Edmunds and Glastonbury). The red hat was solemnly paraded up the central aisle and placed on the high altar.

Three days later, on Sunday 18 November, another grand procession made the short trip to the abbey from Wolsey's palace, York Place (in what is now Whitehall), for a pontifical high Mass of the Holy Spirit celebrated by the Archbishop of Canterbury himself. Wolsey, who as Archbishop of York ranked slightly below Canterbury in the eyes of the world, was leaving no room for doubt that this honour lifted him above all the other churchmen of the kingdom. Parliament was in session that autumn, accompanied as usual by the Convocation of the clergy, so everybody who was anybody was to be found in London or Westminster. Wolsey's splendid train comprised dukes, earls, and barons, knights and gentlemen, bishops, abbots, and ecclesiastical dignitaries galore. Even the archbishops of Dublin and Armagh, rare visitors to Court, were there. A suitably brief sermon was given by the scholarly and fiercely ascetic Dr John Colet, the premier preacher at King Henry's Court, where each year he harrowed the royal conscience with a sermon on Good Friday. While duly flattering the new cardinal on the virtues by which he had merited his distinction, and characterising it as the earthly counterpart to the angelic seraphim, Colet admonished him mildly lest his greatness render him proud, reminding him of the humility of Jesus, who came not to be served, but to serve. After the Agnus Dei had been sung, Wolsey knelt before the high altar in prayer while the Archbishop of Canterbury formally placed the red hat on his head. Then a solemn *Te Deum* was sung and the new cardinal was led out of the abbey by the Dukes of Norfolk and Suffolk – the kingdom's premier duke, the Duke of Buckingham, was not among those present, an absence which seems fraught with significance in the light of his ultimate fate – where a procession formed up to escort him to Charing Cross. Oblivious to Colet's admonitions, Wolsey alone had his ceremonial cross carried before him, while all the attendant archbishops and bishops were denied this customary privilege. The celebrations concluded with a great feast in Wolsey's palace, which the king and queen themselves graced with their presence.[1] Wolsey had made his point: the prince of the Church had arrived. The next fifteen years would be dominated by his relentless ambition and tireless activity, and the five years after that by the consequences of his ultimate failure and fall.

THE COMING OF PEACE AND THE DREAM OF REFORM

The cardinal had surfed to power on the tide of war, but the years of his pomp would mostly be years of peace. A few months before Wolsey's apotheosis, the new King of France had pricked the bubble of Henry's vanity by inflicting a bloody defeat upon a Swiss army at Marignano (now Melegnano), about ten miles south-east of Milan. The grand alliance against France crumbled in the face of this debacle, which left France in control of northern Italy for almost a decade. Henry, his treasury exhausted by the demands of the previous few years, turned his attention to peace and to reform, endeavours in which his chief minister earnestly seconded him. Leo X rushed to Bologna to make a deal with Francis, and France was duly reconciled to the papacy. Henry's discomfiture at the defection of the papacy, however, was mitigated by the birth of a healthy child, his daughter Mary, in February 1516. Mary was not the son he wanted, but her arrival certainly kept his hopes and his marriage alive, at least for a few years.

Reform was in the air all over Europe in 1516, which saw the most fashionable intellectual of the age, Desiderius Erasmus of Rotterdam (as he liked to call himself), publish his vehement appeal for peace, an essay entitled *Dulce bellum inexpertis* ('war is sweet – when left untasted'). The enthusiasm for a fresh start that briefly gripped Europe added impetus to the peace talks, which culminated in the Treaty of London, initially signed between England and France on 2 October 1518, and later ratified by the other major powers. This bound its signatories to refrain from aggression and to come to the defence of any signatory that found itself under attack. England's contribution to this grand reconciliation was to withdraw from Tournai, which had been won and held at such great cost. The militant impulses of Christian princes were purportedly to be sublimated in a crusade against the Ottoman Empire, which was steadily advancing up the Balkans and across the Mediterranean.

Henry's dalliance with peace witnessed apparently serious attempts to embark on political and social reform at home. Two English friends of Erasmus were drafted onto the King's Council, a sharp young lawyer named Thomas More, and the lugubrious Court preacher, John Colet. In 1516 More had published a complex and entirely original work, *Utopia*, which combined a wry critique of contemporary European politics with a beguiling vision of a human society organised on the principles of reason even without the benefit of the Christian revelation. Its instant success (five editions in three years) launched its author onto the political stage, and the next dozen years saw More rise from being the tame intellectual of Henry's Court to becoming his Chancellor. There were perfunctory efforts to mitigate the extravagance of life at Henry's Court. The staffing of the Privy Chamber was taken in hand, and Wolsey seized the opportunity to edge out men he saw as threats to his own position and seek to replace them with more pliable figures. In the public domain, Star Chamber busied itself with bringing to heel disorderly and abusive gentry magnates from the shires. As John Guy has shown, Wolsey's systematic use of Star Chamber made it a magnet for the oppressed and the litigious, but it did have a lasting impact in bringing the English elite rather more, though not yet wholly, under the rule of law.[2]

Most dramatically, Wolsey issued a series of commissions under the Great Seal to investigate 'enclosures' – the practice by which the 'common land' of medieval England was being annexed and taken into private ownership by powerful landowners. Enclosure had been identified in *Utopia* as the premier social evil of the day, a glaring example of the subversion of the common good by naked self-interest. Land that had previously been open for humble freeholders or copyholders to use for grazing their beasts was privatised for large flocks of sheep owned by the wealthy few. Such proto-capitalist enterprise had its role in the long-term development of the English economy, but to those turfed off the commons, the loss and damage to their interests were all too obvious. Wolsey's commissions were empowered to identify unlawful enclosure and refer it to the king's courts at Westminster for remedy. Had they pursued this policy vigorously, Henry might have earned a reputation for justice and for protecting the weak against the strong. But the policy encroached upon the interests of the landed elites. Though everyone agreed in principle that enclosure was wrong, there was in practice always a good reason in one's own case, and reform ran out of steam in the face of special pleading and the risk of alienating landowners as a class. Commissions under the Great Seal, the executive instruments by which Wolsey sought to achieve most political objectives, were also problematic, because they were staffed largely by landowners who had to live with those whose interests they were challenging, and who were sometimes enclosers themselves.

At Court, Henry displayed his commitment to reform through aligning himself overtly with Christian humanism. Thomas More's *Utopia* was just one of a series of programmatic books published in the 1510s by a clutch of authors, among whom the most influential was the Dutch scholar Erasmus. Erasmus's satirical *tour de force*, *In Praise of Folly*, had blazed the trail in 1511, and his handbook of moralistic political advice to rulers, *The Education of a Christian Prince*, had followed in 1515. His many educational publications and his editions of ancient classical and Christian texts (such as the monumental complete works of St Jerome, which appeared in 1516) also gave voice to his aspirations for reform in Church and society, and authors such as Rodolphus Agricola, Juan Luis Vives and Polydore Vergil were lesser lights in an enterprise that embraced much of Europe, at least among the educated elites.

The most significant humanist work of that decade was arguably Erasmus's ground-breaking edition of the New Testament in 1516, in which he published the Greek text for the first time, alongside a new

Winchester Cathedral Round Table
This medieval artefact, which still hangs in the Great Hall that is all that remains of
Winchester Castle, was repainted in the reign of Henry VIII to give it a distinctively
Tudor aspect, with the rose at its centre and the segments in the alternating green
and white of Tudor livery. The king at the head of the table may perhaps be a rather
unconvincing depiction of Henry himself.

Latin rendering of his own, together with extensive annotations. The
study of Greek was a flagship issue for 'humanist' scholars, and Erasmus's
New Testament added impetus to its cause, which was not without its
opponents among some more hidebound sections of the contemporary
academic establishment. His second, improved edition, printed in 1519,
proved more controversial than the first, largely because the emergence of
a very different reforming figure, Martin Luther, was by then fomenting
the suspicion that fashionable scholarship was a hothouse for heresy. At
Henry's Court, however, the Erasmian movement was in high favour.
When in 1519 a hapless theologian preached against Erasmus's New
Testament in the king's presence, Henry rather cruelly unleashed Thomas
More against him in debate.[3] Likewise, when the Court neared Oxford
on its summer tour that year, the king intervened robustly in a typically
academic dogfight that had broken out there between advocates of Greek

scholarship and some diehard opponents who had styled themselves 'Trojans'. Henry liked to present himself as an engaged patron of the latest scholarship. He built up the first royal library worthy of the name, and enjoyed scholarly and theological discussions – from time to time.[4] (Hunting was always a more compelling pursuit.) The role of printed books in fostering a Court climate favourable to reform and scholarship must not be underestimated. Without print, men such as Erasmus could never have been what they were – international celebrities. Royal and princely Courts had long had a place for learned men, to lend a certain tone and lustre on occasion. But now the praise which a writer such as Erasmus could bestow upon a king such as Henry in the dedication to a book such as his *Paraphrase on the Gospel of Luke* (Basel, 1523) could be read within a year, through the wonder of technology, anywhere from Oxford to Olomouc or from Stockholm to Seville.

HENRY VIII AND LUTHER

The kingdom of England's slow awakening to the challenge posed by Martin Luther in 1517 shows how the advent of print was beginning to change society. Henry VIII's famous decision to enter the literary lists against the notorious friar from Wittenberg had a bundle of motives, chief of which was to earn himself a religious adjunct to his royal title, to put him on a par with the Holy Roman Emperor (of, essentially, Germany), the Catholic King (of Spain), and the Most Christian King (of France). Henry's *Assertion of the Seven Sacraments* duly won him the papal soubriquet 'Defender of the Faith'. But far more interesting is the fact that a king had decided to publish a book in print. A few kings had written or translated books, notably Alfonso el Sabio of Castile, but Henry was the first to have one printed. Not that he started a fashion: few reigning kings have followed his example. But the decision shows awareness of the new power in the world. Print had made Luther what he was, so with print he had to be withstood. Henry's contribution to the debate was of no great originality, but it was frequently reprinted, and it certainly heartened and stiffened Catholic opposition to Luther.

When Luther reopened their debate in 1525, Henry wrote against him once more. On this second occasion, his pamphlet was published not only in Latin but in English as well. This marked an important shift. Evidence had come to light of the spread of Luther's ideas in England. At Cambridge, a rising scholar named Robert Barnes, a member of the same religious order as Luther, was investigated for heresy after a sermon he preached on Christmas Eve 1525. The following February he was compelled to do public penance for his errors at Paul's Cross.[5] Still more worryingly, by 1526 William Tyndale had embarked on his epoch-making translation of the New Testament. While Henry's second reply to Luther was in the press that autumn, copies of Tyndale's work began to trickle into London. Issuing an English translation of Henry's reply was an instant response to this new situation, as the king's preface, written specially for the English version, makes clear.[6] Some copies of Tyndale's work were confiscated and burned, but despite these first steps towards a system of censorship, smuggled copies of the English New Testament and of other Protestant pamphlets printed abroad would find their way across the Channel in increasing numbers over the next ten years.

WAR WITH FRANCE

The lull that Western Europe enjoyed in the late 1510s is best understood as a phoney peace. Its fundamental insincerity was evident in its most spectacular moment, the summit meeting known to history as the 'Field of Cloth of Gold'. In summer 1520 the Courts of Francis I and Henry VIII were established in two camps at the edge of the Calais Pale, the English Crown's last foothold in France. Each king attended with his queen and his chief councillors, peers and courtiers, each side over 5,000 strong. They were accommodated in splendid tents, marquees or even prefabricated buildings, gorgeously decorated.[7] Yet for all the high-flown talk of peace, the realities of European politics remained stubbornly familiar. Dynastic dynamics impelled a succession of conflicts in which monarchs accountable only to God sought to vindicate an endless list of clashing hereditary claims on each other's territories. The most abiding symbol of this folly was the inclusion in the English royal title of the empty boast 'King of France' – a claim not actually abandoned until France had ceased to be a monarchy. This was why even as Henry was posing with Francis I at the Field of Cloth of Gold, he was secretly negotiating a fresh alliance against France with Charles V. There is little military significance in the ensuing English campaigns on French soil in 1522 and 1523. A substantial force crossed the Channel in 1523, but there was no realistic strategy and it marched out from Calais too late in the year to achieve anything. Its most significant impact was to persuade the English people that, after ten years, it was no longer worth paying for Henry's bellicose fantasies. The Parliament that met through spring and summer 1523 was induced to finance this last hurrah only with the utmost difficulty. MPs were already aware that the people had been taxed to the limit: Henry had probably extracted more resources from his kingdom over that decade than any previous ruler in a comparable period, with literally nothing to show for it.

So when the capture of the King of France at the disastrous Battle of Pavia in February 1525 offered a genuine opportunity for a strategically decisive intervention across the Channel, Henry and Wolsey did not even consider approaching Parliament for money. Instead, they sought donations, an 'amicable grant' or 'benevolence' by which Henry's subjects could show how much they loved him. This turned out to be not quite as much as hoped. The royal commissioners appointed to solicit donations looked rather like tax collectors, and the donations they solicited were personally tailored to the donors on the basis of the data gathered for tax purposes in 1523. In short, the 'amicable grant' walked like a tax and talked like a tax. A mutiny resulted, as taxpayers protested across the counties of southern, eastern and central England.[8] For once, their protest was not suppressed by their social superiors. At the top of regional society, magnates such as the Earl of Oxford wrote urgently to the king, warning him that they could not hope to pacify this groundswell of resistance and reporting that it was based on lucidly formulated fears that it would set a precedent for unparliamentary taxation that would undermine English property rights forever. Parliament, whose constitutional role was to represent the grievances of the people to a merciful sovereign, depended for its existence on its power to grant taxation. If the king were no longer to need it to raise extraordinary revenue, its future would be bleak. This strong sense of constitutional principle was expressed even at relatively humble levels of society, which shows that the political myth of Parliament as a body representing the entire nation was widely shared, even if that body itself was manned only by members of the elites chosen by narrow electorates. It is evident that the concerns of the demonstrators were completely shared by the gentry and the peerage, who had the most to lose from the prospect of a monarch who could tax at will. What Henry was facing in 1525 was nothing less than a veto from his governing class, voiced by everyone from the Duke of Norfolk and the Archbishop of Canterbury downwards. Fortunately for the king, the scarlet eminence of Cardinal Wolsey made him the ideal lightning rod for the accumulated political tension, and he gracefully took the blame. The grant was off, so too was the invasion, and Henry had to watch his one real chance to recover serious portions of his French 'inheritance' slip away.

War with France and controversy with Luther dominated the early 1520s, but a new concern preoccupied the king in the second half of the decade. In the absence of a legitimate son and heir, the question of the succession was a genuine worry. Henry's own anxiety about it was palpable. In 1521, his baseless fears that the Duke of Buckingham was ruminating on his own prospects for the throne led to that peer's abrupt trial and execution.[9] The 'evidence' against him is scarcely worth discussing. What the episode reveals is that the ascendancy over the nobility achieved by Henry VII had become, if anything, still more complete under his son. Not only was he able to bring down the nation's most powerful magnate, he was also able to elicit this verdict from a jury of peers led by the nation's next most powerful magnate, the Duke of Norfolk, who was in tears as he pronounced sentence. One could not imagine a more vivid demonstration of royal dominance. By this time, too, Henry's youthful passion for his wife had discernibly cooled. His affair with one of the queen's maids of honour, Elizabeth Blount, during Catherine's last recorded pregnancy in 1518, bore fruit the following year in an illegitimate son, Henry Fitzroy, a poignant contrast to the loss of Catherine's child. Another affair, with Mary Carey (the elder sister of Anne Boleyn), followed in the early 1520s, by which time it was clear that Catherine's childbearing years were over. There is every chance that Mary's daughter Catherine, born around that time, was also the king's, and there are even questions over her son, Henry Carey, born in 1526.[10] These proofs of Henry's fertility outside marriage may have stirred his first doubts about his marriage to Catherine.

Henry's grand passion for Mary's sister, Anne, which perhaps began as early as 1526, crystallised those doubts. His decision to disencumber himself of his first wife was taken in spring 1527, when he authorised Cardinal Wolsey to enquire into the lawfulness of his marriage to Catherine in the light of the biblical prohibitions on marrying a brother's wife (Lev. 18:16 and 20:21). Cardinal Wolsey convened a select group of canon lawyers and theologians in May to consider the king's case, and on 22 June Henry told Catherine that they had been living in the gravest sin for 19 years and that they would never again sleep together.

Over the next few years, Henry's conscience sank its teeth into these biblical texts, in particular Leviticus 20:21, which foretold that if a man married his brother's wife, they would be childless. His conscience developed a death-grip when he was assured by England's only expert in Hebrew, Robert Wakefield, that the true meaning of the Hebrew text was that such a couple would have no male heirs. The king was therefore able to see Catherine's tragic history of miscarriage and infant mortality as the inexorable working of divine providence in chastisement of their incestuous relationship.[11] Catherine of Aragon was, if anything, even more pious and conscientious than her husband. If the biblical texts had really been as straightforward as Henry imagined, she might have felt compelled to take his strictures to heart. But while Leviticus left no room for doubt about sexual relations with a brother's wife, another book of the Bible indicated flexibility in the case of a brother's widow. Deuteronomy 25:5 actually commanded a man, under certain circumstances, to marry his brother's widow if that brother had died childless. For Catherine's spiritual and legal counsel, such as Bishop John Fisher of Rochester, that instruction, even though it was no longer binding on Christians (because Christian theologians defined it as part of what they called the 'judicial' law of the Old Testament, rather than of the perpetually binding 'moral' or natural law), that instruction showed that Leviticus forbade only marriage to a brother's wife – not marriage to a brother's widow. God, Catherine's supporters argued, could not have positively commanded his chosen people with one law to do something that he had absolutely forbidden them with another. Marriage to a brother's widow could not therefore be absolutely contrary to natural and moral law, and was therefore permissible through a papal dispensation.

It should all have been plain sailing. Among the manifold responsibilities of the late medieval papacy, one was resolving the matrimonial embarrassments of European royalty. The complexities of medieval canon law ensured that, in the marriages of the mighty, there were many obstacles to clear away before they could take place, and many opportunities, should need arise, to discover later that they should be annulled. Since late medieval Christianity still upheld the uncompromising exclusion of divorce and remarriage handed down from its founder, annulment offered the only escape from an unsatisfactory marriage for those powerful enough to secure it.[12] The popes were usually happy to accept the get-outs offered by the lawyers, and discarded queens were usually pragmatic enough to accept their fate.

In Henry's case, his enthusiastic endorsement of papal authority against Luther amid the crisis of the Reformation enhanced his innate sense of entitlement. The Defender of the Faith expected the gratitude of the Supreme Pontiff. Unfortunately, the kaleidoscope of European politics had spun an unfavourable pattern. The Emperor Charles V had gone on from his victory over France at Pavia in 1525 to dominate Italy, and papal hostility to his dominance had led to the imperial assault, capture and sack of Rome itself on 6 May 1527. Thus, at the very moment Henry was giving Wolsey his momentous instructions, his wife's nephew was taking virtual control of the only institution that could give the king what he wanted. It will never be certain that, under other circumstances, Henry's annulment would have wound its way through the curia to the consummation he so devoutly wished for. What is certain is that there was no way it would happen with the papacy under the imperial thumb. For the next two years, though, every resource of English power was devoted to this goal. Wolsey manoeuvred to encourage French military intervention in Italy with a view to breaking the imperial grip, and Henry contemplated an invasion of Charles V's territories in the Netherlands. He was deterred only by London's merchants, who feared the impact on the wool trade of a conflict that would cut them off from Antwerp, their chief market and the hub of north-west European finance.

Success seemed within Henry's grasp when his emissaries bullied Pope Clement VII into sending a papal legate, the anglophile Cardinal Lorenzo Campeggio, to preside with Wolsey over a formal hearing of the case in London in 1529. The pope had empowered Campeggio to give the king what he wanted, but his secret instructions were more nuanced. The outcome of the hearing, should it take place, would depend on political circumstances. There was no rush, and Campeggio was to seek some kind of compromise with the queen – urging her to seek retirement in a nunnery and sorting the mess out with unprecedented papal dispensations. Catherine, however, was having none of it. A new French invasion of Italy in 1529 gave the king hope, and the hearing finally opened in June. But the proceedings were soon bogged down in legal minutiae and theological disputations, and when rumours arrived of the defeat of the French at Landriano, Campeggio was swift to act on his secret instructions and wind things up. Catherine gave him the pretext he needed by making a formal appeal to the pope, and Henry was faced with one of the most infuriating disappointments of his life as Campeggio solemnly revoked the case to Rome.

That was the end for Cardinal Wolsey. Henry spent August and September taking out his frustrations on the animal kingdom in some late summer hunting, before ensconcing himself in Windsor Castle at Michaelmas to arrange for life after Wolsey. The first step was to summon Parliament. Wolsey was still going through the motions of governing, but in October he was charged with the ancient and somewhat obscure

– but nonetheless potent – offence of *praemunire*. Within a few weeks he had resigned as Lord Chancellor, surrendered all he owned into the hands of the king, and accepted his conviction, humbly begging pardon for offences which, however absurd, it would have been suicidal folly to deny. He felt fortunate to be allowed to retain the archbishopric of York, to which he duly retreated in public disgrace. King Henry came up to London for the opening of Parliament on 3 November. Proceedings began with a spasm of anticlerical outbursts sparked off by the cardinal's fall, and went on with a legislative assault on the privileges of the clergy that would, over the ensuing seven years, permanently diminish the significance of the Church as an institution in the English polity.

THE 'REFORMATION PARLIAMENT'

The fall of Wolsey in autumn 1529 promised a reshuffle of patronage and officeholding after fifteen years in which he had dominated both. The death in 1528 of Henry's foremost courtier, Sir William Compton, who had been the head of the Privy Chamber until 1526, also helped open up the patronage market. Around Henry himself, the next few years saw England's dukes, Norfolk and Suffolk, assume brief political ascendancy. Norfolk was uncle to Anne Boleyn, while Suffolk was husband to the king's younger sister, Mary Tudor (still generally known as the 'French Queen' owing to her brief teenage marriage with the aging Louis XII of France). However, these two caricatures of military aristocracy – they both had experience of command in the field, but one was a comic-book conservative, the other a more ordinary buffoon – were unequal to the complexities of Henry's quest for his annulment.

With Wolsey gone, Henry needed a new Chancellor. It was symbolic that he chose a layman. The chancery had been in the hands of bishops for all but a few years since 1400, and no one alive could remember a lay Chancellor. The appointment was in some ways a harbinger of the surge of parliamentary anticlericalism. However, the layman was carefully chosen. It was Sir Thomas More, already Chancellor of the Duchy of Lancaster, a layman certainly, and one who was quite ready to lambast or lampoon the excesses or failings of the clergy.[13] Yet he had also been a loyal lieutenant of the king in his labours against Luther since 1521, and had himself, at the request of England's bishops, written his lively *Dialogue concerning Heresies* in an attempt to counter the influence of Luther and Tyndale on English readers.[14] Nobody could impugn More's orthodoxy, and while Henry wanted to put pressure on the clergy in order to extort their support for his divorce, he did not wish to alienate the first estate. Although he was enraged at the way the pope had treated him, and allowed blowhards such as Norfolk and Suffolk to recall that it was 'merry England' when it was not cluttered with cardinals, there was still no imaginable exit strategy that did not involve some level of papal collaboration.

Blaming Wolsey for the fiasco of the divorce tribunal, though, did not bring Henry any closer to his goal. It did not help him that his policy was far from popular with his subjects. In a monarchy such as Tudor England, of course, popularity was not as potent a consideration as in a modern consumer democracy. There was little that 'the people' could do about things they collectively disliked. But unpopularity did not help, and people liked Catherine of Aragon. Henry had sought to keep his quest for a divorce secret at the start, anxious about the public reaction. But news inevitably leaked out, and by 1530 it was common knowledge that, however the king might rationalise things in terms of divine law and the national interest, the driving force of his policy was his desire for Anne Boleyn. Women, in particular, sympathised with Catherine in her capacity as wronged wife. Moreover, even among the ranks of the king's councillors, Catherine had her sympathisers. Her leading adviser, Bishop Fisher of Rochester, had been a councillor back at the start of the reign, though it was long since Henry had sought his views on anything except perhaps Luther. But Cuthbert Tunstall (Master of the Rolls and Bishop of London) also took the queen's side, and Thomas More, in his subtle way, kept a meaningful silence. The king had pressed him for an opinion, but More had dodged the issue. His unexpected elevation to the Chancellorship was a crude attempt to manhandle him into line behind the king. Henry was personally hurt by the fact that his kingdom's three foremost scholars did not see the case the way he did. He would have given anything to have their favourable opinion, and he waited a very long time to get it. Fisher and More never fell into line, and were to pay the price with their heads. But Tunstall eventually capitulated in 1534, when the intimidation became too much.

Henry's breach with Catherine gave rise to something like a popular movement of disquiet and discontent, an effect only previously seen in English history in reaction to excessive fiscal demands. It was also, revealingly, reflected in print. The discontent crystallised around the strange persona of a young nun of Canterbury, Elizabeth Barton, known as the 'Holy Maid of Kent', who gained a reputation in the later 1520s as a visionary favoured by God with spiritual insight. The public career of this rural domestic servant had begun with experiences of seizures that today might be classified as epilepsy, in the midst of which she spoke of visions and made pronouncements on a range of religious topics, including pilgrimage and the intercession of saints, which were then being called into question. In accordance with her own predictions, her seizures were cured after visits to the nearby chapel of Our Lady at Court-at-Street (a wayside chapel on the old Roman road from Aldington, her home village, to the Kent coast). On the strength of this, she became a nun at St Sepulchre's convent in Canterbury, with the learned Edward Bocking, a senior monk in the cathedral priory, as her confessor. From the outset Elizabeth had attracted the attention of influential clergymen, starting with Richard Master, the Oxford MA who was her vicar at Aldington. The venerable Archbishop of Canterbury himself, William Warham, took a personal interest in her case, and often discussed it with his episcopal neighbour, John Fisher.[15]

What made Barton a national and not merely a local figure was that her early visions and miraculous cure were reported in a pamphlet, *A Marvelous Work of late done in Court of Street in Kent*, probably printed in 1527. She was famous enough for William Tyndale, who had been out of the country for five years, to disparage her in his *Obedience of a Christian Man* (1528). Her denunciations of heresy and her affirmations of traditional Catholic doctrines and practices are sufficient to explain his hostility. But she did not stop there. By 1530, she was venturing comments on the king's matrimonial plans and on the pressure his regime was putting on the institutional Church. Nor was her audience confined to credulous rustics. Learned clergymen and prominent members of the gentry and nobility were among those who sought her guidance and heeded her predictions. She had audiences with Warham, Wolsey, and even the king himself. We cannot know what she told him. But her public message was one of warning: against the rise of heresy, against infringements of the liberties of the Church, and against putting asunder what God had joined together in matrimony. It is unlikely that she changed her tune for the king. Most probably he tried to persuade her to lend her renown for sanctity and divine favour to his agenda. If so, he failed.

Henry's meeting with the Holy Maid of Kent came at a moment when, having cast aside Wolsey, he had decided to take government in hand himself and rule with the advice of a council. Even in Wolsey's pomp, of course, the king had his council: no respectable monarch could be without one. But through the 1520s it had mostly been an echo chamber for Wolsey. When the imperial ambassador's despatches fell by chance into the cardinal's hands in 1525, and it transpired that they offered a frank account of Wolsey's political dominance, he was summoned before an imposing collection of royal councillors – who remained silent but censorious as Wolsey himself gave him a thorough bawling out for his temerity. Even as he reported this to Henry's ambassador at Charles V's Court, Wolsey could not help letting the truth slip out in his anxiety to put the record straight. Listing the names of various prominent Privy Councillors present for another discussion the next day, he described them as having 'heard my conference the day before with the said ambassador'.[16] His fellow councillors were not actors but audience. There is a widespread belief among historians that the 'Privy Council' was a creation of the 1530s, appearing in practice in 1536 and receiving formal institutional establishment in 1540. However, it was certainly older than that, at least in name. Wolsey referred to it in 1525, and Sir Robert Wingfield (named as a member of it in Wolsey's letter), told Thomas Cromwell in 1535 that he (Wingfield) had been a councillor of the king for over twenty years, and had been sworn in as a Privy Councillor over fourteen years ago.[17] There was evidently a real distinction between these two levels of conciliar status if they involved separate oaths. Privy Council status entailed a genuine advisory role, while that of King's Councillor was largely honorific (it was granted to all ambassadors).

After Wolsey's fall, then, Henry intended to rule in person, not through a proxy, and he symbolised by this by taking up residence in the palace that the cardinal had turned into the virtual seat of government: York Place, later known as Whitehall. From there he kept a close eye on proceedings in the Parliament of autumn 1529. He was there again in May 1530 for something to which he still attached the highest priority, the struggle against heresy. A committee of learned clergymen met to discuss the spread of Lutheran books, with Henry presiding in person at least some of the time. He was clearly the driving force of this initiative. The outcome was a proclamation printed in June. There were further personal interventions that year. Also in June, Henry convened a Great Council at Windsor to gather signatures for a letter imploring Pope Clement VII to grant the king his annulment. Another council was convened at Hampton Court when news came that the Sorbonne had backed his case. The Faculty of Theology at the University of Paris (known for short as the Sorbonne) was widely viewed as the most authoritative body of theologians in Christendom, so Henry hoped that its favourable judgement would sway some of the more dubious of his subjects. The possibility was also mooted that his divorce might be secured by unilateral action in England. But the feeling of the meeting was against this radical solution, and the king was advised that a decision was needed from Rome. A group of lawyers and theologians was gathered at Hampton Court in October to discuss whether Parliament could empower the Archbishop of Canterbury to hear the case in England.[18] Asking the pope nicely had got the king nowhere, so he was now considering more direct options. But the first and second estates of the realm were not prepared as yet to defy the authority of the universal Church. Public opinion, or at any rate elite opinion, had to be shifted.

Popularity mattered enough to the king to ensure that the divorce project led to the first effort by an English regime to reshape public opinion, an endeavour in which print naturally played a prominent part. After Henry's matrimonial case had been revoked to Rome in summer 1529, it was not immediately obvious how to maintain momentum. Pope Clement VII was in no hurry. One idea, later credited to Thomas Cranmer, was to solicit scholarly opinion in the king's favour from universities across Europe and thus build an intellectual consensus in his favour. Emissaries were despatched abroad for this purpose from late 1529 onwards. Dr Richard Croke, who had entered the king's service as tutor to his illegitimate son in 1526, was rescued from that purgatorial task and sent to Italy to canvass opinions and to ransack libraries for ancient Christian writings on Leviticus and Deuteronomy.

Politics in 1530 had been very busy, but there was little to show for it beyond a folder of somewhat pricey legal and theological opinions. Parliament reconvened in January 1531, amid rumours that it would legislate for a local solution to the divorce, but that policy was not yet ready to launch. However, with many among the clergy deeply opposed to the divorce and some even preaching openly against it, a move was made to bring them into line. The tool selected was the ancient statute of *praemunire*, which had brought Wolsey down in 1529 and had also been used in 1530 against a handful of high-profile targets, notably Bishop Fisher of Rochester, who had opposed Parliament's anticlerical laws. Now, in January 1531, the representative institution of the Church of England, Convocation, was presented with a charge of *praemunire* directed against the entire personnel of the Church, on the grounds that they had collaborated with Wolsey in his unlawful exercise of authority as a papal legate. The threat was effective: *praemunire* was the sort of law against which it was virtually impossible to make a defence. Many years later, Stephen Gardiner ironically recalled his bafflement at the way the statute had been used against Wolsey, who was charged with treason for having been made a cardinal and a legate – which had been done at the king's express request.[19] The penalties of *praemunire* included confiscation of all property and imprisonment at the king's pleasure. Convocation crumbled, crawled and coughed up. Their petition for the king's pardon was accepted at the price of a tax of £100,000 – which was close to the value of a single 'subsidy', the standard unit in which Parliament voted national taxes to the king. This bitter cup, however, was to wash down a still more bitter pill. The king's agents demanded that the text of this grant should include the astonishing acknowledgement of the king as the 'protector and supreme head' of the Church of England. This was the first sighting of the doctrine of the 'royal supremacy'. In the event, the king did not quite get it all his own way. The title as finally agreed acknowledged him as the 'singular protector, the unique and supreme lord, and even, as far as the law of God allows, the supreme head'. That little caveat 'as far as the law of God allows' expressed a distance as ill-defined as the title itself, but assuaged many consciences. Even so, a group of middle-ranking churchmen, distinguished by their opposition to the divorce and their fervent hostility to Protestantism, went so far as to sign a secret protest against the new title. The whole episode boded ill for the traditional 'liberties' of the Church of England.

According to G. R. Elton, royal policy between the fall of Wolsey and the rise of Thomas Cromwell was mere drift. An alternative view, advanced by J. J. Scarisbrick and more recently by G. W. Bernard, was that from 1530 Henry's heart was set on a break with Rome and an English resolution to his matrimonial problem.[20] Both interpretations find some support in the evidence. Antipapal sentiments were in the air at Court from 1530, and there was a ratcheting up of pressure on the clergy. Yet the criss-crossing of Europe by royal emissaries and the endless round of inconclusive councils and committees are an impressive record of activity without achievement. It was plain from the start that the desired outcome to Henry's case was most likely to result from a process held in England – hence the Blackfriars tribunal in 1529, and the concern thereafter to prevent the case from being heard at Rome, where imperial influence would swing things in favour of the emperor's aunt. Yet the challenge was to imagine how a local solution could be achieved once the pope had formally revoked the case to Rome.

The shift from vague hopes to an active policy looks as though it coincided with the emergence of Cromwell as Henry's most trusted councillor. The year 1531 saw numerous meetings of an expanded royal council at which conflicting views were expressed and from which nothing new materialised. The despatch of a conciliar delegation in summer to bully Catherine into accepting that the case should be heard in England looks like nothing more than wishful thinking. All it achieved was a final breach in relations between king and queen. They had not shared a bed since 1527, but had mostly lived together for the sake of appearances. Now Henry, enraged by her obstinacy, abandoned her at Windsor in July and went off with Anne Boleyn. He was never to see Catherine again.

The change of gear came in autumn 1531, and was related to the fortunes of the two men then vying for the role of Wolsey's political heir. They were the learned clergyman Stephen Gardiner, the strong favourite in the race, and Thomas Cromwell, a late starter. Gardiner had followed a classic path: legal studies at Cambridge, headship of his college (Trinity Hall), and promotion through Wolsey's household. He had been involved in the divorce case from the start and had talked the pope into authorising the tribunal held in London in 1529. By that time, he had become the king's Principal Secretary, and was perfectly placed to leave his former master to his fate and flourish as the king's man from October that year. With his appointment as Bishop of Winchester in September 1531, his triumph seemed assured. Cromwell was a very different proposition, with little by way of formal education. A hard-headed man of business, he had got something of the common law by practice, and joined Wolsey's household in the 1520s, becoming his chief agent in all matters to do with estates and properties, a role that left him almost as widely hated as the cardinal. His decision to do what he could for Wolsey when the ship went down, however, earned him some respect, and his practical talents and command of the cardinal's affairs made him useful to the king and his courtiers in the scramble for the spoils. By the end of 1530 this usefulness had brought him onto the King's Council, which gave him value to those in need of a friend at Court. He also secured a seat in Parliament. Cromwell's rise, however, was thus far steady rather than spectacular.

What changed the situation was that, shortly after his elevation to Winchester, Gardiner was sent on a diplomatic mission to the French Court. While he was away, Cromwell's star rose rapidly. Over autumn and winter he became one of the king's real advisers, and this coincides with the beginnings of more purposeful activity in January 1532 at new sessions of Convocation and Parliament. At the centre of events was a parliamentary document known as the 'Supplication against the Ordinaries', an extensive statement of the grievances (real or purported) of the common people of England against their bishops. This paper, the product of endless parliamentary drafting apparently supervised by Cromwell, assaulted the theory and practice of ecclesiastical jurisdiction over a wide front, ranging from the allegedly excessive level of probate fees to the conduct of heresy investigations. The supplication was finally presented to the king in mid-March, as the first session of Parliament was nearing its end.

Its purpose became apparent when Parliament and Convocation reconvened in mid-April. The supplication was presented to Convocation by Archbishop Warham, and the task of drafting the clergy's response fell to Gardiner, just back from France in early March 1532 and presumably unaware of the new currents at Court which had given rise to this astonishing text. Expert canon lawyer that he was, Gardiner drew up a robust exposition of the divine right of ecclesiastical authority and of its complete autonomy from royal power. This brought down the king's wrath upon him, and he was obliged to apologise in short order, though he compounded his offence by citing Henry VIII's *Assertion of the Seven Sacraments* in his own defence. Gardiner's false move probably cost him his chance of succeeding to Wolsey's mantle. He had shown that he was not entirely aligned with the king's thinking, and although his sheer capacity rendered him all but indispensable, Henry would never entirely trust him again.[21]

Meanwhile, Henry's delegates had gone back to Convocation with the demand that in future all its proposed legislation should be, like that of Parliament, subject to royal assent or veto. This meant the abandonment of that fundamental liberty of the Church which been guaranteed for 300 years by the first clause of Magna Carta, though of course the verbal promise to uphold the liberties of the Church remained part of the coronation oath. The changes of the 1530s, however, were to void that clause of any meaning. When Thomas More resigned the Chancellorship in May 1532, this was certainly the reason he did so. The Great Seal, however, remained in lay hands, those of Thomas Audley, another alumnus of the cardinal's household, who would in due course be appointed Chancellor in January 1533.

The 1532 Parliament was frenetic. The first session passed a raft of legislation, starting with a massive curtailment of the traditional 'benefit of clergy', and including several other restrictions on the customary 'liberties' of the Church. A surprising proportion of its legislation was promoted by the Crown, rather than, as was more usual, by members of the House of Commons seeking to remedy problems or grievances. After its Easter break, Parliament reconvened to enact two further statutes. One guaranteed a wide-ranging but carefully defined royal pardon to the clergy (23 Henry VIII c. 19). The other was the Act in Conditional Restraint of Annates (23 Henry VIII c. 20) – a threat to cut off the payment of ecclesiastical taxation to the pope.[22] Newly appointed bishops, and some other senior figures in the Church, were obliged to pay the pope 'annates', a levy equivalent to the first year's net revenue of their office. Henry was now empowered, after the expiry of a year, to terminate such payments if the pope had not persuaded him otherwise. The persuasion that was needed, of course, was the annulment of Henry's marriage. Together, the 'submission of the clergy' and the act against annates posed a profound challenge to the structure and authority of the Church, denying those rights to autonomous legislation and taxation which had made it, in the later Middle Ages, in effect a sovereign body. The papacy still had a year in which to give the king what he wanted and set about some policy of détente. In the midst of all this, on 14 April 1532, Thomas Cromwell received his first significant and remunerative Crown office, as Master of the King's Jewels. The coincidence of this with the sudden recall of Parliament that threw down a direct challenge to papal authority is a clear indication that there was a new mind at the heart of the king's counsels.

The submission of the clergy heralded a publicity campaign designed to rub in the humiliation of the first estate. Once more, Cromwell's hand is to be detected at work. Until this time, little had been done to represent the king's position in print other than to publish the theological and legal opinions elicited from foreign universities. First printed as a proclamation late in 1530, these had been read out to Parliament in January 1531. Subsequently they were supplemented with a scholarly presentation of the case for the king's divorce in book form, the *Gravissimae Censurae* ('very weighty opinions') of April 1531, which was issued in English in November as *The Determinations of the Universities*. But 1532 saw a change in target and tone, most vividly expressed in *A Treatise concerning the Division between the Spiritualty and the Temporalty*. This was the work of a lawyer, Christopher St German, who had made his name in the late 1520s by writing a handbook to English common law. His anticlerical predilections were useful to Henry's regime, and he penned a series of pamphlets against clerical privilege, of which the *Division* was the most successful. Printed five times between 1532 and 1537, it drew him into a bitter controversy with Thomas More. From 1532 to 1535, St German was in effect the propaganda officer for the Henrician regime in its guerrilla war against the English clergy. But his was not the only pen in the king's service, just the most prolific.

The most significant aspect of St German's output was that it was couched in English. It was designed for a literate but not learned readership. It would be too much to see it as aiming to shape 'public opinion' in the modern sense. In the conditions of the early sixteenth century, 'public opinion' was not a thing: information did not circulate far and fast enough for it to exist. But his campaign certainly aimed at shaping parliamentary and elite opinion. If the increasingly anticlerical and antipapal legislation was to get through Parliament in what was still a profoundly Catholic society, then the moral authority of the clergy had to be discredited. Opinion also had to be won round to the divorce, and that received further attention in a lively little dialogue setting out the case in a nutshell, *A Glasse of the Truthe* ('glass' in the sense of looking glass rather than drinking vessel). The *Glasse* spelled out not only the agony of conscience suffered by a king trapped through clerical malice in an incestuous marital bond but also the deadly peril faced by the kingdom should Henry be able to leave only a female heir to inherit his throne.

Any English resolution to Henry's matrimonial problem would always depend on the Archbishop of Canterbury. But the aged William Warham, archbishop since 1504, was a man whose readiness to serve his king was tempered by a reluctance to defy canon law and papal authority as well as by a lifelong devotion to his martyred predecessor, Thomas Becket, who had died rather than sacrifice the interests of the Church to those of the king. Warham's obvious scruples about Henry's policy were aggravated by contacts with two of the queen's most zealous supporters: John Fisher, Bishop of Rochester, whose London residence in Lambeth was just along the river from Lambeth Palace; and the Holy Maid of Kent, whose nunnery was in his episcopal see at Canterbury. The archbishop had shown signs of discontent in the Parliament of 1532, speaking out against encroachments on ecclesiastical authority on 15 March. His opposition, however, soon evaporated, his spirit broken by the familiar threat of *praemunire*. Two months after his outburst in the Lords he had led the bishops in subscribing to the submission that the king demanded of them. Nevertheless, it would have been futile to expect this broken man to preside over the sort of short, sharp hearing that Henry needed to solve his problem.[23]

It was Warham's death on 22 August 1532 that cleared the way. A summons was sent to Thomas Cranmer, at that time serving as an ambassador to the Court of Charles V. It reached him in Italy in October, and he started a difficult winter journey northwards. In the meantime, a flurry of activity was under way back home. By early September, Henry was blustering to the papal nuncio about the excessive powers that the papacy had usurped. A royal visit to France was arranged in order to seal French diplomatic support for the endgame. Henry crossed to Calais in October with a splendid entourage that included Anne Boleyn, elevated to the rank of Marchioness of Pembroke in her own right for the occasion. Copies of the *Glasse of the Truthe* translated into Latin and French were taken for the edification of French courtiers and councillors.

Further urgency was added by Anne's discovery in January that she was pregnant. A marriage was hastily celebrated, probably on 25 January, and Parliament was recalled for 5 February to enact the enabling legislation. The Act against Appeals to Rome (24 Henry VIII c. 12), which grandiloquently declared 'this realm of England' to be 'an empire unto itself', forbade any sentence passed in an English court to be appealed to any tribunal outside that imperial realm. At much the same time, Convocation was called upon to declare whether a man could marry his brother's widow if her first marriage had been consummated, and whether the pope could issue a dispensation for such a marriage. It came up with the right answers (no and no), and the stage was set. In the meantime, Cranmer had made it back to England, and once the requisite papal bulls had been obtained from Rome, was duly consecrated Archbishop of Canterbury on 30 March. His conscience at this time must have been somewhat vexed. The ceremonies involved swearing a public oath of obedience to the pope. He prepared for this by forswearing it the previous day in secret, making his public oath the first of his many perjuries. Even more astoundingly, while on diplomatic service at the imperial Court in Nuremberg, he had been converted to the new theology of Lutheranism by the local Lutheran preacher, Andreas Osiander, and had sealed this by marrying Osiander's niece, in defiance of canon law.[24]

Now that Parliament and Convocation had paved the way, Cranmer was able to summon his king to appear before an ecclesiastical court to explain why he had married his brother's wife in contravention of scripture and canon law. The outcome was, literally, a foregone conclusion. Two days after Cranmer's summons to the king, the Prior of the London Austin Friars, Dr George Browne, was the Easter Sunday preacher at Paul's Cross on 13 April. Primed no doubt by Cromwell, who had lived next to the Austin Friars for ten years, and with whom he developed a good working relationship in the 1530s, Browne started by inviting prayers for King Henry and Queen Anne – which must have left the crowd stunned – and then embarked on a sermon that, setting aside the traditional Easter topic of Christ's Resurrection, expounded at length the arguments against the lawfulness of marrying a brother's wife. Proceedings in Cranmer's court began on 10 May and concluded on 23 May with the decree of annulment.

This was followed a week later by Anne's formal coronation as queen, a ceremony involving a splendid procession through London and an elaborate liturgy in Westminster Abbey. There was doubtless ribald comment on what must by then have been her very visible pregnancy. Just over three months later she gave birth: not to the boy who was expected to set the seal of divine approval on Henry's proceedings, but to another girl, christened Elizabeth. The birth of a healthy child at least furnished hope that a son might one day follow, so it would be hasty to infer that this disappointment was the beginning of the end for the royal marriage. But it probably took some of the shine off.

The birth of Elizabeth made the task of shaping opinion all the more pressing. Notwithstanding the steps already taken to turn opinion against Henry's marriage to Catherine and against papal authority, there had been public challenges to the trend of royal policy. Catherine enjoyed widespread public sympathy, especially among women and the clergy. As early as March 1532 a priest had been arrested for using his chance to preach at Paul's Cross to attack the king's pursuit of a divorce. In November, an Observant Franciscan named John Forest preached a similar sermon, and as a result was sent to internal exile at one of his order's northern houses. But if royal policy was being challenged in the kingdom's premier pulpit, the level of dissent in the kingdom at large was probably high. The Convocation that endorsed the principles behind the king's divorce saw a small knot of dissidents, led by John Fisher, vote against. Fisher himself spoke out publicly the next day, and was gaoled for his pains. There was even opposition to the divorce in print – though such books could not be printed in England. Following the example of Protestant dissidents, Catholic opponents of Henry's policy had their efforts printed abroad. Fisher's Latin defence of the king's marriage was printed in Alcalá de Henares in August 1530, and Catherine's chaplain, Thomas Abell, produced a work in her favour which, despite its Latin title, *Invicta Veritas* ('unconquered truth'), was a vernacular response to the *Determinations of the Universities*. Given the fictitious imprint of 'Luneburg' ('Moontown'), it was printed in Antwerp, as were two anonymous Latin treatises, one of them refuting Henry's *Glasse of the Truthe*.[25] This opposition campaign, such as it was, appears to have been masterminded by the imperial ambassador, Eustace Chapuys, who arranged for several treatises to be smuggled out of the country.

The loudest voice of opposition to the king remained that of the Holy Maid of Kent. Elizabeth Barton was speaking out with increasing audacity against the threat of heresy and against royal encroachment on the Church. This may have reflected the guidance of her spiritual director, Edward Bocking, and of the Observant Franciscan friars who were busy publicising her visions and predictions. By early 1533, she was foretelling divine chastisement for the king if he repudiated his wife. In autumn, various associates of hers were rounded up, and by November she was under interrogation in the Tower. Within a week or two she had cracked and confessed herself a fraud, and was brought before a Great Council to make this admission before a representative cross-section of the kingdom's elite. On 23 November she was required, with her associates, to do public penance at Paul's Cross while the Sunday preacher denounced her for heresy and treason. The lengths to which the king went to discredit her and her alleged prophecies are testimony to the threat she was felt to pose to his security and credibility.

With the main potential threat thus defused, Henry's Council turned to the wider implications of his drastic resolution of his matrimonial problems. The king's subjects had to be aligned with the new order. The process began with the publication of nine 'articles' by the King's Council. Formulated in December 1533 and printed almost at once, they were designed to 'inform his loving subjects of the truth' – as neat a definition of royal propaganda as one might hope to find. The text began with robust affirmations of the grounds for the annulment of Henry's first marriage and of the principle that all lawsuits should be finally decided within the realm. It then insisted on the superiority of general councils to the papacy and on the king's right to appeal from the pope to a future general council. It pre-emptively denied the validity of any papal excommunication that might be launched against Henry, compared the 'bishop of Rome' disadvantageously with 'our good bishop of Canterbury', and concluded by attacking the papal office and denouncing the pope as a bastard and a heretic. The main lesson of the Nine Articles, however, was imparted by example rather than instruction. The papacy is mentioned eleven times in 16 pages, yet the title 'pope'

Opening of Parliament, 1523 (from the 'Wriothesley Garter Book')
This illustration from a book compiled by the herald Thomas Wriothesley (Garter
King of Arms, 1505–34) depicts the opening of Parliament in April 1523. Henry
VIII is seated on the throne, beneath the cloth of estate, with Cardinal Wolsey and
Archbishop Warham seated immediately to his right (and the Master of the Rolls,
Bishop Cuthbert Tunstall, standing behind them). The spiritual peers are seated to the
king's right (bishops in front, mitred abbots behind), and the temporal peers to his
left (the two dukes, Norfolk and Suffolk, are distinguished by their coronets).

appears only in the phrases: 'by some men called Pope' (once) and 'which calleth himself Pope' (twice). Otherwise the text religiously refers to him as 'the Bishop of Rome', implicitly lowering him to the level of any other bishop by denying the title which expressed his primacy over the Catholic Church. The lesson, which was spelled out by Chapuys in a report to his master, was that henceforth people were expected to talk no more of the 'pope' but only of the 'Bishop of Rome'.[26] It is remarkable just how quickly this was put into effect, not only in official documents but also in commercial publications – though of course it was difficult for many people to break the habit of a lifetime, and 'pope' would pop out when they forgot to self-censor. The Nine Articles were also the first occasion on which an official text deployed the word 'papists', a term of abuse originally coined by Luther – he had applied it to Henry VIII – and until then used in English only in those books that the king had been energetic in burning.

The Nine Articles, which deserve to be better known, set the scene for the year to come, which saw the demolition of papal authority in England. The wrecking ball was Parliament, which had already demonstrated its potency by authorising the Archbishop of Canterbury to pass judgement on the king's marriage. Care was taken to make Parliament amenable. Some key figures were warned not to attend, notably Bishops Fisher of Rochester and Tunstall of Durham, while others were intimidated. Bishop Nix of Norwich was charged with *praemunire* and fined a massive £10,000. The king lobbied and leaned on members of the Lords and Commons to pave the way for the legislative programme. The spring session, ending on 30 March, saw a raft of legislation, notably an act of attainder against the Holy Maid of Kent and her associates (25 Henry VIII c. 12). (Henry met a rare rebuff when the Lords refused to include Thomas More in the scope of the act, even though they agreed to include Bishop Fisher.) Other acts included the Act for Submission of the Clergy (c. 19), which enshrined in law the surrender offered by the clergy in 1532, and acts (cc. 20 and 21) ending the customary papal levy known as 'Peter's Pence' and definitively diverting to the Crown the levies of 'first fruits and annates'.

The most momentous statute, however, was the Act of Succession (25 Henry VIII c. 22), which for the first time made succession to the crown subject to parliamentary definition. Until this time, the succession had been a matter of prerogative and custom. But by inviting Parliament, in however submissive a capacity, to lay down the law on it, Henry gave a hostage to fortune that would trouble his successors. In the short term the act delivered valuable clarity amid the murmuring and discontent over his divorce and second marriage. That said, its passage through the Lords was far from serene, and seems to have required royal intervention. Before it passed, Henry had summoned the Lords and at least some of the Commons to York Place for a lengthy meeting. The resulting statute declared his first marriage contrary to God's law, and his daughter Mary a bastard, excluding her from the succession. The heirs of Henry's body by Anne were to be his lawful heirs. Most dramatically, each and every one of his subjects (at least, the adult males) were to swear an oath to accept and uphold this settlement. The process began even before Parliament was prorogued on 30 March.

Within weeks, the oath had been taken by the king's councillors and the Lords, and started to be rolled out more widely. The clergy of London were summoned to Lambeth Palace on Friday 17 April, and all but a handful of them swore it (the few dissidents were soon in gaol). On Monday it was the turn of the city of London. The citizens were given some encouragement in their duty by the sight of the Holy Maid and five of her supporters being dragged across the city that very morning for execution at Tyburn.[27] Compliance was predictably prompt and dutiful. Over the next few weeks commissions were sent out to administer the oath across England, and we see glimpses of the commissioners in action as far apart as Devon, Hampshire, Kent, Norfolk and Yorkshire through the summer of that year.

June 1534 saw the scope of Henry's demands expand. The Convocations of Canterbury and York had been persuaded to deny that the 'Bishop of Rome' had any more authority in England than any other foreign prelate. And after that orders went out to require all priests in England to renounce papal jurisdiction. As with the earlier oath, resistance was sparse, but embarrassingly for the king it included the Observant Franciscan friars who lived next door to Greenwich Palace. Two cartloads of them were deposited at the Tower in June for refusing the oath. Others of the same order were immured soon after in the Fleet and Marshalsea prisons, and by the end of August practically all the English personnel of that select order were in custody. Otherwise there was general acquiescence. The exaction of these oaths was the regime's top priority that summer, and the campaign was successful. There was discreet dissent. Lord Darcy, a powerful regional magnate with significant military experience, was discussing with the imperial ambassador the prospects of intervention by Charles V. But in Henry's England it was just talk.

Parliament reconvened on 7 November for another short session, to enact the principle of Henry VIII's emerging Reformation, the Act of Supremacy (26 Henry VIII c. 1). One of the shortest statutes ever inscribed among the laws of the land, it was carefully worded to state that it was merely recognising, not conferring, the new dignity. It was followed by a new Treason Act (26 Henry VIII c. 13) which expanded the scope of the offence to include anyone who should 'maliciously' deny any part of the king's title. There was of course only one component of his title that anyone might have reason to deny, and as for the adverb (added to the law by MPs worried at the idea of treason by words), it transpired that any denial of any part of the king's title was by its very nature malicious. As 1534 gave way to 1535, Henry VIII was possessed of wider ranging powers than any previous king of England. It remained to be seen what he would do with them.

3

REFORMATIONS, 1535–1553

On 4 May 1535, four monks and a priest were led out of the Tower of London for execution. Three of the monks were Carthusians, brethren of the most fervent and ascetic religious order to be found in England at that time. Each was the head of his house: John Houghton, Prior of the London Charterhouse; Robert Lawrence, Prior of Beauvale in Nottinghamshire; and Augustine Webster, Prior of Axholme in Lincolnshire. The fourth monk was Richard Reynolds, of the Bridgettines, one of the team of learned priests who served as chaplains to the nuns of Syon Abbey (Middlesex), which, like the Charterhouses, was a beacon in English religious life. The secular priest was John Hale, Vicar of nearby Isleworth. Lashed to crude sleds, they were dragged by horses across the city of London to Tyburn (near what is now Marble Arch), still in their ecclesiastical clothing. This was a calculated display of contempt for their status: by custom, priests were formally stripped of that status and of its symbolic clothing before being handed over to the temporal authorities for execution. One by one, the five were subjected to the gruesome penalties for Tudor treason. First they were 'hanged' for a while from the gallows – carefully, with a thick rope, to make sure they did not die too soon. Cut down alive and preferably conscious, they were stripped for the butcher. Then their genitals were hacked off and cast into the fire, and their torsos ripped open so that their guts could be 'drawn' and similarly disposed of. Finally, they were beheaded and their bodies were 'quartered', so that their heads and dismembered limbs could be used to decorate London Bridge and the gates of the city, to dispel any lingering doubts as to the wisdom of compliance with the royal will.

What awful crime had merited this horrific death? They had denied that Henry VIII was the Supreme Head of the Church of England. For each of them, even at the last minute, a word was enough to save them. Henry's mercy knew no bounds when those mired in error and blindness finally had their eyes opened to the new truth he had proclaimed. Indeed, if we can trust the report of the imperial ambassador in London, Eustace Chapuys, the king himself was present in disguise to see his justice done. This would explain why the onlookers included a throng of councillors and courtiers, who would not usually grace a grisly public execution with their presence. The Dukes of Norfolk and Richmond were there, with Anne Boleyn's father, the Earl of Wiltshire, as well as her brother George. Among other lords and gentlemen in the crowd was Henry Norris, who, as Chief Gentleman of the Privy Chamber, was the king's senior personal attendant and closest companion. Also present were five mysterious masked men, armed and dressed like the 'reivers' or raiders who infested the Scottish Borders. The mask on one of them slipped to reveal the face of Lord Thomas Howard, brother to the Duke of Norfolk and at that moment riding high in royal favour (barely a year later he would be in the Tower).[1] That one of those five was the king himself seems almost certain: he did love dressing up. And no doubt he was ready to unmask and bestow his mercy should any of the victims beg for it at the price of acknowledging his royal supremacy over the Church.

On 15 January 1535, Henry had formally adopted the title of Supreme Head into his official 'royal style', the wording used in royal commissions and in legal documents of all kinds. He made quite a ceremony of it, with the Chancellor (Thomas Audley), Norfolk, Wiltshire, Thomas Cromwell and sundry others witnessing the deed in his Privy Chamber.[2] His realisation that he was Supreme Head (under Christ, he modestly acknowledged) of the Church of England came upon him as, literally, a revelation, one he was consumed with zeal to share. His conscience, which had led him to throw off 'subjection to Rome', was 'enlightened and instructed by the Spirit of God', and he was eager to 'open the eyes of other princes' to the truths it had uncovered. His subjects were expected to follow his conscience dutifully. The final version of the oath that he required of his officials and clergy began by making them acknowledge that 'the veil of darkness of the usurped power, authority and jurisdiction of the Bishop of Rome' had been 'clearly taken away from mine eyes'.[3] It was a particular priority to put the bishops on a tight leash, to show they owed their authority to the king, as Supreme Head, rather than to the pope. So they were commanded to hand over any papal bulls in their possession for burning. New oaths to the king were required of them all, in person, starting with Cranmer and Gardiner on 10 February.[4]

By summer, a two-pronged campaign of terror and propaganda was reaching its height. Another three Carthusians were dragged to Tyburn for butchery on 19 June. The gaoled Bishop of Rochester, John Fisher, and the former Chancellor, Thomas More, were despatched by the axe at the Tower of London on 22 June and 6 July respectively. Their deaths shocked all Europe, and in England people realised that if Henry was prepared to sacrifice two such men, there were no lengths to which he would not go. To deny his new title was death, no matter how important, or unimportant, you were. In Yorkshire, Sir Francis Bigod, a Protestant client of Cromwell's, was escorting one Thomas Garrett on a preaching tour to spread the new word. During Garrett's sermon at Jervaulx Abbey on Sunday 11 July, one of the brethren, Dan George Lazenby, stood up to object (Figure 3.1). Later, under questioning, he denied the royal supremacy and affirmed papal primacy with cool audacity, even putting his signature to a statement of his views. He was executed at the York Assizes in August.[5] Very few, though, refused the oath to the supremacy which was soon required of priests every time they accepted a new benefice. The ruthless executions did their work, inducing a terror sufficient to extort a few simple words.

The next five years saw an avalanche of change sweep away many of the landmarks of England's traditional religion. No one could have foreseen this. And it would probably not have happened had the king been left to himself. That this change reflects the influence of his chief minister, Thomas Cromwell, is agreed by most historians, though not all.[6] Almost the first move was to initiate a nationwide valuation of the property of the Church, the 'Valor Ecclesiasticus'. The main aim of this was to have an up-to-date basis on which to levy taxes on church property ('annates' and 'first fruits and tenths'), which were now payable to the king rather than to the pope. But this was followed up with an inspection (a 'visitation') of all religious houses, purportedly designed to take them back to the pure observance of their founders' times, but certainly with more far-reaching though as yet undefined aims. Cromwell for one appreciated that the monasteries were potential bastions of 'papist' sympathies, and the principal task of his inspectors (the 'visitors') was to ensure that the royal supremacy was acknowledged by every last monk in the land. But while it is impossible to know how many moves ahead he was thinking, it is evident that his visitors were tasked with gathering whatever evidence or gossip they could about any sexual or other misconduct, past or present, on the part of the nation's monks and nuns. His most gifted muckrakers were Richard Layton and Thomas

Jervaulx Abbey
It was in the church of Jervaulx Abbey that George Lazenby became the only man
to openly deny Henry VIII's claim to be Supreme Head on earth of the Church of
England, interrupting a licensed royal preacher to do so. A few weeks later he was
executed for treason in York. The abbey itself was dissolved in 1537 after being
implicated in the Pilgrimage of Grace.

Legh, who covered much of southern England in the second half of 1535
before turning to the north in early 1536.[7]

By spring 1536 it had been decided to close all religious houses with
an income below £200 a year, confiscating their assets and rehousing
their occupants in larger and sounder houses. Under the canon law of the
medieval Church, what was proposed was, in essence, sacrilege. Everyone
knew this because they were told it four times a year in church, in English,
through the public recitation of the 'general sentence', a declaration of
automatic excommunication upon 'all those that any manner goods,
moveable or unmoveable, away bear with strength or wrongfully away
draw or waste': in short, anyone who deprived the Church of its property.[8]
To defuse such a notorious prohibition required special legitimation, and
this was provided by an act of Parliament. A dossier of tales of immorality
in England's religious houses, compiled from the visitors' reports, was
presented to Parliament and prompted a surge of revulsion that gave easy
passage to the first act for the suppression of monasteries.

The headlong rush to Reformation, however, hit a stumbling block in spring 1536: the sudden fall of Anne Boleyn, who had been one of the main patrons of reform. While Henry was already tiring of her, it was the accusation that she had committed adultery with a handful of his own closest male attendants that led to the arrest on 1 May 1536 of the chief of them, Henry Norris. Anne followed Norris to the Tower next day, and her other supposed lovers soon after. With one exception, everyone involved insisted on their innocence to the very end, which given the emphasis at that time on meeting death with a clear conscience is powerful testimony that they were telling the truth. Indeed, the reported details of their alleged assignations show enough inconsistencies with the historical record to give strong indications that the charges were trumped up.[9] Henry's suspicious nature seems to have been played upon by his chief minister, Cromwell, whose grip on power was consolidated by the destruction of Anne and Norris, his chief rivals for the king's trust. The idea that the whole episode was a power-play by Cromwell might seem far-fetched, yet it is perhaps the only explanation that makes sense. Henry's growing disillusionment with Anne, who had failed to provide him with a son, provided circumstances that Cromwell could exploit for his own purposes. Anne was beheaded on 19 May, and Henry was married to Jane Seymour by the end of the month. Their short but happy marriage was to end tragically. She bore him a son, Edward, on 12 October 1537, but the birth was difficult, and resulted in an infection from which she died two weeks later.

Anne had been a keen patron of Protestant clergy and ideas, so her fall from grace in May 1536 heartened the conservative majority of the clergy. Consequently, when Parliament was convened to tidy up after Anne, the Convocation that met at the same time did not go according to plan. The plan was set out by the keynote preacher, Hugh Latimer (appointed Bishop of Worcester in 1535). His sermon, a call for further religious change, was closely attuned to the agenda of Cranmer and Cromwell.[10] The authorities offered the clergy a draft set of 'articles' of religion, to clarify the doctrinal position of Henry's Church. But the lower house of clergy countered with a more conservative paper of their own, offering the bishops a comprehensive list of religious errors (the 'mala dogmata', or evil teachings), culled from recent Protestant texts, for official condemnation.[11] The impasse was resolved only by the intervention of the king, who in July imposed a text comprising ten statements on disputed issues, the Ten Articles, which both Houses of Convocation dutifully endorsed.

The Ten Articles were a setback for the Protestant tendency. But Cromwell snatched victory from the jaws of defeat with the 'injunctions' (ecclesiastical instructions) that he issued in September that year, while the king was enjoying his late summer honeymoon. In his capacity as Vicar-General, he updated the medieval practice by which a bishop issued injunctions for a diocese. Instead, he issued his for the entire kingdom. Ignoring the traditional doctrine that marked the Ten Articles, his injunctions took up the Erasmian tone with which they discussed pilgrimage and the cult of the saints, but turned it in a more radical direction. Where the articles upheld traditional practices but warned against abuses, the injunctions attacked abuses so strongly as to insinuate doubts about the practices. Priests were not to offer relics to pilgrims for veneration, nor to spread stories of miracles, nor to encourage offerings at shrines. Under the pretext of discouraging superstition, this eroded customary pieties. Cromwell knew exactly what he was doing. The regime's first moves against popular devotion had been taken the previous year. When miracles and visions started to be reported after the execution of John Fisher, orders went out that he and Thomas More were to be emphatically and repeatedly denounced as traitors.[12] Henry and Cromwell knew how disastrous the popular cult of Thomas Becket had proved for Henry II, and they did not want history repeating itself with a Bishop of Rochester. The offensive against the cult of the saints in 1536 was a shrewd blow aimed at the taproot of opposition to Henry's Reformation.

The injunctions began to be disseminated at much the same time that the first monasteries were being dissolved, and some pilgrimage shrines were necessarily closed down as a side effect of the closure of monasteries. This meant that popular notions of the sacred were under open attack from two directions, which helps explain the extraordinary volatility of English popular politics in late 1536. With relics being spirited away and monasteries being shut down, the kingdom was ripe for rumour. When royal commissioners enforcing Cromwell's injunctions and subsidy commissioners collecting a tax converged on Louth in Lincolnshire in September, word spread that parish churches too were to be asset-stripped. Churches such as Louth were rich in church plate and ornate vestments, as well as in rents dedicated to supporting chaplains and chantries. Gatherings of angry protesters soon turned into open rebellion.

The rebellion spread rapidly through northern Lincolnshire and then into Yorkshire and beyond. Henry responded with his own call to arms and with printed pamphlets calling his subjects back to obedience. The rising in Lincolnshire was part talked down and part overawed within a few weeks. But the news from further north got worse. By the time Henry's troops were heading northwards under the Duke of Norfolk, with orders to wreak dire vengeance, Pontefract Castle had surrendered to a force numbered in tens of thousands.[13] Nor was this an undisciplined mob. The tenants and labourers of the northern gentry were there for the most part under their accustomed gentry leaders. The rebels had an oath and a cause, calling themselves the 'Pilgrimage of Grace for the Common Weal'. It was to all intents and purposes an army, but it lacked one thing: a commander. Very well disciplined, and knowing what they wanted, but not what they wanted to do, they compiled a wish-list. Their wish-list, elaborated through lengthy discussions in Pontefract Castle, has perplexed generations of historians who have missed the wood for the trees. It was a mixture of outraged protest against the religious changes, economic or social grievances about such issues as enclosures and rents, and gentry concerns over royal plans to interfere with their use of wills and trusts to dodge inheritance dues. It was anything but a coherent package, and has led historians to waste a great deal of ink worrying about whether the Pilgrimage of Grace was a 'religious' rebellion or a more traditional social protest that simply used religion as a banner. But that is not a distinction that would have made any sense to the rebels.

The Pilgrims were too strong for Norfolk to risk obeying Henry's orders by offering battle. But they were too loyal and peaceable to see that the only way to make their wishes come true was to march south and overthrow the king. Negotiations were therefore the only option for both sides. The Pilgrims, and especially their gentry leaders, who had so much to lose, were happy to be talked down, and Norfolk made enough promises to get them home for Christmas. The north had felt neglected for a generation or more, since Richard fell at Bosworth, so they were especially pleased with the promise of a parliament at York, recalling the medieval tradition of a peripatetic parliament that showed it represented the whole realm by meeting at various places within it. They could reasonably feel that they had made a difference and that their grievances would receive a fair hearing.

Henry was relieved from the embarrassment of fulfilling his obligations by the unaccountable behaviour of a man who had hitherto been one of his most zealous servants in the north, the young Francis Bigod. Though he had sought to flee the Pilgrimage by sea, he was captured and compelled to join it, and ended up making ill-judged and unwelcome suggestions at the Pilgrims' council at Pontefract. Rightly doubtful that Henry would keep his promises, Bigod ensured this by trying to relaunch the Pilgrimage on 16 January 1537. His small force was surprised, he was captured, and Henry had the perfect excuse to renege. All Bigod achieved was to show the king that the threat was well and truly past. On the slender pretext that this futile plot somehow implicated the entire body of the Pilgrims, their former leaders were rounded up (even those who had helped suppress the second rising) and submitted to a lengthy series of interrogations and trials that made the Pilgrimage the best documented of all Tudor rebellions.

One of the things revealed by the interrogations was the extent to which monks and friars had thrown themselves into the fray. In many places people reopened recently closed monasteries. At Richmond in Yorkshire they reinstated the displaced Praemonstratensian Canons at Easby Abbey, a mile downstream from the town. The religious orders themselves were understandably committed to the old ways that the king was undermining. Dr John Pickering, a Dominican based at Scarborough, penned a ballad to voice the aspirations of the Pilgrims, and he was loud in affirming papal primacy at the Pontefract Council. He was picked out for special mention in the letter Henry later wrote to the Duke of Norfolk imposing martial law in the north and urging him to wreak 'dreadful execution' upon its inhabitants.[14] Henry's reference in the same letter to 'those persons that call themselves religious in the colours of their hypocrisy' testifies to the bitterness of his disenchantment. In 1536 he seems to have believed his own propaganda about reforming monasticism. Even while closing down inadequate monasteries, he devoted some of the spoils to founding two new houses, to be known as 'the New Monasteries of King Henry VIII', to intercede for him, Queen Jane, and their children. This initiative was entirely serious, and continued into early 1537 even as Henry's own heart was visibly hardening against the very idea of the 'religious life'.[15]

In the immediate aftermath of the Pilgrimage, two new methods for closing religious houses were developed. Both depended on treating a religious house as though it was personal property under English law. So when John Paslew, Abbot of Whalley, was convicted of treason for his role in the Pilgrimage, his abbey was deemed forfeited to the Crown, just like the estates of a layman guilty of the same offence. Jervaulx Abbey fell the same way. Monks and friars, some of them even heads of houses, had been convicted of treason before – most notably the Carthusian Priors with whose fate this chapter opened – but never before had their houses been deemed forfeit for that reason. Still more significant, though, was the fate of Furness Abbey, one of the wealthiest in the land. Here, the abbot and brethren, terrified of the consequences of their complicity in the Pilgrimage, were induced in April 1537 to make a voluntary surrender of their monastery into the king's hands. Several other northern houses were intimidated into following suit. Judicial confiscation and voluntary surrender were both predicated on the notion that monastic lands were property just like any other – an implicit denial of the principle of medieval canon law, that the lands of the Church belonged to God. In a sense, once monastic property was just property like any other, the writing was on the wall. The mystique had been exorcised.

The appeal of voluntary surrender was that its potential was limitless. Proof of concept came towards the end of the year, when one of England's greatest and most ancient monasteries, the Cluniac Priory at Lewes (Sussex), became the first major house to surrender without obvious reason. Lewes was about as far away from the Pilgrimage as it was possible to get and its wealth put it comfortably out of reach of the Act of 1536. But by autumn 1537 no one imagined that a monk's cowl offered any protection against royal displeasure. So when the invitation to surrender came, there was only one safe course of action. The prior and brethren surrendered their house into the hands of the king on 16 November, and were duly compensated for their pains. But Lewes was chosen to make a point: if Lewes could fall, nowhere was safe.[16] People got the message. By January 1538, rumours were rife that the king was going to close down every monastery in England. In response the government announced that it had no such intentions – perhaps the first time in English history that a government policy has been confirmed by official denial.[17] An almost unknown lawsuit a few months later put this beyond doubt. In his chronicle of Henry's reign, Charles Wriothesley reports that in May 1538 the Bishop of London, John Stokesley, found himself on the wrong end of the *praemunire* statute. His offence, to which he pleaded guilty and for which he successfully begged the king's pardon, was that he had veiled (that is, admitted) some young women as novice nuns at Syon Abbey. The offence lay in the fact that this formal procedure was authorised by canon law, the pope's law – which was no longer law in England. Strictly, then, it was no longer legal to admit new nuns to a convent. This whole case was a public signal intended to discourage monastic recruitment.[18]

Voluntary surrender gathered momentum through 1538, and early autumn saw it deployed to close down the most troublesome of the religious orders, the friars. Friars were the populist wing of the clergy in the late medieval Church. They provided the bulk of popular preaching, particularly in the towns, where their friaries were mostly located. It was not uncommon for them to be involved at the start of risings and rebellions, and it is a sign of their influence that so many friars, such as Robert Barnes and John Bale, were prominent in the English Reformation. But others were prominent in opposing it. Several had been involved in the Pilgrimage of Grace, and Henry would not have forgotten how obstructive the Observant Franciscans had been over the divorce and the supremacy a few years before. So although their assets were limited compared to those of ancient monasteries, there was a political dividend in shutting them down. It markedly reduced the latent capacity for resistance to Henry's will.

As the closure of monasteries gained pace, it was accompanied by an unholy onslaught on the great shrines of England and their relics and images. Time-honoured images were transported to London where they figured in public ceremonies of desecration and destruction which punctuated the year. In February 1538 a famous crucifix, the Rood of Boxley (Kent), was torn to pieces at Paul's Cross by a mob that had been brought to fever pitch by a sermon from one of Cromwell's episcopal henchmen, John Hilsey, Bishop of Rochester. The greatest shrine of all, that of St Thomas at Canterbury, was stripped of its fabulous wealth in the presence of the king himself in September, while the saint's relics were exhumed and burned as those of a traitor.[19] (A subsequent proclamation that referred to him only as 'Thomas Becket' – as he is still known to this day – taught that he was no longer to be taken as 'a saint, but rather . . . a rebel and traitor to his prince'.[20]) News of this spectacular impiety flashed across Europe, and precipitated, after years of hesitation, the public excommunication of Henry by Pope Paul III. A second set of injunctions for the English Church issued by Cromwell around this time spelled out the implicit meaning of these iconoclastic performances. Relics, miracles and pilgrimages were prohibited. A part of English Christianity since the arrival of Augustine at Canterbury in the year 597 was brought to an almost instant end. It is truly remarkable that such an integral element in English religion was crushed so easily in just a few years. Although the Catholic faith that engendered such devotional practices can hardly have evaporated instantly, the massive shifting of the boundary between the sacred and the profane that was expressed in their abrupt suppression shook that faith to its foundations, disturbing the ground so thoroughly that the seeds of the new doctrine would find it easier to take root.

Cromwell's injunctions of 1538 set the seal on another religious change that had been gathering momentum for a decade, the authorisation of an English translation of the Bible. English versions of scripture had been viewed with considerable mistrust by the authorities since the early fifteenth century, when they had been associated with the Lollards. Mere possession of the scriptures in English could be grounds in itself for suspicion of heresy. Inspired by the example of Luther in Germany, however, English evangelicals led by William Tyndale had been working since 1525 on a new English version. Henry had initially shared his bishops' hostility towards this enterprise. But the Break with Rome changed everything, and the choice of Cranmer as Archbishop of Canterbury changed the official line. As early as 1534, he sought – unsuccessfully – to engage his fellow bishops in producing an official version. In collaboration with Cromwell, though, he supported the publication of the first complete English Bible at Antwerp in 1535. Next year Cromwell had briefly sought to authorise the English Bible in the injunctions he issued for the Church of England that year, but that initiative was tacitly abandoned in the face of the general reaction against religious change represented by the Pilgrimage of Grace. Certainly there is no evidence that this particular injunction was ever implemented. But Cromwell and Cranmer pressed on, and in 1538 Cromwell's second injunctions required every parish in England to acquire a copy of the Bible in English. At the same time, he was managing a project to have a high-quality edition printed at Paris. The job had to be transferred to London when it fell foul of the French authorities, but was brought to a triumphant conclusion in 1539. Surviving parish accounts show that some local churches were soon purchasing their copy. The fact that Richard Grafton and Edward Whitchurch, the evangelical entrepreneurs to whom Cromwell subcontracted the job, published six editions between 1539 and 1541 indicates that compliance was widespread, even though the price (twenty shillings) and the inevitable delays in producing enough copies made the process of buying bibles much slower than that of smashing statues.

The mid-1530s were a period of uncertainty in religion. Few can have thought that Henry's religious position represented any kind of settlement. Overthrowing the pope, closing monasteries, and chipping away at the cult of the saints pointed down the Lutheran path, as did his reliance on 'evangelical' (i.e. mildly Protestant) bishops and clergy to preach the message of the royal supremacy. But Henry's personal contempt for Luther and his doctrines, his unshakable attachment to the Mass, and his commitment to all seven sacraments heartened those who hoped that the spat with the pope would blow over, as such quarrels had often done before. The 'new-fangled fellows' and the 'papists', as they termed each other, vied for supremacy in Henry's Church. The evangelicals enjoyed the support of Cromwell and Cranmer. The Catholics placed their trust in the king's essentially conventional theology. The Ten Articles had done little to resolve the uncertainty. Evangelicals found solace in their hesitant critique of the cult of the saints, while Catholics delighted in their robust doctrine. Thus, although historians have often misread the Ten Articles as an evangelical victory, the rebel Pilgrims in autumn 1536 happily called for the Ten Articles to be enforced, while Reginald Pole, the king's most outspoken opponent, looked favourably on them.

After the Pilgrimage, confusion continued for years. Protracted discussions between bishops and theologians through spring 1537 resulted in a comprehensive account of Christian doctrine generally known as the Bishops' Book. Like the Ten Articles, the Bishops' Book has been much misunderstood by historians insensitive to theological niceties. They have seen it as more 'conservative' than the Ten Articles because it discusses all seven sacraments while the Ten Articles mention only three. But a close reading reveals a subtly ambiguous text. Its account of Christian doctrine is largely Catholic, yet in language and tone it nods towards evangelical ideas. Even more than with the Ten Articles, both sides could find things in it with which they could be pleased.

Cromwell's diplomacy through the later 1530s shows that he saw the solution in going forwards, not backwards. Frequent negotiations (1534–38) with the princes and theologians of the Lutheran Schmalkaldic League in Germany reflect his realisation that the Henrician royal supremacy would find its most satisfactory theological context in Lutheranism.[21] Luther's idiosyncratic reading of the fourth commandment ('Honour your father and mother') as a divine charter for patriarchal political authority underpinned his teaching that subjects owed their princes an obedience limited only by their duty to disobey any order that went against the law of God. That was the one element of Lutheran doctrine that was, from the start, integrated fully into Henry's Church. Hence the remark of one of his propagandists, Richard Morison, writing against the Pilgrims, 'which of all the commandments is more necessary for us than this, "Obey ye your King"?' The question only makes sense when one realises that 'Obey ye your King' is a paraphrase of the fourth commandment.[22] Cromwell's pursuit of the Schmalkaldic alliance was good policy as well as acute theology. Henry's breach with the papacy set him at odds with Charles V, who ruled Spain and the Holy Roman Empire. And it made for problems with France, troubled by its own burgeoning Protestant movement. Charles and Francis were usually at loggerheads, but Henry feared that they might make common cause with the pope against him. The Schmalkaldic League was the only realistic prospect for a foreign alliance.

The policy foundered on Henry's own convictions. The Schmalkaldic League was defined by allegiance to Luther's doctrine, but Henry's convictions were as uncompromising as Luther's. Transubstantiation, eucharistic sacrifice, clerical celibacy, the binding force of religious vows, and the administration of communion to the laity under only one kind were all red lines for the king, but had all been condemned by Luther. Despite the goodwill of Henry's negotiators, there was no deal to be done. Henry walked away. The collapse of the talks was not as disastrous for Cromwell as the failure to deliver the divorce had been for Wolsey. But it weakened him, and from then onwards Henry's default Catholicism came to the fore. Stephen Gardiner was recalled from the diplomatic exile in France to which he had been consigned, and over the winter of 1538 Catholic elements at Court alerted Henry to what they saw as the rising tide of heresy in the kingdom.[23] The outcome was a draconian law passed in the Parliament of 1539, threatening the death penalty for priestly marriage and the denial of transubstantiation. Though it did claim some victims, the Act of Six Articles was more bark than bite, its enforcement tempered by political caution. It had its own place in Henry's foreign policy. Pope Paul III had finally excommunicated Henry in December 1538, shortly after a Franco–Imperial peace treaty. The nightmare scenario of invasion loomed. Henry responded with a two-pronged strategy: an urgent campaign of coastal fortification, financed by the dissolution of the monasteries and often recycling the very stone from the abbeys; and a pointed display of Catholic piety.

Even now, however, uncertainty persisted. Cromwell was no longer at one with the king on religion or foreign policy, but as the king's most powerful subject, he was no longer content simply to do as he was told. His pursuit of a German matrimonial alliance for the king was to prove his undoing. Anne of Cleves was the daughter of the Duke of Jülich-Kleve, who, while not a Lutheran or a member of the Schmalkaldic League, had close connections with it. The match, in Cromwell's mind at least, was manifestly still looking towards linking Henry with Charles V's German and Lutheran enemies. Unfortunately, when Anne arrived, Henry felt at once that he had been misled as to her personal attractions and, not long after the marriage had taken place, he informed Cromwell that he had been unable to consummate it. Things did not improve, and Henry's insistence on an annulment (straightforward enough, under the circumstances) left his chief minister looking vulnerable, as the man chiefly responsible for his overlord's embarrassing predicament. A power struggle in the early months of 1540 saw Cromwell's Catholic enemies, led by the Duke of Norfolk and Stephen Gardiner, seek to bring him down. But Cromwell fought back hard, putting the Lutheran Robert Barnes into the pulpit at Paul's Cross to attack Gardiner. Although ambassadors to Henry's Court saw his weakness, he nevertheless reached the zenith of his political career in April with his elevation to the earldom of Essex and his appointment to his highest secular office, Lord Chamberlain of the Household. But there was a further twist, and on 10 June the Duke of Norfolk presided over Cromwell's arrest at the Privy Council table. Within weeks the king had been persuaded that his chief minister was both a heretic and a traitor, and Cromwell went to the block on 28 July.

Cromwell's fall ended any further prospect of significant religious change under Henry VIII, though it is not helpful to speak of the last years of his reign in terms of 'reaction', as many historians have done. The year 1538 had marked the high tide of his Reformation: the line was drawn in November when the king manifested his commitment to the Catholic theology of the eucharist by personally presiding at the trial for heresy of John Lambert. But no ebb tide followed. Henry did not retreat from any religious position he had taken up. He tried to rein in access to the English Bible at the lower levels of society, but the English Bible was neither withdrawn nor seriously discouraged. And a revision of the Bishops' Book of 1537, which had already been in hand, advanced slowly, resulting in the appearance of what was called the King's Book in 1543, given statutory force that same year by the Act for the Advancement of True Religion. This Henrician Settlement, as it was evidently meant to be, was hardly a drastic change, though the King's Book was more Catholic in tone than its predecessor. It made it clear that Henry's Church was broadly Catholic in its doctrine, except for such points as the replacement of papal with royal supremacy. But the elimination of monasticism and the attack on the cult of the saints took his Church outside the Catholic tradition in its broader sense – saints and monasticism were common to the Catholic, Orthodox, Coptic and Syriac Churches. The king's chequered matrimonial history, moreover, reflected the continuing religious ambiguity. He married his fifth wife, Catherine Howard, a niece of the Duke of Norfolk's, on the very day of

Cromwell's execution. That alliance marked a decisive shift in religious tone, but not a permanent one. When Catherine's premarital sexual experiences and matrimonial indiscretions came to light, they led her to the scaffold in February 1542. Henry's last wife, Catherine Parr, whom he married in July 1543, was more sympathetic to Protestantism, and her influence gave Protestants hope despite the appearance of the King's Book that year.

The Reformation undertaken in the 1530s initiated deep and lasting changes in the relationship between England and its close neighbours, Wales, Ireland and Scotland. Behind the religious politics stood a succession crisis, and relations with these other polities were all crucial to England's security. Wales and Ireland had each played important parts in the Wars of the Roses, and Scotland was always a thorn in England's side. Henry's Reformation was accompanied by radical changes for Wales. Starting in 1536, a series of acts of Parliament integrated the principality fully into the English realm. Wales was divided into shires and assize circuits, and writs were issued to elect MPs for its shires and boroughs.[24] Civil disabilities that had made the Welsh second-class subjects in England were abolished. Although some deep cultural differences would remain, a political integration was accomplished that would stand unchallenged for the next four centuries. In Ireland, by contrast, an attempt to impose Henry's Reformation was only superficially successful. It provoked fierce resistance from the start, and while Wales was set on a path of unification, Ireland was set on a path of conflict. An immediate rebellion against Henry's Break with Rome, led by 'Silken Thomas', the son of the Earl of Kildare, was suppressed in two years of expensive and bloody warfare (1534–36). This left the Tudor regime with a lasting distrust of the local elites (the 'Anglo-Irish', descended from Norman conquerors of Ireland) as well as of the Gaelic-speaking indigenous Irish.[25] A nominal recognition of Henry's royal supremacy was achieved, and a good many Irish monasteries would be suppressed over the next ten years.[26] But Irish monasticism was marginalised rather than wiped out, and popular devotions were left untouched. The English Bible was an irrelevance to Gaelic speakers, and Protestantism made no headway at all on the island. Henry satisfied himself with formal recognition as King of Ireland in 1541, but this was little more than gesture politics. Henry never achieved the control in Ireland that he had in England and Wales, nor did any of his Tudor successors.

Relations with Scotland were also crucially changed by Henry's Break with Rome. From the start, Henry feared that the 'Auld Alliance' between Scotland and France might work to his disadvantage if an edge of religious division was put onto what was always a tense relationship. So the primary goal of his Scottish policy was to convince James V to follow his example in putting himself at the head of a national Church, tempting him with the prospect of enrichment through suppressing the monasteries. But James had no pressing need for such a measure, and remained a steadfast Catholic. When, in the 1540s, the aging Henry went in search of lost youth by renewing his early wars with France, he sought to insure against the classic threat of a Scottish offensive from the north – the sort of thing that had led to the slaughter at Flodden Field in 1513 – by launching a pre-emptive strike. As so often with Henry's initiatives, this precipitated the threat it had sought to avert, but James V's retaliation misfired and ended in another terrible Scottish defeat, this time at Solway Moss in 1542. The sudden death of James himself three weeks later left Scotland unexpectedly vulnerable under the six-day-old Mary Queen of Scots.

Henry's hitherto impotent assertions of feudal overlordship and English sovereignty over Scotland now took on a more threatening aspect, and he set about a policy of annexation via treaty while also giving voice to more grandiose imperial conceptions of the relationship between the two countries.[27] Judicious pensions and promises created an English party among the Scottish nobility. This opened up the cracks in the Scottish polity which were never more than papered over even during the adult years of strong kings such as James V. Henry was therefore able to secure excellent peace terms in the Treaty of Greenwich (1543), the principal article of which arranged a marriage between the infant Mary and Prince Edward. Had it taken place, this would have brought the union of the crowns forward by two generations. But the turbulence of Scottish minority politics frustrated the plan as the Catholic party in Scotland, led by Cardinal David Beaton of St Andrews, regained power and repudiated the treaty. The infuriated King of England unleashed a brutal war of vengeance against the Scots in 1544 and 1545, sending his son's uncle, the Earl of Hertford, to lay waste to Edinburgh and as much else as he could.

Had Henry possessed a strategic sense of national interest instead of an obsession with personal glory, Scotland would have been a more realistic target for his ambitions than France. But his attention turned back to France once the Scottish threat had been neutralised, and in 1544 he crossed the Channel one last time, in pursuance of a treaty he had made with Charles V. His huge army marched out from Calais in July and laid siege to Boulogne, which fell to him in September. But as so often before, he was left high and dry by his ally. Charles made peace with France. Boulogne became, like Calais, a black hole in royal finances, for Henry was not going to meekly surrender what had been won at such cost. Nor was France prepared to admit defeat. A French assault on the south coast was driven off in 1545, while French intervention in Scotland provoked another punitive raid under the Earl of Hertford. Neither the squandering of the profits of the dissolution nor the levying of prodigious taxes and forced loans sufficed to meet these costs, and from 1544 Henry's Council turned to the last resort of bankrupt regimes, the debasement of the currency.

Even on his last campaign in France, it was painfully obvious that Henry was not the man he had once been. Overweight and afflicted with a deep ulcer in his leg, he had to be hoisted onto his horse with a small crane. Back home in England, he went into a steep decline in 1545. He had never enjoyed penmanship, but now a mechanised instrument for producing his signature, the 'dry stamp', was manufactured because he could no longer wield a pen at all. Its deployment was jealously guarded and carefully minuted, but it put great power literally into the hands of those around him.[28] His will, though, remained law. In December 1545, in his last personal appearance in Parliament, he delivered an agonised expostulation against the religious divisions among his people that he had himself done so much to foment. His actions, though, failed to back up his words. At his command that very Parliament passed the 'Chantries Act', permitting him to dissolve at will any religious institution he chose, putting collegiate churches, almshouses, confraternities and chantries at risk of going the way of the monasteries. That was certainly a measure that heartened evangelicals. Yet his commitment to traditional theology remained adamant.

Factional strife between Catholics and evangelicals therefore continued to trouble his Court. Some of the Catholics at Court sought to implicate Catherine Parr in a heresy case brought in summer 1546 against a gentlewoman named Anne Askew, who had denied the doctrine of the real presence, and who numbered several evangelical ladies of the Court among her friends.[29] That attempt failed, but Anne herself was burned alive on 16 July, and the Catholics seemed to be riding high. But they fell from grace abruptly and late. Henry Howard, Earl of Surrey (son and heir to the Duke of Norfolk) was arrested in December 1546 on ludicrous charges of treason, occasioned by the presence of elements of the royal arms in his personal heraldry. He was found guilty on this count and was executed on 19 January 1547. This reversal put his father in the Tower as well. The duke cravenly pleaded guilty to whatever was charged against him and threw himself on the king's mercy, but in vain. On the strength of his confession, he was condemned for treason by an act of attainder that received royal assent on 27 January, Henry's last full day on this earth. The king's death overnight saved the duke's life. With the lion dead, the new King's Council either lacked the self-assurance to take a duke's life, or was nervous of the implications of doing so, on the strength of such a flagrantly contrived and unjust conviction.

EDWARD VI

Henry VIII died in the early hours of 28 January 1547. As in 1509, the king's death was at first a closely guarded secret, as the regime negotiated the transition to life under a boy king. Henry's will set out very clearly that England was to be ruled during his son's minority by a regency council. On his deathbed he required those councillors to swear a solemn oath that they would alter nothing in Church or kingdom during that time. He certainly imagined he could rule from beyond the grave, at least for a while. But his precautions were self-defeating. His greatest fear was that his Break with Rome might be undone, and this explains his deliberate exclusion from the regency council of the most capable politician in his service, Stephen Gardiner. Henry read his man well: he would certainly have favoured mending fences with Rome once the tyrant was in his tomb. But in excluding Gardiner, Henry removed the one man who might have stopped the subversion of his plans by the young king's uncle, Edward Seymour, Earl of Hertford. Under Seymour's guidance the regency council agreed on 31 January, after formally proclaiming the new king, that Seymour should become Lord Protector of the Realm and Governor of the King's Person. A few days later they approved a distribution of lands and titles among themselves, purportedly authorised by the late king. Edward Seymour became Duke of Somerset, but the Lord Chancellor Thomas Wriothesley, despite receiving the earldom of Southampton, was still reluctant to issue the letters patent confirming the Protectorate. So Somerset accused him of exceeding his authority and he was compelled to resign on 5 March, for fear of a worse fate. William Paulet, Wriothesley's successor in charge of the Great Seal of England, promptly issued the letters patent confirming Somerset in his new office. Henry's plan for the government of the realm had been overturned.

Somerset turned next to the Henrician Settlement of 1543. While Henry had reined in religious change since 1540, the new regime spurred it on. The path of travel was signposted when Nicholas Ridley began the series of Lenten sermons at Court on Ash Wednesday (23 February) with a fierce denunciation of images and ceremonies (especially holy water, which had an important part in that day's liturgy). Among his audience was Stephen Gardiner, who wrote at some length to take issue with his dismissal of all images as 'idols' and to remind him of 'the doctrine set forth by our late sovereign lord' in the King's Book of 1543 – which he would defend for the rest of the year.[30] Encouraged by such clear signals from the Court, zealous reformers were soon busy in print and in direct action. Iconoclastic incidents multiplied, and Protestant pamphlets proliferated.

Official change began in summer 1547 with the promulgation of a new set of injunctions for the whole Church, accompanied by a Book of Homilies, prepared by Cranmer, to help less educated clergymen preach the appropriate doctrine to their parishioners. The injunctions were a radicalised edition of Cromwell's 1538 injunctions, echoing their polemic against pilgrimage, relics and images, but broadening it into a frontal assault on the cult of the saints and popular religion. The traditional procession around the parish church, with hymns and chants, which preceded high Mass on Sundays and feast days, was prohibited. The candles that burned in front of the crucifix and the Blessed Sacrament were extinguished. All remaining images in churches were to be removed or whitewashed, with edifying sentences from scripture the only mitigation of the new minimalist aesthetic. Even stained-glass windows were whitewashed. The visual and social experience of going to Mass changed completely, even though the Latin service itself remained unchanged. Although it took many months, the injunctions were implemented rigorously. Robert Parkyn, an obscure parish priest just outside Doncaster (Yorkshire) who wrote a poignant account of these troubled years, recorded that in Lent 1548 'all images, pictures, tables, crucifixes, tabernacles, was utterly abolished and taken away'.[31]

Throughout 1547, Stephen Gardiner fought a rearguard action against religious change in a series of eloquent letters to Somerset, Cranmer and the Privy Council. He took his stand on statute, prudence and the late king's will, and his case was strong in law and logic. He pointed out the seditious character of early iconoclasm, complained about the way authors such as John Bale were now being allowed into print, and catalogued the ways in which the Homilies and injunctions contradicted the doctrine that Henry VIII had promulgated in the King's Book and enshrined in statute. These laws were still in force, and the regime was therefore acting *ultra vires*.[32] But for Somerset the law was a tool, not a rule, and Gardiner's arguments secured only his own committal to the Fleet Prison on 25 September, to make sure he was not available for the Parliament in November that was to repeal those irksome laws.

The one aspect of Somerset's policy that Henry certainly would have applauded was his continuation of the war against Scotland. A renewed attack was being planned even as Henry lay dying in late 1546, and early next year Somerset reiterated the demand that Scotland hand over Mary in accordance with the Treaty of Greenwich. Scottish resistance was stiffened by military aid from France, so in September 1547 the duke led an army north from Berwick and cut a Scottish force to pieces just outside Edinburgh at Pinkie. Scottish losses, as so often in these Tudor encounters, were devastating – some 6,000 Scots were killed that day. Somerset returned home in triumph in October, but over the next few months his forces occupied a number of strongholds such as Arbroath, Dundee, Dumfries and Haddington, in the hope of enforcing a settlement on the northern kingdom. But in 1548 the Catholic party in Scotland spirited the young queen away to France. That left a planned withdrawal as the only sensible option, but Somerset was not sensible, and went on pouring resources into defending his pointless Scottish outposts.

The Lord Protector was back in London for the opening of Edward's first Parliament on 4 November. Meeting for less than two months, it was mainly occupied in repealing Henry VIII's recent laws on religion and in passing a new Chantries Act (the 1545 act had lapsed with Henry's death). The repeal was essential to legitimise, albeit retrospectively, the reforms already introduced by the 1547 injunctions. The revised Chantries Act not only empowered the Crown to confiscate colleges and confraternities, but swept up every imaginable devotional fund, all the payments for prayers and Masses established under the terms of people's wills. Interestingly, it attempted a distinction between religious funds and those with secular purposes. The latter were in theory to be spared, as a concession to the major urban guilds, especially the livery guilds of London, whose interests were fiercely defended in the Commons. But the distinction was hard to define and harder to defend. The chantry commissioners were soon at work, and it was through concealment or corruption that towns had their best chances of salvaging something from the wreck.

The most significant act of that Parliament, however, was its very first, the long-windedly entitled 'Act against such as shall unreverently speak against the sacrament of the body and blood of Christ, commonly called the sacrament of the altar, and for the receiving thereof in both kinds' (1 Edward VI, c. 1). This Janus-faced statute began by addressing the concerns of those who deplored the rising tide of Protestant polemic and iconoclasm against the Catholic Mass. It threatened severe punishment for any such behaviour perpetrated after 1 May 1548. But this provision, which was never put into practical effect, was followed by clauses of a very different tone. These stipulated that, with immediate effect, holy communion would be administered in both kinds (that is, under the forms of both bread and wine) and that priests were not to refuse communion to anyone who presented themselves for it. This was a double blow to traditional religion. Communion 'under both kinds' was an emphatically Protestant custom in early sixteenth-century Western Europe. Henry had forbidden it in the Act of Six Articles. Moreover, the new law implicitly dispensed people from the need to go to confession before taking communion – another open move away from Catholicism towards Protestantism. An act which had probably been introduced by conservative religious interests had, it seems, been hijacked by the regime for a very different purpose.

The original inspiration of the Communion Act seems to have been a response to the way that popular print was harnessed to the cause of Protestantism in the first year of Edward's reign. In the wake of Ridley's Lenten sermon, a series of pamphlets appeared attacking the Catholic doctrines of the sacrifice of the Mass and the real presence under the pretext of the official campaign against 'idolatry'. In the meantime, the regime made it clear that print was now out of bounds to defenders of the traditional faith. The author of two heavyweight defences of those Catholic doctrines, Dr Richard Smyth, the Regius Professor of Divinity at Oxford, was forced to make a humiliating public recantation at Paul's Cross on 15 May, while a heap of his books was burned.[33] Dozens of Protestant preachers were granted royal licences to preach anywhere they liked, while Catholic preachers were denied the pulpit, especially in London. The campaign against the Mass intensified in 1548, paving the way for the culmination of Cranmer's Reformation, the appearance of the Book of Common Prayer in summer 1549.

Thomas Cranmer had probably dreamed for years of reforming the worship of the Church of England in line with Protestant doctrine.[34] Henry VIII's death gave him the latitude to do so, and by late 1548 he had, almost single-handed, boiled down and translated the multifarious Latin church services of medieval Catholicism into a single vernacular

Edward VI overthrowing 'popery'
This portion of a painting done in Elizabeth's reign shows Edward VI completing
the overthrow of popery begun by his father. At the king's feet, the pope falls dead,
his neck very obviously broken by a well-thrown Bible. At the table, the king's
councillors look on, the more Protestant ones (facing, and including a wispily
bearded Archbishop Cranmer) with grim satisfaction, but their more 'popishly'
inclined counterparts (opposite, and including a shaven and tonsured bishop, perhaps
Cuthbert Tunstall) with evident consternation. Outside, the work of iconoclasm goes
ahead apace.

text for public worship, the Book of Common Prayer. Cranmer's
Protestant liturgy offered a single form of prayer that would be the same
in any church in the realm. Uniformity was the watchword of the new
service, and it was imposed by the Act of Uniformity, which passed into
law early in 1549 after some divisive debates. The new service was to
come into force on Whitsunday (9 June) 1549.

Historians have failed to recognise the full significance of this wholly
unprecedented event. It was not just that Cranmer replaced a Latin liturgy
older in its essentials than English Christianity itself with a slimmed

down version in English. It was that this was done across an entire nation on one and the same day. The logistical effort alone is staggering. Thousands of copies of the Book of Common Prayer had to be printed and distributed in time for the launch. Richard Grafton and Edward Whitchurch were given the lucrative contract to print it. It accounted for nearly half their total output that year. But the most important thing to notice is that this was not only impossible but unimaginable before the invention of print. Medieval liturgical change was slow, laborious and incremental, limited by the speed of handwriting. No medieval reformer could have dreamed of transforming the entire liturgy of the English Church on a given Sunday. Print alone loomed behind Cranmer's greatest achievement.

The direct consequence of this was a rash of rebellions across most of the country. The most threatening uprisings were in the far south-west and in East Anglia, but there were also outbreaks in Buckinghamshire, Cambridgeshire, Dorset, Gloucestershire, Hampshire, Kent, Oxfordshire and Sussex. Historians have argued pointlessly over how 'religious' these rebellions were. Social and economic grievances such as enclosures, rising prices and punitive taxation were prominent everywhere, but while the headline issue in the West Country was undoubtedly the new church service, which rebels dismissed as a 'Christmas game' (i.e. a pantomime), in East Anglia the religious posture of the rebels was more complex. On the one hand, rebel leaders allowed a sermon to be preached during a Book of Common Prayer service held in their camp at Mousehold Heath, yet on the other much of the initial disorder was clearly reacting against recent religious changes.[35] Seen in a wider perspective, though, the outbreaks of 1549 were manifestly the result of Cranmer's radical disruption of the sacred order. One or two of these risings broke out before Whitsunday, but most of them began within the following fortnight, which included the festival of Corpus Christi. This feast, a celebration of the Catholic doctrine of transubstantiation, summed up everything Cranmer and the Book of Common Prayer were against. Its abrupt abolition and redefinition as a working day was as disruptive and unpopular as the abolition of Christmas by Oliver Cromwell's regime a century later.

A major limiting factor for the rebellions of 1549, as for every Tudor rebellion, was their inability to access print. The Peasants' War, which convulsed large areas of the Holy Roman Empire in the mid-1520s, owed much of its brief success to print, which enabled its message of radical social challenge to reach far wider audiences than ever before with texts such as the Memmingen Articles. And the Wars of Religion which tore France apart in the second half of the century were waged as fiercely in print as on the battlefield. But the preternatural 'centralisation' of England, with its solitary metropolis, weighed decisively against rebels, because all the printing presses were in London. Tudor governments might not have been able to exert absolute control over the press. But with all the presses within just a few miles of Westminster, the voice of violent protest could never get into print. Royal answers to rebel grievances, however, were routinely printed from 1536 onwards, ensuring that it was the royal message that was dinned into most people's ears. The rise of print simply added still more to the preponderance of London in English politics. Not until the English Civil War was armed opposition to the Crown able to access print in England, and even then only because the epicentre of rebellion was London itself. In 1549, the relative isolation of England's regions from each other and their inability to access print meant that there was nothing like the later 'public sphere' within which grievances could circulate so as to forge a national movement out of disparate local uprisings.

The rebellions of 1549 took a couple of months to suppress, which many of Somerset's colleagues blamed on his populist reluctance to clamp down hard. The rough work was handled by Lord Russell in the south-west and by John Dudley, Earl of Warwick, in East Anglia, both of them deploying German and Italian mercenary troops originally hired for service in Scotland. Somerset's authority was seriously undermined. It had already survived one challenge. His younger brother, Thomas Seymour, resented the fact that, though just as much the king's uncle as the duke was, he had nothing like the same power or reward. He pursued his own ambitions first by marrying Henry VIII's widow, Catherine Parr, and then, when she died in September 1548, by seeking the hand of the young Elizabeth, the king's sister. Even during his wife's lifetime, his interest in Elizabeth (who was then living in their household) had led to behaviour which today would have put him on the register of sex offenders. But Seymour's dreams were too much for his colleagues, and he was prosecuted for a range of offences typical of the corruption of Court politics during a royal minority. His execution in March 1549 probably did as much to weaken Somerset as his success would have done. After the risings of 1549, those who had brought down Seymour and suppressed the rebels saw their chance to deal with Somerset as well. Sensing the tide turn, Somerset retreated to the fortress of Windsor at the start of October, taking the young king with him and calling on lords and commons alike to take up arms on their behalf. The denouement was swift. Lord Russell, whose army had been mopping up in the West Country after slaughtering the main rebel force at Sampford Courtenay on 17 August, now threw his weight behind the regency council, and Somerset, facing inevitable defeat, surrendered. He was in the Tower by 14 October.

Somerset's fall opened a brief window of opportunity for religious reaction. Even foreign ambassadors, prone to take the temperature of the kingdom from the somewhat misleading thermometer that was London, felt that things had gone too far and would have to go back. Henry's last Lord Chancellor, Thomas Wriothesley, made a comeback to the Council table, and it was not certain which way Dudley would jump. Wriothesley was gaining ground in autumn 1549, but made a false move in seeking the immediate destruction of Somerset, in revenge for his own humiliation at Somerset's hands in 1547. But the precocious king was now 12 years old. Well drilled in Protestantism for three years by his tutor John Cheke, Edward was moving from childhood piety to adolescent zeal. Over the winter of 1549–50 Warwick charted his own course by the compass of his young sovereign's inclinations. When Wriothesley made his move against Somerset at the Council table, Dudley took the duke's side and faced him down. His stand may have been strengthened by the knowledge that for religious reasons Edward would not tolerate Wriothesley's presence in the Privy Chamber. Wriothesley's comeback, then, was brief. He was back in political retirement by the end of January 1550, and he died in July. The king's burgeoning commitment to Protestantism can be seen in his journal, which shows close interest in the fact that George Day (Bishop of Chichester) was induced to preach against transubstantiation in April and in Gardiner's grudging acceptance of the Book of Common Prayer in June 1550. By December, he was becoming irked by his sister Mary's insistence on retaining the Mass in her private chapel. In March 1551 she was summoned to the royal presence to hear his Council declare to her his displeasure at her obstinacy.

Dudley's need to get rid of Wriothesley made it politic for him to allow the fallen Duke of Somerset to make something of a comeback. Despite his escapade at Windsor in autumn 1549, Somerset escaped serious sanction. By February 1550 he had been released from the Tower, and by April he was once more attending the Privy Council. For the moment, as he stamped out the briefly glowing embers of religious conservatism, Dudley perhaps found Somerset's surprising popularity a political asset amid the continuing instability occasioned by religious change, financial meltdown and recurrent epidemics. Both the Privy Council records and the king's political diary testify to the frequency of plots or riots through these years. Dudley's shrewd policy for rebuilding revolved around a temporary expedient which had a long future ahead of it: the Lord Lieutenancy. The appointment of a nobleman or other substantial landowner as the king's lieutenant in a county was an implicit recognition of the way regional politics had changed since the 'bastard feudalism' of later Plantagenet England. The pressure Henry VII put upon traditional magnates and their practice of retaining had to some extent both required and empowered more of the gentry to take a role in regional and local government. But at times of crisis, leadership of the kind that came from powerful magnates was crucial. Its absence in East Anglia and the south-west surely accounts for the greater severity of the rebellions there in 1549: the Duke of Norfolk and the Earl of Devon were both in the Tower of London throughout Edward's reign. Appointing a royal lieutenant to coordinate local government at critical junctures was an effective solution, and thus, for example, John Russell had been appointed lieutenant for Devon after the rebellion there broke out.[36] Candidates had to be men of sufficient weight and authority to command the respect of their gentry colleagues, but armed with a royal commission the right man could do the job. Thus it was that the Duke of Somerset found himself Lord Lieutenant for Berkshire and Hampshire in 1551 (the death of Wriothesley in July 1550 having left something of a power vacuum there). Under Dudley, the county lieutenancy was very much *ad hoc*. Yet from the 1580s it would become a key element in England's governance.

Dudley was a more clear-headed leader than Somerset. He appreciated that royal finances were in meltdown and that militaristic policies in France and Scotland were unsustainable. Loyal to Henry VIII's memory, Somerset had clung grimly to his last conquest, Boulogne, regardless of cost. Henry II had seized the opportunity to invade and retake the Boulogne hinterland during England's summer of discontent, but the citadel held out through winter. Dudley therefore opened negotiations with France and cut the best deal he could get. Boulogne was handed over in exchange for cash compensation. This reduced Crown debt and released useful troops to help keep order back home. Garrisons were likewise withdrawn from the Scottish strongholds, and royal expenditure was brought under control. Dudley's own growing security, though, reduced his need for Somerset's support and made the duke look increasingly like a potential rival. Exploiting his emerging ascendancy over the young king, whom he flattered by involving him much more than Somerset had done in the business of government, Dudley consolidated his grip on power in October 1551, procuring his own promotion as Duke of Northumberland and bestowing grander titles on key cronies. Somerset was arrested within the week, tried and convicted on 1 December, and beheaded on 22 January – the day before the opening of a new Parliament.

That Parliament added new impetus to the headlong rush of the Edwardian Reformation. The first Book of Common Prayer had been in place for little more than a year before it was under revision, with the active involvement of two theologians of European stature, Martin Bucer and Peter Martyr Vermigli, who had fled to England to escape a short-lived Catholic resurgence in the Holy Roman Empire. The outcome was the second Book of Common Prayer, which systematically excised those residual Catholic elements that had enabled Stephen Gardiner to reconcile himself to the first book in 1550. Completed in 1551 and authorised by the new Parliament of January 1552, it came into force on the feast of All Saints (1 November) 1552. In theological terms, it rejected any notions of real presence, eucharistic sacrifice or a special ministerial priesthood. No one, however wilful or optimistic, could mistake the new communion service for the Mass.

Meanwhile, a commission of lawyers and theologians was established in March 1552 to draft a new canon law for the Church of England. The outcome of their labours, the *Reformatio Legum Ecclesiasticarum* ('Reformation of Ecclesiastical Laws') was ready in 1553, but amid increasing anxiety over the king's health it was shelved. The other project of that last year was the drafting of the Forty-Two Articles of Religion (precursor of the more famous Thirty-Nine Articles). This unmistakably Protestant account of Christian doctrine was promulgated with unseemly haste just weeks before the king's death. It is only through the weight of a much later tradition that Edward's Reformation is seen as in some sense 'over' by the time he died. The idiosyncrasies of the Church of England in 1553 were first fixed in shape when Mary I halted the Reformation in its tracks, and were then baked hard by the fires of her campaign against heresy. Even the second Book of Common Prayer betrayed its ancestry in the 'popish' Mass and Hours, while the retention of episcopacy was almost unique in sixteenth-century Protestantism. It is unlikely that either would have survived had Edward reigned another dozen years. Hallowed by the blood of the Marian martyrs, however, they became part of the heritage of the Church of England.

Though it has sometimes been said that he was a sickly child, Edward had been fit and healthy until 1552. He seems to have avoided the scourge of the Sweat, which burned across England for much of 1550–51. The king's diary for 1551 shows a boyish enthusiasm for martial exercises such as running at the ring and archery. But he himself reports falling ill with measles and smallpox in April 1552, and the lengthy summer tour which the Court undertook that year was obviously aimed at building him up with fresh air and regular changes of residence. Winter took its toll, though, and by March 1553 it was obvious to the Venetian ambassador that the king was ailing fast. An apparent rally in April, however, served to conceal from his Council the urgency of the situation. The heir presumptive under the terms of Henry VIII's last Act of Succession was Mary, and everyone knew that her accession would mean a reversal of the Reformation and political eclipse (or worse) for those who had advanced it. Though Edward had been contemplating the problem of the succession for some time, the plan to change the course plotted by Henry's act can only have been worked out in the final weeks of his reign. The plan was to bypass not only the Catholic Mary but also the entirely conformist Protestant Elizabeth and even the next in line, Frances Grey, now the only surviving child of Edward's aunt, Mary (Queen of France and Duchess of Suffolk). All this was to clear the way for Jane, Frances's eldest daughter – who happened to have married Northumberland's son, Guildford Dudley, on 21 May. There is no doubt that Edward was heart and soul behind this plan. When his judges baulked at authorising such a blatant contravention of statute law, he browbeat them into acquiescence. Yet it would be naïve to suppose that Jane's marriage to a son of the most powerful man in the kingdom was a pure coincidence. Equally obviously, the plan was not in place in March, for a parliament met on the first day of that month, only to be dissolved on the last. Northumberland would never have dismissed Parliament, which alone had the unquestioned power to override the 1544 Act of Succession, had he known that the king was dying and that the succession would need to be altered.[37]

The succession is the most delicate of all topics in any true monarchy. To meddle with what was seen as the working of divine providence was problematic enough, though Henry VIII's three acts of succession had set the precedent for this. But to challenge not only the unwritten law of God but also the written law of man was even more risky. When Edward died on 6 July, the regime therefore sought, as was by now customary, to keep his passing a secret. Northumberland made his plans, and on

10 July Jane was proclaimed queen. Unfortunately for both of them, there was a leak. Mary had the news even before Jane, and proclaimed herself queen on 9 July at Kenninghall, her Norfolk residence. She sent out letters calling for aid and the provinces rallied to her cause. A large army assembled at Framlingham, with the traditional East Anglian clients of the dukes of Norfolk at its core: Mary had in effect succeeded to the ducal position there when Edward's government bestowed upon her the Howard estates in fulfilment of Henry VIII's will (the duke himself was in the Tower after confessing to treason). Northumberland raised a force against Mary, and set out to give battle. But there was little enthusiasm for Jane's cause, and he was unable to hold his troops together as rumours of the size of Mary's army reached their ears. Retreating to Cambridge, he was ignominiously arrested by the mayor on 23 July, and Mary triumphed without a blow having to be struck.

The disastrous course of Edward's reign had done little to win support for his attempt to divert the succession. The futility of the costly entanglements in France and Scotland was made manifest by the eventual surrender of Boulogne and by the Scottish decision to send Mary Queen of Scots to safety in France. Poor harvests had piled agony on the back of swingeing fiscal demands and the confiscation of charitable resources from the Church. The abolition of the Mass in 1549 had set a spark to a powder-keg of resentment across much of southern England. After the massacres that terminated the largest and longest of those rebellions (in Norfolk and Devon), a particularly lethal visitation of the Sweat in 1551, one in a sequence of epidemics that had started in 1543, can hardly have convinced the people of England that God was smiling upon the helter-skelter religious change they had witnessed. Although historians used to imagine that the Protestant Reformation of Edward's reign enjoyed widespread popular support, such evidence as is available suggests rather the opposite. The nearest proxy that historians can find for quantitative evidence of the beliefs of individuals is that provided by their wills, which customarily began with Christian formulae and often included bequests for devotional and charitable purposes. The evidence of wills shows some advance of Protestantism, mostly in towns, and especially in London. But the overall frequency of Protestant wills rarely touches even 5 per cent. England was in law a Protestant country in 1553, but the English people as a whole were nowhere near being Protestants. It was through that gap between theory and practice that Mary marched to an easy victory.

4

REFORMATIONS REVERSED,
1553–1568

On the evening of Thursday 3 August 1553, Mary I rode in triumph through Whitechapel to Aldgate. Gorgeously arrayed in purple velvet embroidered with gold and pearls, she was accompanied by her sister Elizabeth and followed by a mounted entourage of thousands – nobles, ladies, gentlemen and guards. She was greeted at the city gate by the Lord Mayor, Sir George Barne, and the Aldermen. The Lord Mayor, who had signed up to the succession of Jane Grey, had every reason to shed tears of gratitude when she graciously restored to him the sceptre that he ritually surrendered into her hands. The splendid cavalcade then made its slow way down Leadenhall, left onto Gracechurch Street, and left again into Fenchurch Street, before turning right, down Mark Lane, towards the Thames and the Tower of London. The houses along the streets were decked with hangings and streamers, and bands of musicians played and sang at points along the way, though they can scarcely have been audible over the thundering of the guns of the Tower, which had been firing continuously since the queen entered the city. At the Tower Mary was greeted by Sir John Gage, whom she had restored to office as Constable there in reward for his refusal to acquiesce in the usurpation of Jane. There too she acknowledged the Duke of Norfolk, Bishop Stephen Gardiner, and young Edward Courtenay, who had been immured in its cells for years.[1] Within days the Tower was emptied of one tranche of inmates. Gardiner emerged on 9 August to be made Lord Chancellor, Norfolk was released and reinstated, and Courtenay was soon restored to the family earldom of Devon. The Tower needed space for new cohorts of political prisoners. Northumberland and his henchmen had been brought there within days of his capture at Cambridge.

Mary's triumph led at once, as everyone expected, to the restoration of Catholic worship in England. She herself had retained a Catholic chaplain to say Mass throughout her brother's reign, in defiance of the law and of Edward himself. Rosary beads, omnipresent in England until banned in 1547, had remained the livery badge of her retinue, ostentatiously worn by her escort of over a hundred knights and gentlemen when she had ridden into London in strength on 15 March 1551 to be lectured about religion by the King and his Council.[2] So it was with the strongest royal encouragement that the Latin Mass returned, like the onset of a thunderstorm – first just scattered drops here and there, then, almost before it could be realised, on all sides. Mass was restored in St Paul's Cathedral on 27 August and work began on rebuilding the high altar.

There were two remarkable features in the restoration of Catholicism. The obvious one is that it was accomplished entirely without statutory change, in flagrant disregard of the Act of Uniformity of 1552, which was not repealed until the autumn. The other is that this was not the manifestation of pure 'popularity' that it might seem to a modern observer. The Yorkshire priest Robert Parkyn, even as he wrote of the Marian Restoration with unconcealed glee, guilelessly acknowledged that the Mass was restored 'by command of lords and knights Catholic'.[3] The social reality of Tudor England is summed up in those seven words. The will of the people was as nothing to the power of the landed elite. If a monarch enjoyed the loyalty of the lords and knights, then their rule was unshakable.

Robert Parkyn's words also sum up the new religious reality. Under Henry VII it was unnecessary to specify that any English lord or knight was 'Catholic': there was no alternative. But by the 1550s a religious fissure ran through the land, dividing Catholics from Protestants. Although it has been suggested that the words 'Catholic' and 'Protestant' only gained general currency in the latter part of Elizabeth's reign, it is evident that both were current in the reign of Mary in the same sense in which they are used today.[4] The words were of course contested. At first, Protestants bridled at that name, though as so often with such things, it soon became a badge of honour. And they spoke resentfully, as the Catholic pamphleteer Miles Huggarde noted, of 'you which call yourselves Catholics'.[5] But while Protestants managed to popularise 'papist' as a pejorative name for Catholics, they never quite wrested 'Catholic' from the hands of their opponents. In Mary's time the division was still far from equal. Her easy victory is testimony to the massive imbalance. Yet Parkyn's need to specify 'Catholic' lords and knights shows how clear it was, even in Yorkshire, that there were other kinds.

Mary's first Parliament opened on 5 October with the traditional Mass of the Holy Spirit. Most members of the Lords would have been in London anyway, such had been the political drama of the summer. Mary's splendid coronation on 1 October, the first of a reigning Queen of England, added to the appeal of the capital for the nation's elite. Her Parliament worked at breakneck speed. It lasted barely two months, and debate was apparently not endemic. Few if any acts required a formal vote. One of its top priorities was the personal vindication of the queen. All the legislative and judicial acts purporting to invalidate her mother's marriage to Henry VIII, and thus to render her illegitimate, were repealed or annulled. The preamble to that act opened with the portentous observation that 'truth ... cannot but by process of time break out', paraphrasing the motto, *Veritas temporis filia* ('truth is the daughter of time'), which Mary had just adopted (it was engraved on her Great Seal). Another act repealed the statutes with which Edward's regime had imposed 'new things imagined' in place of the time-honoured liturgy of the 'Catholic Church', emphasising the 'strange opinions' and 'discord' that those innovations had fomented.[6] With these two laws, however, an uncomfortable new truth was tacitly acknowledged: both religion and the succession were proper subjects for parliamentary adjudication. Thanks to Henry VIII, this was no longer quite the kingdom Henry VII had taken over in 1485, in which both the succession and religion were beyond the reach of common law.

The great repeal of 1553 restored Catholicism, but not *Roman* Catholicism. In strict law what was restored was what Henry VIII had left standing in January 1547. Ridding the realm of the Book of Common Prayer was straightforward. The first book had been in use for just over three years, and its successor less than one, nothing like enough to etch the rhythms of Cranmer's prose into people's minds and hearts. The prohibitions on processions, crucifixes, devotional images and the rosary had been in place a little longer, but the vast majority of Mary's subjects remembered the old ways and were presumably happy enough to see them back. The wills made during her reign show that the personal paraphernalia of Catholic devotion were still abundant, even if we should recall that wills are, as a historical source, biased towards an older rather than a younger demographic. But the surviving accounts of England's parishes show how vast was the material damage inflicted upon institutional Catholicism.

There was opposition to the restoration, especially in London. The authorities put up a series of learned preachers at Paul's Cross, starting with Dr Gilbert Bourne on 13 August. But the youth of London, well drilled in Protestantism since 1547, regularly disrupted proceedings with catcalls and heckling, and violence was only narrowly averted. Armed guards were needed at Paul's Cross for weeks, and while Catholic rites were being restored from the end of August, occasional Protestant clergy were speaking out against the changes until at least Christmas. However, the open practice of Protestant worship was eliminated and, as a result, many of those who repudiated the Mass as a blasphemous parody of true religion fled the country for places such as Emden, Frankfurt, Geneva, Strasbourg and Zurich. Many hundreds of refugees have been identified, so their true numbers were probably in four figures, and it should be emphasised that most of them left before Mary's regime began burning religious dissidents as heretics.[7] It was not fear of persecution that motivated the exodus but a desire for the freedom to practise their faith.

The Mass was one thing, but the papacy was another matter, as were pilgrimages and monasteries. The monasteries had all been closed down by 1540, pilgrimages had been banned for 15 years, and the papacy had been vitriolically denounced since 1535. No more than half Mary's subjects would have known the pope as anything other than a hate figure, at best the 'usurping' Bishop of Rome, at worst the Antichrist. There was still enough left of the cult of the saints to provide the basis for a full revival (such as was achieved in many parts of Europe over the next century). People would be using Catholic swearwords for generations to come; oaths and curses are among the hardest things to change. But a full revival of the cult of the saints would have taken a long time – which, it turned out, Mary did not have.

The other urgent necessity of Mary's reign was to get the queen married so that she could give birth to an heir. At the age of 37, as the daughter of a woman who had had the last of several pregnancies at the age of 35, Mary's chances were never good. The first task was to find a husband. Lord Chancellor Gardiner and many of her councillors favoured an English candidate, Edward Courtenay, Earl of Devon, who had spent fifteen years in the Tower after the execution of his father in 1538. Mary herself favoured the more prestigious and traditional path of marriage to royalty, in the person of Philip of Spain, the elder son of her mother's nephew, Charles V. She wished to emphasise her Habsburg connections as well as to resume the familiar English alliance with Spain and the Netherlands. Her choice was contentious, however, and as a result she faced an unusual situation on 16 November 1553, when a joint delegation from the Lords and the Commons petitioned her not to marry a foreigner. Parliament would never have dared offer her father unsolicited advice on such a matter, but the dynamics of politics under a female monarch were subtly different. Of course Mary's will prevailed, and the marriage to Philip was swiftly arranged.

Mary's decision precipitated the great political crisis of her reign. Hatred of foreigners is always a rallying cry for malcontents, and members of the English elites who were inclined towards Protestantism planned a rising against the queen, ostensibly to stop her marrying Philip and thus subordinating England to a foreign yoke. The rebellion misfired, and most of its leaders were rounded up in January 1554. However, it gained traction in Kent, from where Sir Thomas Wyatt marched on London with several thousand men. A small force sent against him defected to his side, and he reached Blackheath by 29 January. This threat to the city and the Court unnerved the Queen's Council, but she herself rallied Londoners with a spirited address at the Guildhall on 1 February, and London Bridge was held. In another world, it might have been Mary at the Guildhall in 1554, not Elizabeth at Tilbury in 1588, who became an emblem of Tudor courage and the common touch. The men of Kent, who crossed the Thames upstream at Kingston, were put to flight in skirmishing around St James's Park on 7 February. The real significance of Wyatt's rebellion is not that Mary's position was especially vulnerable: it wasn't. Nor is that Catholicism was associated with Spain: that came later. It was that a group of rebels of evidently Protestant sympathies, who aimed at restoring the shattered fortunes of their faith, saw no political advantage in advertising this. They appealed to patriotism, or xenophobia, not religion. Politically, there was no mileage in Protestantism in 1554.

Mary's speech at the Guildhall, however, was likewise fairly discreet about religion. While she alluded in passing to the suspicion that the rebels were making her marriage 'a Spanish cloak to cover their pretended purpose against our religion', it was Tudor loyalism and obedience to which she appealed in her stirring peroration:

> And now as good and faithful subjects pluck up your hearts, and like true men stand fast with your lawful prince against these rebels, both our enemies and yours, and fear them not, for I assure you, that I fear them nothing at all.[8]

Protestantism had made more of an impact in London than anywhere else in England, and Mary's failure to play the Catholic card in this speech is revealing. Treason trumped heresy as a charge with which to damn her enemies. From 1535 onwards the religion of monarchy commanded wider allegiance than the religion of the monarch in England. About fifty rebels were executed at sites all over London on 14 February.[9] This mass execution, on a scale exceeding anything seen even under Henry VIII, was a Tudor lesson in obedience which quieted the disorders that had hitherto accompanied the restoration of the old faith. But the episode left the Queen's Council highly sensitised to 'seditious words' and suspicions of treason, and a steady stream of offenders were pilloried or mutilated during the rest of the year. Heightened anxieties are also attested by the frequency with which Mary's Council authorised the use of torture for those guilty or vehemently suspected of treason or other crimes (such as coining) that trespassed directly on royal authority.

In the wake of the Wyatt rising, the Marian regime set about taking the Catholic restoration beyond the reintroduction of the Mass. The other big symbolic achievements of Edward's reign were the whitewashing of the churches and the marrying of the clergy. The redecoration of churches was bound to be a slow process. But the perceived pollution of the blessed sacrament by consecration at the hands of priests rendered unclean through sexual relations with their unlawful wives was a sacrilege that could not be countenanced. Purging the Church of its married priests was accomplished with rapidity – thanks to the royal supremacy. Royal injunctions for the Church of England were issued under Mary's name in March 1554 with a view to reframing it once more as a Catholic institution. Clergy were instructed to revert to the liturgical and ceremonial order that had prevailed when Henry VIII died. But the three most substantial injunctions concerned married priests. They empowered bishops to remove married priests from their benefices, gave them discretion to redeploy elsewhere such married priests as were willing to renounce married life, and ordered them to separate any former monks or nuns from their spouses and punish them for breaking their solemn vows.

The purge was comprehensive. It has left few direct records, but its traces are all over the episcopal registers, as record numbers of parochial vacancies had to be filled that year, most of them reported as arising from dismissal. (Under normal circumstances, most vacancies arose through death or resignation.) Something like a third of the parish clergy had married in the diocese of London, and not much less in other nearby counties. But the further away from London, the lower the rates of clerical marriage, with vanishingly small numbers in the north. The deprivations are to be counted in hundreds, and the total probably reached four figures. The task began promptly. Lawrence Saunders, rector of All Hallows Bread Street, had been dispossessed by 2 April. But it stretched over months, and vacancies were still being filled the following year. Even so, the process shows what Tudor administration could achieve, in England at any rate, when pursuing a defined goal with firm royal backing.

Meanwhile, plans for the royal marriage went ahead. Parliament was summoned to enshrine in statute the terms of the marriage treaty, which made Philip king alongside Mary, but stipulated that his reign in England would not survive her death. The opportunity was also taken to clarify, in the novel situation of a female monarch, that the 'regal power, dignity, honour, authority, prerogative, pre-eminence, and jurisdictions' which the laws of England ascribed to a 'king' were as 'fully, wholly, absolutely, and entirely' vested in a female as in a male ruler. Philip, freshly invested by his father with the kingdoms of Naples and Jerusalem to put him on the same level as his future wife, had disembarked at Southampton on 20 July and made his way to Winchester, where the wedding was celebrated on the feast day of St James the Great, Santiago, the patron saint of Spain (25 July). The full royal title of the married couple was magnificent (Figure 4.1).

King and Queen of England, France, Naples, Jerusalem, and Ireland, Defenders of the Faith, Princes of Spain and Sicily, Archdukes of Austria, Dukes of Milan, Burgundy, and Brabant, Counts of Habsburg, Flanders, and Tyrol.

When Bishop Bonner set out his injunctions for the diocese of London in September 1554, he ordered that this title be recited in full in English as part of the bidding prayers read aloud at every high Mass.[10] Mary's subjects were to be relentlessly reminded of the extent of the royal dominions and thus of the power and divine favour enjoyed by their king and queen. After the abdication of Charles V in January 1556, the title received an upgrade: Spain was placed before France, and 'both the Sicilies' after it (Figure 4.1).

Attention now turned to the final act of the restoration – reconciliation with the papacy. Reginald Pole, the exiled cousin and enemy of Henry VIII who had been made a cardinal in the 1530s because of his public defence of papal supremacy, had been appointed papal legate to England for this purpose by Pope Julius III within weeks of Mary's coup. However, his rigid views on the return of confiscated monastic property set up political obstacles that took months to clear away. It was over a year before he crossed the Channel to Dover, where he landed on 20 November 1554.

Medal of Philip and Mary

This reverse side of a medal celebrating the joint reign of Philip and Mary shows them on horseback, with Mary bearing the sceptre of power and Philip the sword of justice. The inscription shown gives their lesser titles: Archdukes of Austria, Dukes of Burgundy, Milan, and Brabant, Counts of Habsburg, Flanders, and Tyrol. The obverse gives their full royal titles: King and Queen of England, the Spains, and France, the Two Sicilies, Jerusalem, and Ireland, Defenders of the Faith.

Parliament expedited a reversal of the attainder that had condemned him to death as a traitor in 1539, and on Saturday 24 November he disembarked from a river barge at Westminster and greeted the queen with the words 'Blessed is the fruit of thy womb' (Luke 1:42). At this, a pamphlet printed a few days later reported, Mary, who was by now believed to be pregnant, felt her baby kick.[11]

This carefully choreographed reminiscence of the New Testament scene of the visitation of Elizabeth by the Virgin Mary might sound like pure fiction, but it is a typically Tudor contrivance. It was followed by days of tough negotiations which made it clear that a return to papal obedience would be untroubled – as long as England's newly enriched landowners were licensed to retain their former monastic estates. Reassured that they could have the best of both this world and the next, those landowners, in the persons of the Lords and Commons, not only repealed the Act of Supremacy but crossed over from Westminster to the palace of Whitehall where, acting in their mystical capacity as the realm in microcosm, they formally repented their sins of heresy and schism and received the cardinal's declaration of national absolution. Lord Chancellor Gardiner himself read out their petition

> that we may, as children repentant, be received into the bosom and unity of Christ's Church, so as this noble realm, with all the members thereof, may in unity and perfect obedience to the See Apostolic and Popes for the time being, serve God and your Majesties to the furtherance and advancement of his honour and glory. Amen.[12]

This took place on 30 November. Although it has been suggested that this was not a 'parliamentary' proceeding, because it took place in Whitehall rather than in the parliament chamber of Westminster, it was only in Whitehall because the queen was unwell. Parliament therefore had to attend on the king and queen, rather than the monarchs gracing the parliament house with their presence. The significance of this event was expounded to the citizens of London the following Sunday (2 December), when Gardiner himself preached at Paul's Cross. He told how 'the three estates assembled in the parliament, representing the whole body of this noble empire of England and dominions of the same, have submitted themselves to his holiness and his successors forever'.[13] He was one of the most eminent figures to preach at the Cross in its 200-year history, to perhaps the most eminent audience ever assembled there, since it included both King Philip and Cardinal Pole.

This third Parliament of Mary's reign marked a shift to a distinctively confessional politics, at once divisive and effective. The writs for its elections had pointedly instructed her subjects to choose men of a 'Catholic sort'. The terminology of 'Catholic' and 'Protestant' thus became a tool of political discernment, distinguishing 'them' from 'us'. This is not to say that her instructions were uniformly heeded. A few Protestant MPs were still returned, among them the wealthy printer Richard Grafton. But the point was made; favour and patronage were for 'us' and not 'them'. Known Protestants faded from public life as the reign progressed. The full impact is difficult to measure, because Mary's reign was short, and shifts of religious position by landowners and officeholders in the next reign make it harder to tell precisely where men stood in the 1550s. But the anecdotal evidence is abundant. When Elizabeth came to the throne there were loud complaints about undue influence brought to bear upon parliamentary elections under Mary, and William Cecil himself, in the policy brief he drew up in 1559 on the 'alteration of religion', stated as a bald fact that opposition was to be expected from 'all such as governed in the late Queen Mary's time, and were chosen thereto for no other cause. . . [than] for being hot and earnest in the other religion', as well as from 'men which be of the papist sect; which late were in manner all the judges of the law; the justices of the peace, chosen out by the late Queen in all the shires'.[14] When Mary died in November 1558, England was on the way to becoming a Catholic 'Confessional State'.

The third Parliament passed the two acts that defined Mary's reign: the one repealing the antipapal legislation of Henry's reign, and the other reinstating the old Plantagenet heresy laws. Despite the efforts to ensure a compliant House of Commons, neither act was passed without debate, sometimes sharp. Yet while it is tempting to see the rough passage of these laws in religious terms, the nub was rights of property. Even the heresy laws provided for the confiscation of the property of heretics (though this had not often been done, because late medieval heretics were mostly persons of modest means), and this caused anxiety. The repeal of antipapal legislation was likewise beset by anxiety over the fate of secularised church lands and of the rights to tithes which had come into lay hands in such quantity after the dissolution of the monasteries. The pope had already issued a dispensation for the laity to keep the booty of the previous twenty years. But landowners were not wholly reassured. What was granted by one pope might be rescinded by another. So this dispensation was written into the statute, and hedged about with clauses putting it beyond question that matters relating to former monastic property were matters of English law. The insistence of an essentially Catholic Parliament on their right to keep what they had plundered from the Church is the best measure of how much damage had been done to England's Catholicism in one generation. The doctrine and discipline of Catholicism might be the same as before, but its social fabric in England could never again be what it had been before Henry and Edward had ripped it asunder.

It used to be a common criticism that Mary and her regime failed to understand the power of the press. But as Eamon Duffy demonstrated, the notion that Protestants outpublished Catholics under Mary is a category mistake that depends on counting only polemical writings. In this market niche, Protestants were indeed busier than Catholics. But Protestant polemic had to be printed overseas and was far less readily brought to market. Meanwhile, Catholic printing in England focused on traditional service books, devotional works, and orthodox sermons and catechetics. Edmund Bonner produced a statement of religious belief closely modelled on the King's Book of 1543, but with the pope put back. He accompanied it with a Book of Homilies more loosely modelled on those of Cranmer. Both texts were frequently reprinted, as was a devotional 'primer' that supplied prayers for the laity to use in parallel Latin and English versions – a response to Protestant jibes that Catholics preferred to bury their teaching in the obscurity of a language unknown to ordinary people. A regular series of high-profile Catholic sermons by Mary's bishops also found its way into print. There was plenty of Catholic literature available under Mary, in both Latin and the vernacular.[15]

The Marian regime was from the start fully alive to the value of print. One of Mary's first moves was to dismiss the previous royal printer, Richard Grafton, and to replace him with the stoutly Catholic John Cawood. Grafton, a committed Protestant, had actually printed the proclamation of Jane Grey as queen in July 1553 – a broadsheet that also proclaimed himself as that queen's printer – and found himself in the Tower before the month was out. Cawood was soon busy, publishing the Duke of Northumberland's edifying last words on the scaffold, including his helpful declaration that he died 'in the true Catholic faith'. Proclamations were used more than ever to communicate government to the queen's subjects. As well as the 'sessional prints' which made the latest parliamentary legislation available in handy booklets, laws that the regime considered particularly important were printed or summarised individually as broadsheets or leaflets for dissemination and display throughout the land. The 1553 acts against unlawful and rebellious assembly and against the disruption of sermons or church services are typical examples.[16]

Marian censorship is likewise testimony to the regime's appreciation of the power of the press. Attempts to control print were not entirely successful, but they were by no means futile. The chartering of the

Stationers' Company in 1557 was meant to limit the trade to known and licensed tradesmen whose work could thus be policed. This institution would underpin the largely successful control of the English press that persisted until the collapse of Charles I's government in 1641. But under Mary, as under Edward, the real bite of censorship lay in the power of the authorities simply to confiscate and destroy seditious or heretical literature. Booksellers and printers could ill afford to see high-value product go up in smoke, and were therefore careful about what they produced. Like all the Tudor regimes, Mary's also realised that the pulpit was at least as important as the press. Here, control was almost total from Christmas 1553. The old system of episcopal licences for preaching was revived, and the pulpits were closed to heretics.

The publication of three now famous anti-monarchical treatises by Protestant authors is sometimes seen as evidence for the ineffectiveness of Marian censorship. John Ponet's *Short Treatise of Politike Power* (1556), Christopher Goodman's *How Superior Powers Ought to be Obeyed* (1558), and John Knox's *First Blast of the Trumpet against the Monstrous Regiment of Women* (1558), however, assumed far greater significance in the minds of later historians than they ever held in the sixteenth century. All three had to be printed abroad, and none achieved wide circulation. None was reprinted until the 1640s, in the context of the English Civil War. Knox's pamphlet did elicit a refutation – from an English Protestant, John Aylmer, in 1559, out of concern to refute arguments which told as heavily against Queen Elizabeth as Queen Mary. In short, these works were a hideous embarrassment to English Protestants. John Foxe, the first historian of Marian Protestantism, never refers to those books, and hardly ever to their authors. Under interrogation in Star Chamber in 1591, the leading Puritan Thomas Cartwright disclaimed any sympathy with Goodman and his 'seditious book'.[17] Thanks to the Civil Wars, the Glorious Revolution and the American Revolution, these texts much later achieved canonical status in some versions of the confessional history of liberalism and republicanism. But the keynotes of political thinking in Tudor times were kingship and obedience, not resistance or republicanism.

The heresy laws were no sooner reinstated than put to work. The act itself came into force on 20 January 1555, and the first man to go to the stake under its authority was John Rogers, on 4 February. He was to be followed by nearly 300 others over the following four years. Lawrence Saunders was burned at Coventry on 8 February, having been arrested the previous October for giving an unauthorised sermon at his former London parish church. The most illustrious victim was Thomas Cranmer, burned at Oxford on 21 March 1556 despite having signed a series of ever more grovelling recantations in the hope that his life might be spared as, in legal terms, a first-time offender. That particular act of terror was a wasted opportunity. A penitent Cranmer kneeling before the sacrament would have done as much to discredit his teachings as his heroic demeanour at the stake did to hearten its later adherents. The last victims were a group of five men and women from Kent, burned at Canterbury on 15 November, just two days before the queen herself died.

The Marian martyrs were memorialised and made famous by the Protestant historian John Foxe, who published the first edition of his 'Book of Martyrs' in 1563, and followed it up with augmented new editions in 1570 and 1583.[18] It has often been suggested that the ferocity and scale of the burnings alienated the English people from the Catholic faith and Church. In the long perspective of the ensuing centuries there is real truth in this. But while the Marian repression of heresy was ferocious even by the standards of the sixteenth century, there is little evidence that it alienated the population at the time. Foxe reports a few displays of sympathy or even support for the victims, and in London it was necessary to take precautions against possible violence. But most burnings were carried out with no more fuss than the far more numerous but mostly unreported hangings that were a feature of Tudor and Stuart England. It was Foxe's careful curation of the memory of the martyrs, not the events themselves, that made the Marian burnings one of the best known episodes in English history and marked Catholicism, in England, with the taint of cruelty.

The disappointment of Mary's pregnancy probably did her more damage than the burnings at the time. Although rumours of the birth of a son sparked rejoicing in London on 30 April 1555, the story was known next day to be false, and as weeks turned into months it became apparent that so too was the pregnancy. Her husband, who had been with her the whole time, left for the Netherlands in August and was not to return to her for two years, long enough to show that he now doubted she would ever bear him a child. With no prospect of a certainly Catholic heir, her reign took on a different aspect.

Mary's reign reminds the historian that the papacy was much more of a problem for Catholic monarchs than for Protestant ones. It was Catholic rulers who could find ecclesiastical matters in tension with national interests. Through her marriage to Philip II of Spain, Mary was also caught up in a conflict between her husband and the erratic and irascible Pope Paul IV, who probably did more damage to the Church and much else than any other pope that century. Paul IV resented Spanish hegemony in Italy, and pursued an alliance with France in the hope of overthrowing it. His doctrinal rigidity, extraordinary even by the standards of sixteenth-century intolerance, led him to nurse profound suspicions of the orthodoxy of the primates of both the Spanish and the English Churches. He wanted to bring both Bartolomé Carranza (Archbishop of Toledo) and Reginald Pole to Rome to face charges of heresy. Mary's flat refusal to hand over her archbishop paralysed English relations with Rome for the last year of her reign, which delayed the appointment of new bishops – a matter that took on special urgency in the catastrophe which engulfed her final years.

That catastrophe was not, as one might imagine, the war with France into which England was dragged by Philip II when he briefly returned to the country in 1557. The fall of Calais in January 1558 marred what was otherwise a successful campaign. Of course it damaged Mary's prestige, and the war was a waste of money. But the real catastrophe was that, from late 1557, a pandemic more deadly than that which swept the world in 2020–22 decimated the English people. A recurrence of the English Sweat, maybe jostling with some variant of influenza and other infections, caused the biggest demographic shock since the Black Death. England has never seen the like of it since – not even in the plague of the 1660s or the influenza of 1919. Thanks to Thomas Cromwell's introduction of parish registers in 1538, historical demographers have been able to reconstruct the terrible story. The two years from July 1557 to June 1559 saw mortality respectively 60 and 120 per cent higher than the 25-year trend (which was in any case high).[19] Mary, of course, was afflicted with what we have learned to call 'pre-existing conditions', and it is no surprise that the fever ended her life on 17 November 1558. Reginald Pole, by a fateful coincidence, died the same day, probably of the same cause. Thus the queen and the nearest thing she had to a chief minister left the scene together, clearing the way for the peaceful accession of Elizabeth. Pole's death was especially helpful to the latter. The man who promulgated Henry VIII's excommunication and had laboured to overthrow him was not the man to shy away from a confrontation with his daughter. The 'Elizabethan Settlement' of religion in 1559 would have a faced a far rougher ride from a hostile Cardinal Archbishop of Canterbury.

Although she knew she was dying, Mary made no moves to block her sister's accession, satisfying herself with securing from Elizabeth what proved to be equivocal undertakings to uphold the Catholic faith. Her

Lord Chancellor, Nicholas Heath, Archbishop of York, led a delegation of Mary's councillors to Hatfield where they paid homage to Elizabeth as their lawful queen. Heath was an old hand from Henry's reign, and while this time he followed his conscience and set his face against religious change, he was not, like Pole, a man to upset the good order of the kingdom and the succession over a question of faith. The religion of monarchy once more proved to be the defining religion of Tudor England.

The kingdom of England which Elizabeth I inherited already looked rather different from the one her grandfather had known. It was inconceivable in 1485 that a woman might ascend the throne. John Knox's now infamous denunciation of female rule – 'the monstrous regiment of women' (by which he meant that the rule, or 'regime', of women was contrary to nature) – was an extreme formulation of a common prejudice. Yet Elizabeth was the second woman in a row to wear the crown, and just as the likeliest alternative to Mary I had been Lady Jane Grey, the likeliest alternative to Elizabeth was Mary Queen of Scots. Things were also different in the ranks of the aristocracy. Elizabeth's England was down to its last duke. She never created a new one, and was to execute that last one, albeit reluctantly, in 1572. Except for a handful of religious houses insecurely refounded by Mary, the vast infrastructure of medieval monasticism, that once stretched like a web across the kingdom, was no more. The thousands of guilds and confraternities that had formed the fabric of much of England's social life were likewise gone. Partly as a result of these suppressions and partly because of economic change driven by an expanded class of more exploitative rentier landlords, the problem of poverty was becoming more painful and more visible. After her long reign, the kingdom Elizabeth bequeathed in 1603 would be as different again.

Elizabeth was not always fortunate in her judgement of men, but she had for some years accepted the advice and guidance of William Cecil, a shrewd and considered politician who had risen rapidly under the Protector Somerset and the Lord President Northumberland. After he had helped her navigate the aftermath of the fall of Sir Thomas Seymour, she had appointed him her estate manager in 1550. Betting on Elizabeth rather than Mary, Cecil had served her loyally throughout her sister's reign. He won his bet the day Mary died, and was immediately sworn in as Elizabeth's first Privy Councillor, holding the office of Principal Secretary. For forty years he would quietly dominate English politics, sometimes guiding and sometimes pushing his sovereign – who often pushed back. To the extent that there was government policy in her reign, its general direction was largely charted by Cecil, but the queen was no mere puppet. She had to be persuaded to authorise action, and she had a considerable capacity for digging in her heels where she saw avoidable risk or expense. Elizabeth did not so much set policy as set its limits.

The first priority of Elizabeth and her government was, as it had been for Mary, religion. However, unlike Mary, Elizabeth charted her course cautiously and hesitantly. There was no royal licence to abandon the Mass, nor did Elizabeth set any such example. For the first six months of her reign, the Latin Mass remained the liturgy of the English Church, although the use of English was permitted for the readings and the litany. There were hints of impending change. The queen made a few public gestures, objecting to what she saw as the excessive use of candles, and walking out of a Mass at the elevation of the consecrated host. But it was also made clear that change, when it came, would be transacted in an orderly fashion under the guidance of the law of the land, and not, as under both Edward and Mary, in defiance of it.

Plans were soon being made, as one can see from the 'Device for alteration of religion', the first in a sequence of policy papers that Cecil produced at critical junctures in the reign, papers which embodied a new approach to politics. The 'Device' was drawn up in advance of her first Parliament, which convened shortly after the coronation. In the statute book, the two chief acts of what has come to be called the 'Elizabethan Settlement' look straightforward. The acts of supremacy and uniformity head the booklet as chapters 1 and 2 of her laws. Even the curious 'Act of Recognition', which formally recognised Elizabeth's right to the crown 'by the laws of God and the laws and statutes of this realm', took third place behind them. Yet the records of proceedings in Parliament, sketchy though they are, show that it was no straightforward story.

The surviving evidence does not permit a definitive account of what happened, but the bills were drafted and redrafted, discussed in committee and amended, and sometimes voted down before they were finalised in April. This has given rise to diverse interpretations. John Neale believed that the agenda for her reign was set by a 'Puritan choir' in the House of Commons which forced upon the queen a settlement more Protestant than she desired. But subsequent research has found no trace of any 'Puritan choir'. Norman Jones offered a more persuasive reinterpretation, seeing Elizabeth as determined from the start upon something very like the settlement she secured, and facing opposition not from Puritans in the Commons but from Catholic bishops and their allies in the Lords. This opposition, he argued, extorted concessions to conservative opinion, such as the conflation of the different version of the words of administration of communion used in the 1549 and 1552 Books of Common Prayer, and the abandonment of the title 'Supreme Head'.[20]

Jones was certainly right to see the bishops in the Lords at the heart of opposition to change. Thus Bishop Cuthbert Scott protested that Parliament simply had no authority to 'meddle' in 'matters of religion'.[21] And the bishops led Convocation, which met at the same time as Parliament, in promulgating an uncompromising statement of traditional Catholic doctrine – the only time in Tudor religious history that the representative body of the clergy frankly defied the will of the monarch.[22] However, there is no reason to think that this opposition won any concessions, for the changes made did nothing to mollify Catholic opinion. Notwithstanding the 'concession' on the words used at communion, the Act of Uniformity only passed the Lords by three votes, because not only the bishops but also several Catholic peers opposed it. It does not look as though they were impressed by any tinkering with the words. As Diarmaid MacCulloch has argued, this change was probably intended to mollify Lutheran, not Catholic, opinion. Likewise, the title of 'Supreme Head' was abandoned to please returning Protestant exiles, who knew how offensive it was to Calvin and other leading Reformers.[23]

The 'Elizabethan Settlement' was a compromise in two respects, but not between Catholicism and Protestantism. First, it was a compromise between past and future, a snapshot of a Church in transit, frozen into a lasting pattern by the queen's aversion to change. It was the enshrining of Protestant doctrine within a Catholic ecclesiastical structure, and it established a Protestant liturgy carved out of Catholic raw materials rather than created from scratch. But the Settlement was also a compromise with reality. Elizabeth's was a Protestant Church staffed by Catholic clergy. Catholic priests in their thousands were the majority of Elizabeth's clergy into the 1570s, and a sizeable minority even into the 1580s. These men were at best reluctant missionaries, at worst a fifth column; and if the clergy were predominantly Catholic, so too were the laity. Some further concessions made in the Settlement perhaps sugared the pill for some of her Catholic subjects. Rogationtide processions were allowed (having been prohibited under Edward), organs were not actually banned and were often retained, and for many years the queen herself kept a crucifix and candles on the altar in the Chapel Royal. Yet these were concessions made to Elizabeth rather than by her. She had a taste for decorum and even beauty in worship. She had no time for Calvin or the sort of discipline and liturgy he promoted, and she preferred worship to sermons. Unlike her father and brother, she was not much interested in theology. Continuity of personnel in the parish churches was far more important in securing widespread gradual acceptance of the latest religious change. Pragmatic Catholics did not need subtle or ambiguous concessions to square their consciences, but just told themselves that their Protestant parish ministers were doing no more than handing round bread for people to eat. Nor did the changes of 1559 leave anyone under any misapprehension that the new service was in some way the same as the old. As John Whitgift put it a dozen years later, 'the most ignorant and simplest Papist that is, knoweth that the Communion is not the Mass'.[24]

The Elizabethan Settlement was not just about legislation: it was also about implementation. This began almost immediately, by means of a nationwide visitation of the Church, reforming it in accordance with new royal injunctions – a slightly revised version of those issued under Edward VI. The primary purpose of these injunctions was to impose the royal supremacy upon the clergy, or to dismiss from their posts in the Church any priests who refused to take the oath. Hundreds of refuseniks were dismissed – including all but one of the surviving Marian bishops, high proportions of the cathedral chapters, and a good many college heads and fellows at Oxford and Cambridge. Dozens of these dissidents made their way abroad as refugees.[25] A minority were held in prison or under house arrest for the rest of their lives. Still others melted away into private life, sometimes ministering clandestinely to those who remained committed to the traditional faith. The remaining injunctions were enforced with enormous variations in enthusiasm and thoroughness. What mattered in 1559 was ejecting irreconcilable Catholic priests and securing at least nominal compliance from the rest.

The ejected priests came predominantly from the upper levels of the hierarchy, and needed to be replaced fast. Probably Elizabeth would have preferred more of them, especially of the older, Henrician bishops such as Tunstall and Heath, to conform once again to the supremacy and thus temper the Protestantism of her Church. But the lines were drawn more clearly by 1559, after a generation of controversy and coercion, and the old compromises no longer seemed so acceptable to the learned. This situation had an enormous impact on her Church, for she was compelled to look to the returning exiles to fill the vacancies. At the highest level, she preferred men who had, like her, conformed outwardly under Mary rather than fled the country: her chief minister, William Cecil, and her first Archbishop of Canterbury, Matthew Parker, had both stayed in England, keeping their heads down. But the list of churchmen which Brett Usher persuasively argues Cecil offered Elizabeth as prospective bishops in July 1559 had numerous former exiles on it, and even more of them were needed to fill the gaps in the cathedrals and colleges.[26] The necessity of looking towards men of this stamp pulled Elizabeth's Church in a more Protestant direction, and led to long-term tensions between her and her bishops, and within her Church.

As in 1553, so too in 1559 it was thought vital to get the queen married so that she might bear children and secure the succession. Although the precedent set by Mary Tudor might seem unhappy, a foreign prince remained the almost universal choice over the alternative, an English nobleman. The lengthy list of Elizabeth's potential husbands only ever included one Englishman, Robert Dudley, Earl of Leicester, and the nobility and Privy Council opposed that idea almost to a man. To see one of their own, a man with friends and enemies already made, raised up over themselves was intolerable. With an outsider, at least, everyone would start on an equal footing. With one exception, everyone wanted the queen to marry. The exception, though, was important: it was the queen herself. Elizabeth rarely had a good word to say for the married state, and only twice displayed any serious interest in actually marrying someone, in each case someone whom she knew was fundamentally unacceptable to her leading subjects: Leicester, as already mentioned; and the Duke of Anjou, Francis of Valois. Her policy over her own marriage sums up the nature of her ultimately rather limited political gifts: she was very good at saying no, but found it much more challenging to make positive decisions. Delay and deflection were her default tactics. Beyond that, she never had a strategy.

At first, the question of the queen's marriage was uncontroversial. When Elizabeth's first Parliament petitioned her to marry, it was the polite voicing of a general expectation, not an expression of anxiety. Of course the queen would marry. Nor did her gracious response give any cause for alarm, though a careful reading of her words betrays, in hindsight, her reservations. By the time the 1563 Parliament convened, there was a new sense of urgency: Elizabeth was still unmarried. Her romance with the safely married Robert Dudley had done nothing to dampen expectations of her taking a husband in due course. Indeed, the unwitnessed death of Dudley's wife Amy in September 1560 had given rise to rumours that he had put her out of the way in order to free himself to marry the queen. This made his rivals and enemies all the keener to see her married to a foreign prince. Other deaths sharpened their anxieties. The death of

Henry II of France in July 1559, following a jousting accident, made Mary Queen of Scots and France a more threatening contender for the crown. And if the death of her husband, Francis II, in December 1560 reduced the immediate threat, her return to Scotland in August 1561 put her in a good position to launch a bid for the English throne in the event of Elizabeth's death. Elizabeth's own brush with death in October 1562, an attack of smallpox that saw her life despaired of, showed how slender was the thread on which the regime dangled.

The summons for a new Parliament that went out in November 1562 reflected this sense of insecurity and urgency. The opening of Parliament on 12 January 1563 took place amidst a veritable campaign of lobbying, doubtless incited by worried Privy Councillors. The Dean of St Paul's, the devoutly Calvinist Alexander Nowell, preached the opening sermon, and he used this opportunity to call upon the queen to marry. An MP moved a petition on the subject in the House of Commons within a week, and Cecil himself was busy in the manoeuvres that followed. Confidence in the queen's intentions was by now less than total. In March, there was debate in Parliament over a succession bill, and it is now known that Cecil went so far as to draft unprecedented clauses that would empower the Privy Council and Parliament to decide upon the rightful heir in the event of the queen's death with the succession unresolved. What is most remarkable about this bill is not that it sank without trace, but that it was moved at all without royal authorisation. The three acts of succession passed under Henry VIII (in 1534, 1536 and 1544) had all emanated from the royal will. No mere subject would have dared move a bill to regulate the succession in Henry's reign without his direct command. Ironically, however, the fact that these three acts were all widely available in print fostered in Members of Parliament the notion that legislating on the succession was part of their job. This notion gained plausibility under the rule of a woman, who, their worldview assured them, stood in need of male advice and guidance in politics. Elizabeth was acutely sensitive on all these points. When John Hales, who as an MP had no doubt been involved in the debates of 1563, penned a treatise on the succession in 1564, he was promptly consigned to the Tower.

The 1563 Parliament mostly kept its nose out of religion, but the Convocation that met at the same time was vociferous in calling for further reform. Alexander Nowell was the proctor of the Lower House and thus its spokesman in dealing with the bishops of the Upper House, and he played a leading role in formulating demands for change. These included many initiatives later associated with Puritanism, such as an end to elaborate choral music, a prohibition on organs in church, and the abandonment of traditional vestments. Not that this was controversial within Convocation. The bishops and the lower clergy were in broad harmony on almost everything. They agreed the Thirty-Nine Articles (a slightly edited version of the Forty-Two Articles defined under Edward VI), authorised a second Book of Homilies (including a massive polemic against religious images), approved a strongly Calvinist catechism drafted by Nowell himself, and drew up a 'book of discipline' for the Church, an attempt to implement the moral substance of Calvinist Presbyterianism within the framework of episcopacy. The entire programme was stopped in its tracks by the royal veto.[27] This check was the first time that Elizabeth publicly displayed her lifelong sense that what had been done in 1559 was a settlement and not a staging-post.

By the middle of the 1560s, it was becoming apparent that Elizabeth I had no appetite for further religious change. There had been no reason to think this in 1559. Imperfections in the religious order established that year could easily be viewed as unavoidable compromises with reality: most English people were still Catholics, as were most of their parish priests. But even then Cecil had foreseen trouble from such as 'shall see peradventure that some old ceremonies shall be left still' in the English Church. And the experience of the 1563 Convocation had alerted zealous Protestants to the queen's attitude. Soon after that, the Church of England came under pressure from below – or at least from halfway down. Fired up by young dons in the universities, students at some of the colleges began to rebel against the obligation to wear clerical dress in chapel, baulking even at a white surplice and a square black cap. Other distasteful ceremonial elements, such as kneeling to receive communion or bowing the head at the mention of the name of Jesus, were likewise discarded in a calculated display of disobedience.

When news of such demonstrations reached the queen she told her bishops to suppress them, in a letter of 25 January 1565. Many of the bishops were unwilling agents, sympathising more with the students than with their queen, but when Parker and his colleagues drew up a plan of action for her approval, they were dismayed to find that she would not lift a finger to help them. The measures they proposed were eventually issued under the title 'Advertisements' (which then meant a warning, not a commercial), but some proved all but impossible to enforce: kneeling for communion was soon a dead letter in the English Church. Non-compliance was particularly marked in London, where the wealthy parishes lured talented young ministers fresh from university.

In March 1566, as the 'Advertisements' were going to press, Parker and the Bishop of London summoned all 110 or so London parish clergy to Lambeth to demand their conformity. A third of them refused and were promptly suspended, leaving many churches with difficulties providing religious services at Easter.[28] The clampdown was either not necessary or not possible outside London, Oxford and Cambridge, and the furore gradually died down as hot-headed ministers toned down their resistance while shrewd bishops picked their battles. But from this time forward, the Church of England was troubled by such low-level recalcitrance in matters of ritual.

Elizabeth's chief minister, William Cecil, saw as clearly as Henry VIII and Thomas Cromwell before him that the security of the English Reformation was imperilled by a Catholic Scotland. A Catholic Scotland ruled by a Catholic rival for the throne of England was still more of a threat, as was a Catholic Scotland in alliance with Catholic France. It is hardly surprising then that from the start, as Stephen Alford has shown, Cecil had a clear 'British policy', namely the promotion of the Protestant cause in Scotland with a view to breaking up the 'Auld Alliance' with France and aligning the kingdom instead with England.[29] When Elizabeth came to the throne, Scotland was under the effective rule of Mary Stewart's mother, Marie de Guise, as Regent. Regent Marie faced a powerful faction of Scottish Protestant noblemen, backed by a popular Protestant movement inspired by John Knox. She depended on military assistance from France to resist this pressure. Reluctant though Elizabeth was to encourage rebellion against lawfully constituted rulers, Cecil and the Council persuaded her that the time was ripe for military intervention because of the risk that a French Scotland posed to her personally. It helped that Mary and her young husband, Francis II of France, had started to quarter the royal arms of England into their own heraldry when their marriage was celebrated back in April 1558. Once Francis had succeeded his father in July 1559, it was entirely reasonable to foresee that a Catholic triumph in Scotland might lead to a two-pronged assault on England.

An expeditionary force therefore headed north from Berwick at the end of March and besieged the French forces at Leith in April, with tacit support from most of the Scottish nobility. By June the Regent was in active negotiations with the English invaders, and peace terms were agreed in July 1560. By the Treaty of Edinburgh, Scotland was made safe for a Reformation which rapidly outpaced that of England. The death of Francis II in December 1560 reduced the immediate threat posed by the potential claim of Mary Queen of Scots to the English crown. The militantly Catholic Duke of Guise, her cousin, was no longer master of France, and the risk of French Catholic power reversing the Reformation in Scotland and making it a launchpad for an assault on England was gone. But Mary's own return to Scotland in 1561 changed the problem. Should Elizabeth die, Mary was now extremely well placed to pursue her claim, and even Scotland's Protestants saw advantage in that prospect. Scottish diplomacy was therefore orientated towards securing recognition for Mary as Elizabeth's heir. Mary's own policy in Scotland, where she made no serious efforts to advance Catholic interests against the recently successful official Reformation, was likewise calculated to allay English anxieties about her Catholicism. But neither Elizabeth nor Cecil, for different reasons, had any intention of acknowledging Mary's claim.

Mary's potential as a challenger was diminished by developments in France in the 1560s. Her immensely powerful cousins there, the Duke of Guise and his brothers, were sympathetic to her cause, but were soon more than fully occupied in the series of conflicts now known as the French Wars of Religion. French Protestants, like those of Scotland, looked to England for support against the Catholics and the Guises, and the idea that this offered a way back to the glory days of the Hundred Years' War briefly seized even Elizabeth herself. In return for English aid, the French Protestants offered Le Havre (which the English then called Newhaven) as a surety for the restoration of Calais in the event of their triumph. In October 1562 a force was sent under the Earl of Warwick (Robert Dudley's elder brother) to hold the port. But the peace which ended the first phase of France's civil wars was celebrated by a French siege of Le Havre by a force that combined Catholic and Protestant troops in common hatred of the English. Warwick surrendered towards the end of July 1563, and Elizabeth, her fingers thus burned, was henceforth reluctant to commit troops to battle outside her domains.

When Mary herself married for the second time in 1565, the succession question took on yet more urgency. The weight of opinion at Elizabeth's Court favoured marrying her to Archduke Charles of Austria, one of the sons of the Emperor Maximilian, which had been under discussion since 1563. But the Habsburg ambassadors soon realised that Elizabeth was not in earnest. The birth of Mary's son James in summer 1566 heightened English anxiety to fever pitch, and advocates of a royal marriage persuaded the queen to recall Parliament that autumn. It immediately resumed lobbying the queen to marry, now adding the suggestion that if she wouldn't marry, an act should be passed settling the succession. The debate was now becoming public, as pamphlets appeared urging the queen to do her duty. A delegation from both houses attended her on 5 November to make this case, only to be told by her in no uncertain terms that the succession was none of their business and that naming her own successor would only foster treasonous plots against her. They had to be satisfied with her announcement that she was 'determined to marry'. But her professed determination was, characteristically, hedged about with qualifications and equivocations: 'if Almighty God should not take away either her own person or the person of him with whom she meant to marry'.[30] Ructions followed in the Commons over what some saw as her infringement of their freedom of speech. Negotiations for the Habsburg marriage staggered on into 1567, but the Catholic Charles was not prepared to forego the Mass. The Earl of Sussex went to Vienna for one last effort, offering a religious compromise the Habsburgs could accept. But back home the idea of concessions to Catholicism was opposed in private at the Council table and then, in public, by Bishop John Jewel (virtually the official voice of the Church of England) in a sermon at Paul's Cross on 29 November 1567.[31] Elizabeth grabbed the excuse to reject the treaty and the marriage.

Cecil's priority was to manage the threat of Mary by supporting Protestantism in Scotland and thus reducing her personal power. Mary herself had delivered the means into his hands when, in July 1565, she married Henry Stewart, Lord Darnley, a Scottish descendant of both the Stewart and Tudor lines who had been brought up in England. Darnley soon alienated not only the Scottish nobility but also his wife, though not before he had made her pregnant. He arranged the murder of her secretary, David Rizzio, before her very eyes in March 1566, but she survived the shock unharmed and gave birth to her son, James, in June. James was christened, unusually late, in December that year, and soon afterwards Darnley was assassinated while staying at Kirk O'Field, just outside Edinburgh, a short distance from Holyrood Palace. The house itself was blown up, and his corpse was found nearby. From an early stage Mary herself was publicly blamed for his murder, but it is most likely that this was the work of those Scottish nobles who were loudest in pinning the blame on her. It did not help that a few months later she was abducted and probably raped by Earl Bothwell (who, although formally acquitted by a court, was one of the prime suspects in Darnley's death) and then felt obliged to accept his offer of marriage.[32] In the ensuing eruption of civil war her forces were defeated at Carberry Hill in June

1567 and she was induced to abdicate in July. Escaping from captivity in 1568, she was finally defeated in battle at Langside (near Glasgow) in May 1568.

English policy towards Scotland in the 1560s was a triumph, but in Ireland the attempt to impose England's Protestant Reformation was a fiasco. As Henry Jefferies has shown, the Reformation legislation enacted in Elizabeth's first Irish parliament, in January 1560, was a dead letter from the start. Not even the oath to the supremacy was successfully administered. There was no hope at all for the Book of Common Prayer – and not only because no Irish version was produced. The Old English were just as hostile as the Irish to the new religion, which seemed inextricably associated with a policy designed to eradicate their political influence. Lacking preachers and patrons, Protestantism could not even find a foothold. Nor did the passage of time mitigate this failure. As late as 1600, genuinely Irish Protestants were only to be numbered in dozens, while Irish preachers could be counted on one's fingers.[33]

The regime hardly even bothered to attempt a religious reformation. Instead, its stated aim was the reduction of the kingdom to order, though even this was but a scanty veil under which landless Englishmen of 'gentle' birth sought to make their fortunes. The Lord Deputy, the Earl of Sussex, was in almost permanent competition with the Irish chieftain of Ulster, Shane O'Neill, Earl of Tyrone, which kept the island in disorder through the early 1560s, even though at times O'Neill was granted some recognition by Elizabeth. Under the next Lord Deputy, Sir Henry Sidney, O'Neill was put under greater pressure, and during a fight for survival generally labelled a rebellion, he was murdered during negotiations with a rival clan, the MacDonalds. Such tensions between Irish clans were a condition of survival for the flimsy sphere of real English influence known as the Pale. The tragedy of Ireland throughout Elizabeth's reign was that regional identities and personal loyalties were too deep-rooted to permit the success either of English government or of Irish resistance.

After the disasters of the late 1550s, the 1560s were for England itself a decade of recovery and growth, both demographically and economically. The epidemic of smallpox that almost killed Elizabeth in autumn 1562 was nothing to the horrors of the late 1550s. And after that England was blessedly free from major visitations of disease until the 1590s, allowing the kind of steady demographic growth without which economic growth is all but impossible. Harvests, likewise, did not fail badly enough or often enough to cause crisis. One of the other brakes on economic growth, war, was largely avoided until the 1580s. The invasion of Scotland and the fiasco in France were modest enterprises that did not put undue strain on Crown finances. The loss of Calais proved a double boon. It could be blamed on Mary and it slashed recurrent military expenditure. Moreover, English merchants had for decades been focusing more profitably on the Netherlands, and the military commitments of other European nations provided openings for English merchants.

But there was more than this. The 1560s might be the first time in English history when government policy significantly promoted the kingdom's economic interests. It began with the restoration of the currency after the radical debasements under Henry VIII and Protector Somerset. A plan already roughed out under Mary to restore the value of the English coinage brought much-needed stability and confidence to the money market and thus to trade. The mastermind of this was Sir Thomas Gresham, a successful merchant who from 1551 had been the English Crown's main financial agent on the Antwerp money market. When permitted, he exercised his financial acumen to keep the service costs of Crown debt as low as he could and even to reduce the debt. Situated as he was more on the Protestant than the Catholic side of the emerging divide (he had been educated for a time at Gonville Hall, one of the more evangelical of Cambridge's colleges), he was not entirely trusted by Mary's regime, which tried to replace him a couple of times, with disastrous consequences. Yet he not only served Mary faithfully, but even cleared up the mess when they had to reinstate him. Under Elizabeth, however, his career reached its zenith, and he had Cecil's complete confidence. Within five years he had sorted out the currency and settled the overseas debt, and after that he turned his attention to the domestic scene. His commercial vision led him to establish in London a forum in which merchants could strike deals and trade in lucrative goods, along the lines of the Antwerp Bourse. With the aid of the City of London and then the patronage of the queen, work started in 1566 on the construction of a venue which was formally opened by Elizabeth as the Royal Exchange in 1571. This magnificent Renaissance edifice was perhaps as much a symbol as a cause of the growing prosperity of London. But under Elizabeth London emerged as a major centre for international as well as national trade, as English shipping achieved a worldwide commercial reach it would retain until the twentieth century.

The new trading vehicles, joint-stock companies, that had begun to appear in English commerce around the middle of the century, were to dominate the business transacted in the new Royal Exchange. Most of these companies were transient affairs, brought together for specific ventures rather than for long-term purposes. But the Muscovy Company was perhaps the first attempt in England to establish a commercial corporation that was less a trade union of independent merchants and more an entity with a corporate business strategy. Elizabeth's own financial straits tempted her to invest in the privateering enterprises she herself licensed with 'letters of marque', and she made healthy profits from state-sponsored piracy on several occasions. The joint-stock company was not the only aspect of the Elizabethan economy with a long future ahead of it. As English merchants and privateers variously preyed upon or dabbled in Spanish transatlantic trade, they were tempted by the high profits in trading slaves from Africa to America. The papal decrees that had presumptuously divided the 'New World' between Spain and Portugal had been followed by further judgements that recognised the humanity of the indigenous peoples of America and instructed their new masters to set about their evangelisation. This prevented those peoples from being enslaved (though not from being expropriated and exploited), but the demographic catastrophe inflicted upon them by lethal viruses from the 'Old World' left the colonists in need of labour – which was supplied by slaves from Africa. Into this profitable trade such seadogs as Jack Hawkins and Martin Frobisher intruded themselves in the 1560s. England itself had no transatlantic colonies as yet, so this element in English trade was only small, but the 1560s sketched the outlines of what by the 1670s would be a potent engine of wealth.

The greatest boon for England and its people was the lengthy interlude of peace they enjoyed under the rule of a woman who had opted against marriage. A sample of two is hardly statistically conclusive, but Mary had been drawn into war against France only at the instigation of her husband Philip, while Elizabeth showed no enthusiasm whatsoever for military adventure after the ignominious surrender of Le Havre in 1563. Royal women simply were not imbued from earliest youth with dreams of martial glory. The military intervention in Scotland in 1560 was not a return to the hubristic war of conquest initiated by Henry VIII and blindly continued by Somerset in the 1540s. Cecil's policy of alignment went with the grain of Scottish politics rather than against it, and was infinitely less expensive and more effective than that of annexation. Additionally, the international situation gave little reason to spend heavily on defence. France was torn apart by internecine conflict almost throughout Elizabeth's reign, while Spain was soon bogged down in a war of attrition against the rebel provinces of the Netherlands. Peace meant low levels of State expenditure and therefore low taxes. Labour was not diverted to

View of Hampton Court Palace
Sketched by the Flemish artist Anton van den Wyngaerde (d. 1571), who specialised in townscapes, this view shows Hampton Court from the river, including the ornate gatehouse on the bank of the Thames, from which royalty or nobility could board a boat to make the journey downstream to Westminster.

military service, but left available for agriculture or craft industry. It left English traders in a much more favourable position than those of Spain, France or the Netherlands. Through the 1560s and 1570s, therefore, as bullion shipments from America swelled Spanish coffers and thus fuelled aggregate demand in Western Europe, the economy of England enjoyed a largely uninterrupted boom. A religious age inevitably interpreted this as a providential blessing, and England's preachers were eager to remind their captive audiences, in an early version of 'you've never had it so good', that peace and prosperity represented the seal of divine approval for the restoration of true religion under Elizabeth.

Cecil brought something new to English politics. Though he was to some extent simply another chief minister in the tradition of Wolsey and Cromwell, the archive he has left displays a new approach to the task. Unlike them, he ran a system predicated on a functioning executive body in the Privy Council. The Privy Council had existed under Cromwell and even under Wolsey, but Wolsey used it as an echo chamber, and Cromwell used it for political cover. Executive action under both of them was run from their personal households. It was only after Cromwell's fall that the Council was set on a permanent institutional footing, and only over the next twenty years that it became the ordinary instrument of central executive power.

Cecil brought more than policy papers and bureaucratic tidy-mindedness to government. He also brought a vision, as Stephen Alford has demonstrated. That vision was political, but not in the contemporary sense of the term. His vision was a matter of religious politics, very much a matter of this world, yet with an other-worldly dimension that lent it a coherence transcending the mere opportunism of most politics.[34] Twentieth-century views of Cecil as a cool exponent of secular politics mistook him for a mid-twentieth-century British Prime Minister, perhaps because of a confusion between religion and theology which also distorted views of Elizabeth. Like Elizabeth, Cecil was not theologically driven. Like his sovereign, he did not get excited over justification, predestination, transubstantiation, or any of the other polysyllabic buzzwords that spilled so much ink and blood. But religion remained for him, as for her, as fundamental to politics as to private life. He could never have understood the exclusion of religion from politics that characterises the modernity, or postmodernity, of the contemporary West.

Religion alone can explain the sudden démarche which Cecil sprang on his queen as 1568 turned into 1569. Religious tensions had risen in the Netherlands through the 1560s, and after the widespread Protestant iconoclasm at Antwerp and elsewhere in August 1566, Philip II despatched his top commander, the Duke of Alva, to take over as governor there. Alva brought some 10,000 troops to overawe Philip's unruly subjects. But troops had to be paid, and in December 1568 a Genoese flotilla was transporting a cargo of bullion that had been borrowed from Genoa's bankers for this purpose when it found itself obliged to take refuge from a storm at Plymouth. In flagrant breach of law and custom, Cecil gave orders that the bullion was to be seized, risking the ire not only of

Philip but also of Elizabeth, whom he consulted only afterwards. English ships in Dutch ports were immediately impounded in reprisals, but that could not compensate Alva for the loss of nearly half a million ducats. Protestants in the Netherlands had been put under huge pressure by Alva, and in France, likewise, the Protestant interest was facing pressure from the regime of Charles IX and Catherine de Medici. Cecil subscribed to the conspiracy theory which held that the kings of France and Spain had made a secret alliance to extirpate Protestantism in a summit meeting at Bayonne in 1565.[35] From that point of view, it was vital to defend Protestant interests across the Channel, and thus reduce the risk of a Catholic crusade against England. Cecil may well have been shrewd enough to calculate that Spain was in no position to respond in kind to what was an act of war. But it was still a risk only to be taken for an end of overriding importance. From that time on, relations between England and Spain varied between cold war and proxy war, until the conflict became open in 1585. In 1568, however, England was the aggressor, and remained so until the later 1580s. Cecil's New Year's gamble in 1569 set the tone of foreign relations for the rest of Elizabeth's reign.

5

THE ELIZABETHAN EXCLUSION CRISIS, 1568–1587

Towards dusk on Sunday 16 May 1568 a small fishing-boat approached the shore in the Derwent estuary, a little downstream from Workington in Cumberland. It had crossed that day from the Kirkcudbrightshire coast, a few miles south of Dundrennan. From it disembarked a party of 16 persons: Mary Queen of Scots and a small retinue, headed by Claude Chatelherault (the son of the Duke of Hamilton) and Lords Fleming and Herries. Mary had crossed the Solway Firth in a desperate bid to escape the clutches of her half-brother, the Regent James Stewart, Earl of Moray, who had inflicted a final defeat on her forces at the Battle of Langside just outside Glasgow a few days earlier. The fleeing queen was housed overnight at Workington Hall, the seat of Henry Curwen, the local squire (who happened to be away in Bath at the time, thus missing what would otherwise have been the highlight of his career). From there she wrote a lengthy letter next day to her cousin, Queen Elizabeth, relating her misadventures, begging assistance in regaining her kingdom, and bewailing her wretched condition. In the meantime, rumours of this strange landing had spread, and a posse of local gentry assembled to investigate. On reaching Workington they discovered just who it was that had come ashore, and they escorted her further inland to Cockermouth, where she was installed in the castle of the Earl of Northumberland, feudal overlord of the area. Word was sent to the earl himself, then residing at one of his favourite Yorkshire manors, Topcliffe, and also to the highest local holder of royal authority, the Deputy Captain of Carlisle Castle, Richard Lowther. It was from the earl that news was sent post haste to the Court at Greenwich. Meanwhile, Lowther hurried down to Cockermouth, assured himself of the Scottish queen's safety and comfort, and ordered a muster of the county gentry to escort her with all possible honour to Carlisle on the Tuesday.[1]

The way in which Mary's advent upset the delicate balance of English politics was evident from the start. The Earl of Northumberland's first thought was that, as Mary had landed in his domains, he should be granted the honour of being her host. As he spelled out to Cecil in a note accompanying his report to the queen, which he sent as soon the news reached him on Tuesday 18 May, it would be detrimental to his reputation if Mary were to be entrusted to anyone else's care. In York he found it easy to persuade the Council of the North of this, but the officers whom he sent on ahead with the Council's instructions to the sheriff, justices and gentry of Cumberland to follow the earl's orders discovered that she had already been spirited away to the royal castle at Carlisle. And Lowther, the Deputy Captain, was not going to diminish his own authority by handing her over. In the event, despite the earl's plea to Cecil, it was decided that Mary's custodian would be Henry, Lord Scrope, Captain of Carlisle and Warden of the Western Marches, who was ideally placed at Court in Greenwich when Mary arrived in England. Scrope was reliably Protestant, while Northumberland was a known Catholic. And while Mary was accommodated for a couple of months at the royal castle in Carlisle, her transfer in July to Scrope's family seat at Castle Bolton (near Leyburn, in Wensleydale) made the mistrustful regime's slight to Northumberland still more hurtful. For nearly twenty years, Mary would remain the apple of discord in English politics, the self-evident yet unacknowledged heir to the throne who stood for everything that England's official religion was against.

If Mary's arrival caused a commotion in Cumberland, it provoked consternation at Court. While she was in Scotland, the problem of Mary had been chronic. Now she was in England, it was acute. Cecil had no doubt expected her to meet a violent death at the hands of her enemies, for assassination was then a routine feature of Scottish politics. So her arrival in England was an unwelcome surprise. However, he soon compiled a substantial file on the matter, and his papers show him weighing the pros and cons of various options.[2] What Mary wanted above all was access to Elizabeth at Court, to present her case to the queen in person, win her sympathy, and secure English support for her restoration. What Elizabeth wanted is far from clear, and the complexities of the situation gave ample scope to her talent for creative inaction. What Cecil wanted above all was Mary's destruction, and at the very least her permanent exclusion from Scottish politics and the English succession. The blizzard of accusation and defamation which the Scottish regime had unleashed against Mary gave him the excuse to assure Elizabeth that she could not receive her unbidden guest at Court until and unless her name was cleared. In October 1568 a commission of enquiry was therefore set up at York, under the presidency of the Duke of Norfolk, so that the two sides could be heard. Norfolk, however, proved a little too sympathetic to Mary, and the hearing was revoked to Westminster. Before long her representatives realised that the odds were stacked against her and withdrew from the process. That left the field to the Regent Moray, who now lay before the queen's commissioners the notorious 'Casket Letters', a dossier of carefully curated and redacted documents purporting to show that Mary had intrigued to bring about the assassination of her husband, Henry Lord Darnley, in 1566. In the light of modern critical scholarship these documents are fairly transparent and at times crude forgeries, patched together from a variety of sources. But they were good enough for Cecil, good enough to keep the Scottish queen at a safe distance from her English cousin.

The prospect of a Catholic successor to Elizabeth seemed if anything closer once that successor was resident within the kingdom, despite the fact that she had lost her former power as Queen of Scotland. William Cecil, who had signed up to the unlawful attempt to frustrate a Catholic succession in 1553, would have seen only too easily the parallels between Mary Tudor and Mary Stewart. Mary Tudor had shown what a woman could achieve with a sound claim to the throne and some solid gentry support. So Cecil continued to argue, as he had already done, that Mary was excluded from the succession by Henry VIII's statute of 1544 and by his will, which had lawful authority under that act. But this claim, though it has routinely been accepted by many historians, was not true. If it had been, then James VI of Scotland, Mary's son, could never have become James I of England, which he did with serene ease in 1603. In fact, the Stewart line was not excluded by the 1544 statute: it was merely passed over in silence. Indeed, when that law was made, Mary Stewart was expected to marry Henry VIII's son Edward under the terms of the Treaty of Greenwich (1543). That expectation explains why there was no mention of the Scottish line in the 1544 statute. And it would have been a logical impossibility to exclude her descendants from the succession. Cecil was merely scrabbling together whatever arguments he could find to block Mary Stewart's claim.

It was vital to Cecil and his allies that Mary's very real claim to the throne and on popular loyalty be weakened as much as possible. Print provided the perfect medium for this, and the arrival of Mary Stewart therefore opened a new chapter in English politics. The discrediting of Mary had already begun in Scotland, where the mudslinging focused on her alleged responsibility for the assassination of her second husband, Darnley, in a gunpowder plot at Kirk O'Field in Edinburgh. Mary was quite possibly the only major figure in the Scottish political elite who was not involved in the plot against Darnley, but making her the fall guy for it doubled its value to the conspirators. The dossier of forged or redacted documents that was put together to justify the outlandish theory of her involvement was compiled by scholars working for her half-brother, the Earl of Moray, who had probably masterminded the plot itself, which made him the virtual ruler of Scotland. This bundle of falsehoods and half-truths, which has long since been unpicked, was easily believed at least on one side amid the bitter religious divisions of the age. It was taken up with alacrity by Cecil and was put into print in London as early as 1571.

Mary did not lack for defenders and supporters. Her closest ally, John Leslie, the refugee Catholic Bishop of Ross, wrote tirelessly in her cause. His writings, too, made it into print, and the controversy about Mary was perhaps the first occasion on which real political debate was pursued in English print. Hitherto, print had served to communicate the royal view to English subjects. Now some of them were able to see two sides of an issue in print, and this kind of debate would recur more and more frequently through the later sixteenth and seventeenth centuries. Political debate remained, for the moment, intractably religious. Most political arguments in the later sixteenth century were in effect religious anyway, and most political debate retained a religious dimension until early in the eighteenth century. Leslie's defence, even though it had to be printed overseas, went through three editions in as many years, an indication that it was getting to market in England. His nimble and persuasive rebuttal of the arguments against Mary's right to succeed to the English crown displays a mastery of English common law that cannot represent the unaided efforts of a man whose legal training was in Roman law and canon law. It is presumably based, directly or indirectly, on the advice of the prominent Catholic lawyer Edmund Plowden, whose own treatise in favour of Mary's claims was itself unprinted, but survives in manuscript.[3]

Nor was the English Reformation yet such a complete success as to make the idea of a Catholic monarch unthinkable. Ten years of the chronically understaffed Elizabethan Church of England were hardly enough to have made England a 'nation of Protestants' by 1569. Protestantism had taken huge strides in those ten years, but the arrival of Mary Queen of Scots offered an alternative path to the road England was to take, the road to the Anglican 'Confessional State' that historians locate in the period from 1689 to 1828. That other path offered an attractive solution to the chronic Elizabethan problem of the succession by marrying off the Scottish Catholic Mary to some eligible English Protestant nobleman. And none was more eligible than the youthful yet thrice widowed Thomas Howard, 4th Duke of Norfolk, the kingdom's premier peer. A marriage was quickly arranged, and the engagement enjoyed a fair degree of support among some elements of the Court and aristocracy. Mary's fertility was proven (there were whispered doubts about Elizabeth's), and to some this marriage was a dream solution, promising a secure English succession and offering the prospect of religious peace between Protestants and Catholics, albeit under a Protestant establishment. Mary Stewart had shown herself sympathetic to a tolerant religious policy in Protestant Scotland. The large body of Catholics, would-be Catholics, or Catholic sympathisers that still existed in England could hope for a happier future with a Catholic queen or queen-mother. This dream solution, however, was a nightmare for Cecil and his allies, for whom it would have meant political eclipse. Also, Cecil's own position in 1569, though powerful, was not unchallenged, and there were many among the queen's courtiers and England's lords who saw the Norfolk marriage as a way to trim Cecil's sails.

The marriage was mooted, welcomed by some, and feared by others, but without anyone consulting the only person whose opinion mattered: Queen Elizabeth. Hearing vague rumours late in 1568, she asked Norfolk about it directly, but he evaded the issue. By June 1569, Mary herself had consented to the proposal, but still no one was willing to broach the matter with the queen. When Leicester finally told her what was afoot, she flatly forbade the duke to contemplate the marriage any further, and he fled from Court to his Norfolk home at Kenninghall – a move which looked threatening, though he was far too indecisive to have meant anything by it. Summoned back to London, he obeyed, but in the north his Catholic noble allies, the earls of Westmoreland and Northumberland, stumbled rather than marched into open rebellion with vague aims of liberating Mary and restoring Catholicism. Appealing to the pope to excommunicate Queen Elizabeth – which the pope, in a fit of credulous insouciance, promptly did, making life for English Catholics hell for the next thirty years – the earls failed to raise adequate forces or define achievable strategic goals. Northumberland could not even raise all his own tenants. Thousands of men did take up arms across Durham and North Yorkshire, but this was not the wildfire rebellion of 1536. Far fewer gentry were involved, and the rising did not sweep the countryside as the Pilgrimage had done. Rebel forces restored the Mass briefly in Durham Cathedral and burned a few Protestant books, and similar gestures were made elsewhere. At Kirkbymoorside the Protestant communion table was taken down.[4] The recently appointed Lord President of the Council of the North, the Earl of Sussex, rallied gentry support in Yorkshire and was soon reinforced by troops from the south. As a substantial force gathered against them, the rebel earls' troops melted away, and the earls themselves fled into Scotland before the end of the year. This half-cock rebellion, though, was what Cecil and his allies had been waiting for, ideal material with which to pressure Elizabeth into clamping down on England's still numerous and often locally powerful body of Catholics. The regime authorised reprisals on an unprecedented scale. Under martial law, about 600 were executed in pairs at towns and settlements from Wetherby in Yorkshire to Newcastle upon Tyne. Given that the rebel force was estimated at around 6,000 men, the punishment may have been quite literally decimation.[5] More men were executed for treason in four weeks than had been burned for heresy under Mary in four years.

The rebellion was over before the pope's supremely ill-judged call to arms, the papal bull *Regnans in Excelsis*, was even drafted. It was officially published on 25 February 1570, and copies reached England a few months later. One English Catholic, John Felton, went so far as to nail a copy to the door of the Bishop of London's house beside St Paul's, on 25 May. The ensuing investigation soon traced this outrage to him, and it is a fair summary of what the papal bull achieved that Felton was the first (though not the last) Catholic subjected to torture under Elizabeth. Besides making it easy for the English authorities to believe that Catholics as such were now necessarily traitors, the papal bull also seemed to confirm everything that Henrician or Protestant polemicists had been saying since 1535 about the 'usurped' authority of the 'Bishop of Rome'. The pope had not only painted his English subjects into a corner, he had presented himself in the colours of a bloodthirsty meddler and a fomenter of rebellion – the most heinous crime of all in the eyes of the Tudors and most of their subjects. This futile papal challenge to the Tudor religion of monarchy can only have weakened English Catholicism at this point. There is no way to document how many Catholics or sympathisers were alienated by this edict, but there is no doubt that many were. For Protestants, the bull was a gift. A plethora of sermons, pamphlets and ballads excoriated the papacy as the Antichrist and denounced Rome as Babylon. European reformers such as Heinrich Bullinger seized the opportunity to join in the chorus of denunciation.

The other effect of the rebellion was to add an unmistakable taint of treason to Norfolk's faint-hearted courtship of the Queen of Scots. Despite that, Norfolk was a good Protestant, and neither Cecil nor the queen was anxious to destroy him. He was, after all, literally the queen's cousin (not merely metaphorically, as all dukes and earls were by courtesy), and it is unlikely that he had envisaged actual treason. What did for him was that, despite this narrow escape, and despite his own renunciation of any aspirations to marry Mary, before long he was once more dallying with the idea, giving an ear to the flattering insinuations of a Florentine moneylender called Roberto Ridolfi, who doubled as an agent for the pope but may also have been 'turned' by the Secretary of State, Francis Walsingham, who had arrested and interrogated him in 1569. By spring 1571, Ridolfi was hawking a list of potential English rebels around European Catholic Courts, but Cecil soon received intelligence about the plot and spent the summer exploring its ramifications. Second time around, Norfolk had certainly dabbled in treason, and he was duly convicted of it in January 1572. In a conversation reported while he was on death row, he repented his matrimonial ambitions and offered an intriguing insight into the emerging power of print, reflecting glumly that Mary was now so 'openly defamed with so many books, as by no means possible' could she ever recover her lost reputation.[6] His execution was delayed for several months, and was expedited only when pressure was brought to bear from the Parliament that convened on 24 May. His beheading on 2 June was the price Elizabeth paid for sparing her royal cousin Mary.

Elizabeth's tenderness towards Mary seemed almost suicidal to her councillors, whether churchmen or statesmen. As Edwin Sandys, the Bishop of London, wrote to Cecil in September 1572, the first step towards guaranteeing the security of the queen was 'Forthwith to cut off the Scottish Queen's head: *ipsa est nostri fundi calamitas*' ('for she is the overthrow of our State', a punning use of a tag from the Roman dramatist Terence).[7] Admittedly this was written as news was coming in of the appalling massacres of Protestants by Catholic mobs in Paris and elsewhere in France. But it is still odd advice from the lips of a Christian bishop, and needs to be weighed in the scale with the fact that earlier in the same letter he had requested guidance from Cecil for the preachers at Paul's Cross, whom he described as 'young men, unskilful in matters political, yet so carried with zeal that they will enter into them and pour forth their opinions'. Sandys evidently considered himself a man of mature years and judgement (which was half true). Not that his robust pastoral approach was unique. He was one of eight bishops on a committee of the House of Lords which spent the summer of that year lobbying Elizabeth to send Mary to the block.

While the arrival of Mary and the subsequent machinations at Court and among the nobility dominated English politics from 1568 to 1572, developments with profound implications were taking place within the English Church. These developments, which posterity has lumped together under the label of 'Puritanism', reflected in various ways an aspiration to a more thoroughgoing Protestant Reformation than had been achieved in or since 1559. This owed something to the political context established by Mary's arrival, which set the widespread survival of Catholic practices and sympathies in a disturbing light. But it was born partly out of disappointment with progress so far and partly out of the progress made so far – a classic revolution (or attempted revolution) of rising expectations. Ten or fifteen years in, the reign of Elizabeth was seeing the emergence of committed Protestants in large numbers. Those reaching adulthood in the 1570s had no memory of the Mass in the parish church, and had been brought up on Protestant preaching, whether it was the milk-and-water variety of the official Homilies or the headier stuff served up by returned exiles or by eager graduates fresh from Oxford and Cambridge. Terms such as 'Puritan' and 'Precisian' were becoming current to describe those whose zeal inspired them to call for further reform in the life and liturgy of the Church of England, a group of men hard to define but easy to identify.

In a kingdom in which religious policy was determined by the Crown, the obvious way to achieve change was by speaking truth to power and hoping to bend its ear. It was the appropriately named Edward Dering who dared to deliver a seasonable message to the queen in a sermon in Lent 1570. He started happily enough by discoursing on God's favour to King David. Before long, though, he was taking a common enough parallel between the English monarch and the kings of the Old Testament in a more censorious direction, reminding Elizabeth how God dealt with those kings 'when they began to fall away'. Urging her to 'do his prophets no harm', he went on 'I need not seek far for offences whereat God's people are grieved; even round about this chapel I see a great many'. He was referring to the crucifix and candles that Elizabeth was still trying to keep on the altar there, despite the regular iconoclastic vandalism they underwent. Likening her tactlessly to 'an untamed and unruly heifer' (Jer. 31:18), Dering untruthfully promised that he would 'not with many words admonish Your Majesty'. She was not amused. He was never invited back, and died in 1576 as a man with a bright future behind him.[8] But his sermon lived on in print, reaching at least sixteen editions by the time the queen died, testimony to the size of the market for his ideas.

Dering was a fellow of Christ's College in Cambridge, and his performance was a sign of the ascendancy that Calvinist theology, which underpinned Puritanism, had achieved in the two universities. In both Cambridge and Oxford, keen young Protestants were being imbued with the idea that the imperfections in their Church were the consequence of its failure to embody the 'discipline', that is, the form and pattern of church life and government discerned by Calvin in the pages of the New Testament. According to him, it taught that the Church ought to be ruled not hierarchically, by bishops, but more horizontally, by committees ('consistories' or 'presbyteries') composed of pastors (preaching clergy) and elders (senior lay figures – male, of course). The ministry of the Church consisted not of the threefold ministry of bishops, priests and deacons, which the Church of England had retained in line with medieval and ancient custom, but of a fourfold ministry: pastors, elders, deacons (managers of church funds and goods) and doctors (teachers or catechists). This innovative system, which Calvin had implemented in Geneva from the 1540s, was adopted or adapted by all the 'Reformed' churches of Europe except for the Church of England. England's failure to introduce the 'discipline' offered a seductively simple explanation of the shortcomings of its reformation.

The first person on record as putting these disruptive thoughts into words in England was a difficult but popular academic in Cambridge named Thomas Cartwright, who became Lady Margaret Professor of Theology there in 1569 (Figure 5.1). His first lectures in that role espoused a faithfully Calvinist account of the early Church and advocated the replacement of English episcopal government by Presbyterianism. This was too much for the university authorities, led by the ambitious John Whitgift, Master of Trinity College (where Cartwright was a fellow). Under new statutes for the university which had been introduced that year on royal authority, it was an offence to indulge in public criticism of the Church of England's rites and orders. These new statutes were put to immediate use in removing Cartwright from his professorship. Having made Cambridge too hot to hold him, he decamped for a while to Geneva.

Thomas Cartwright
Thomas Cartwright (1534/5–1603) became the figurehead of the Elizabethan Puritan movement after making his name in the early 1570s with his controversial lectures at Cambridge and his voluminous printed defence against John Whitgift of the Puritan manifesto, *An Admonition to Parliament* (1572). Although he was frequently in trouble with the authorities, and often found England too hot to hold him, he also had many friends and patrons in high places, most notably Robert Dudley, Earl of Leicester.

In the meantime, the ideas Cartwright had aired in 1570 were finding a wider audience. They featured in a provocative pamphlet published in 1572 in a hopelessly optimistic attempt to bring about further reformation from below via Parliament. The anonymous *Admonition to Parliament* combined a detailed critique of the Book of Common Prayer (which it damned as 'culled and picked out of that popish dunghill, the Mass Book, full of all abominations') with a wider diagnosis of the ills of the Church of England, which it traced entirely to the failure to implement the discipline.[9] The idea that Parliament might be influenced from below by means of the press was one with a great future, though its time had not yet come. John Whitgift, however, saw in the *Admonition* an opportunity to make a name for himself beyond Cambridge, and before the end of the year issued *An Answer to a Certain Libel*, a needlessly verbose but nonetheless clever refutation. In the meantime, Cartwright had returned to Cambridge, only for Whitgift to dismiss him from his fellowship at Trinity. Unwisely, he pursued his grievance against Whitgift by countering him in print. His *Reply* to the *Answer* appeared in 1573, Whitgift's *Defence* against the *Reply* in 1574, Cartwright's *Second Reply* in 1575, and in 1577, piling tedium on tedium, *The Rest of the Second Reply*. The controversy worked for Whitgift. In 1574 he was invited to preach before the queen at Court, in 1575 he was considered for a bishopric, and in 1577 he became Bishop of Worcester. When Whitgift preached before the queen, his sermon was very different from the reformist hectoring of Dering in 1570. Whitgift's effort was a jeremiad on the inconstancy of the people, their endless hankering after 'novelties', and their ready ear for critiques of 'the magistrates and such as be in authority'. His refrain was the duty of obedience, the danger of 'popularity', and the hypocrisy of self-seeking under the 'shadow of reformation'.[10] This was a political message of a deeply conservative nature, calculated to appeal to the queen.

Elizabeth's own religious prejudices were if anything hardened by the Puritan agitation that commenced from 1570, and it is likely that Whitgift's officially sponsored elaboration of an anti-Puritan ecclesiology for the Church of England rendered them still more adamant. This may help explain why, in summer 1576, she ordered her new Archbishop of Canterbury, Edmund Grindal, to clamp down on 'prophesyings'. Prophesyings were meetings, originally for clergy, at which the scriptures were expounded by learned ministers for the benefit of their less well-educated colleagues. They had been developed in Zurich and Geneva earlier in the century as a means for improving the education of pastors, many of whom had been brought up and first ordained as Catholics. The system was particularly suitable for churches in the throes of 'reformation'. Prophesyings were introduced in England in the 1560s by the former Marian refugees, often with tacit or even explicit episcopal support, and they sometimes expanded to bring in interested layfolk as well. Elizabeth became increasingly irritated by reports of such exercises in places as far apart as Norfolk, Hertfordshire and Warwickshire. However, she had chosen the wrong man in Grindal. A keen Protestant under Edward and a refugee at Strasbourg under Mary, he may not have been a Puritan himself, but he had every sympathy for the Puritans' agenda, and shared to the full their commitment to preaching. He refused point blank to implement the queen's instructions and wrote her a lengthy explanation of his position, which was founded on his prior obligation to God and his Word. He simply could not enact a policy which would obstruct the training of zealous preachers. His obduracy resulted only in his own suspension from office. Elizabeth commanded her bishops to take measures against prophesyings, which they implemented with varying degrees of zeal, and the Church of England lacked an effective primate until Grindal's death in 1583.

By the 1570s many towns and villages across England had Puritan preachers ensconced in the parish church, such as John Oxenbridge at Southam in Warwickshire (1571–97), Richard Greenham at Dry Drayton near Cambridge (1570–92) or William Horne at Hemel Hempstead in Hertfordshire (1571–78). By the 1580s, Puritan influence was widespread. The collegiate church in Manchester was a hotbed of Puritanism from the late 1570s. In some regions, such as the Stour Valley (Suffolk and Essex), the Puritans were so numerous and confident that they set up a version of Presbyterian discipline on a voluntary basis. A tiny minority, led by figures such as Henry Barrow or Robert Browne, despaired of changing the Church of England and broke away from it to form clandestine independent congregations, which the authorities disparaged as 'conventicles'. But most Puritans were determined to stay in the Church of England and reform it from within. Some of the young lions of this generation would still be active in the 1630s, as religious tensions reached fever pitch under Charles I. Humphrey Fenn, Puritan Vicar of Holy Trinity in Coventry from 1578 until his deprivation in 1590, was still describing himself in his will as a preacher when he died there in 1634, affirming the sinfulness of separation from the Church of England even as he reiterated his trenchant critique of it.[11]

Puritanism was by no means an exclusively clerical movement. Puritan ministers could attract large followings and powerful patrons, and the message about the need for further reform in the Church of England won considerable lay support. Frustration with the lack of further progress in the 1560s had surfaced in Parliament in 1571, when William Strickland and Thomas Norton (the translator of Calvin's *Institution of Christian Religion*) put forward a clutch of bills aimed at further reformation, earning themselves rebukes from Privy Councillors. Less ambitious but still markedly reformist petitions were floated in the Parliaments of 1576 and 1581, and were again stymied by intervention from the Court. Although they went nowhere, these bills showed that there were laymen of sufficient substance to gain election to Parliament who felt strongly enough about religion to lobby for further reform despite being fully aware of the queen's views. There were Puritans at the highest levels of the social hierarchy, among the gentry and even the nobility. If men such as William Cecil and Francis Walsingham were hardly Puritans themselves, they respected the commitment and zeal of men such as Cartwright and John Reynolds, and did their best to shield them from the attentions of hostile bishops such as Whitgift. The Earls of Leicester and Huntingdon were renowned patrons of Puritan ministers, and in Huntingdon's case at least that reflected a deep vein of personal piety.

Even while Norfolk had been contemplating marriage to Mary, Elizabeth's councillors were still hopeful of marrying off their queen to some eligible prince. Some of them may even have believed that she might yet bear a child, though by 1571 she was 38, the age at which her sister had married Philip II. In an era of relatively low life expectancy and limited medical knowledge, 38 was an unlikely age at which to bear a first child. The most plausible candidate for a marriage to the queen in 1570 was the then Duke of Anjou, Henry (who was to become Henry III of France in 1574). However, negotiations broke down in 1571 over his insistence that, even as the consort of a Protestant queen, he should retain the right to the public exercise of his Catholic religion. The idea of a matrimonial alliance with the Valois of France was renewed early in 1572 for his younger brother, Francis, who was at that time Duke of Alençon, but succeeded his brother as Duke of Anjou in 1574. The on-off courtship between Francis and Elizabeth (known by historians as the 'Anjou Match'), would last a decade. For much of the time, it was simply a diplomatic game, in which England and France somewhat desultorily sought an alliance with a view to assisting the rebels against Spanish rule in the Netherlands. But at times it was serious.[12]

If the arrival of Mary, the subsequent rebellion in the north, and the papal bull deposing Elizabeth had not done enough to stoke fear of popery in England, the task was completed by the horrific news that reached London in the last week of August 1572. In the wake of the assassination of the leader of France's Protestants, Admiral Gaspard de Coligny, Paris had erupted in communal violence as Catholic mobs raged through the city hunting out the hated Huguenots, beating them to death, and looting their homes in the infamous Massacre of St Bartholomew. Thousands died in Paris, and in copycat outbreaks in other cities. Francis Walsingham, who was next year to join Elizabeth's Privy Council, was at that time her ambassador in Paris. Though unharmed, he was not unmarked by the experience, and returned to England consumed with hatred and revulsion for the faith whose followers had perpetrated such atrocities (though he was to be less censorious towards the actions of English soldiery in Ireland). The events convinced him and many other Protestants, including William Cecil, that the French and Spanish monarchs had made a secret alliance at Bayonne in 1565 with a view to the extermination of Protestantism throughout Europe. The age knew all about conspiracies, but nothing about conspiracy theories. Back home, the bishops issued, in the queen's name, special prayers to be used throughout the land, for the safety of the queen and deliverance from enemies.[13] The massacre interrupted the marriage negotiations. Elizabeth could not be seen to contemplate marriage to a member of the French royal house in the immediate aftermath of a sectarian bloodbath that English opinion blamed on the French Crown and Court.

Elizabeth's government did what it could to succour the cause of Protestantism in France throughout the 1570s, assisting the Huguenots with clandestine aid or by hiring German mercenaries, but without going so far as to commit English troops. However, as Francis was happy to present himself in French politics as the figurehead of moderate Catholicism, the prospect of his marriage to Elizabeth was soon back on the table, though negotiations were intermittent. Only later in the decade, when Henry III had succeeded Charles IX, and Francis, now Duke of Anjou, was next in line to the French throne, with the position of the Dutch rebels against Spanish rule starting to weaken, did these negotiations become serious. Francis himself was angling for a role in the Netherlands in support of the rebels, and offering the prospect of marriage with Elizabeth was a cheap way to encourage French intervention against Spain. Elizabeth herself appeared to take his courtship seriously, and for a time it looked as though they were betrothed. The idea of the marriage was divisive, however. Many even on her council looked askance at it, and it became the stuff of popular political discussion to an even greater extent than Mary I's marriage to Philip II in 1554. An obscure Puritan lawyer called John Stubbs (brother-in-law to Thomas Cartwright) went so far as to publish a vitriolic pamphlet against the marriage in August 1579. It would be 'a great and mighty sin', he urged, 'to give one of Israel's daughters to any of Hamar's sons . . . to couple a Christian Lady . . . to a good son of Rome, that Antichristian mother city'. The very publication of the pamphlet is an index of how royal power had declined since the days of the queen's father. No one would have dared offer Henry VIII matrimonial advice of this kind in print. A ferocious proclamation was issued within weeks to call copies in and punish those responsible for it.[14] Stubbs was prosecuted for his effrontery in October, but it is a sign of the unpopularity of the marriage in London that the jury could not be induced to find him guilty (something else that would never have happened under Henry). That led Elizabeth to have him dealt with in the Court of Queen's Bench, where the panel of judges were not impeded by the inconvenience of juries. He was duly sentenced, under a law passed by Philip and Mary, to have his right hand cut off, and was not released from imprisonment in the Tower until 1581. But the favour he was shown not only by the crowd that witnessed his punishment but also subsequently by William Cecil, and his election as an MP for Yarmouth in 1585, show that there was considerable sympathy for him and probably also for his political and religious views.

The 'Anjou Match' never went ahead (Figure 5.2). There were those on the Queen's Council, chief among them the Earl of Sussex, who promoted it keenly. But the majority were in their hearts opposed. None of them can have entertained any hope that the union would be fruitful, so the issues at stake were the queen's own happiness, the possible political dividend in foreign relations, and the price of allowing the Catholic faith to be practised in close proximity to the queen herself, which would undermine the goal of religious uniformity and give England's Catholics new heart. She doubted her councillors would let her marry a Catholic, and she was probably right – but they doubted she was serious, and they were definitely right. Even Stubbs had been well enough informed to refer in his pamphlet to the queen's 'constant dislike and indisposed mind towards marriage from the flower of her youth'.[15] In the end, the councillors called Elizabeth's bluff. They acknowledged that it was her prerogative, as a woman and a queen, to decide about her own marriage, and they thus allowed – or rather, forced – her to choose. She had hoped they would stop her, so that her failure to take a husband would be their fault. But she blinked first.

Elizabeth I 'Sieve Portrait'
This is one of the many versions or copies of portraits that show Elizabeth holding a sieve. The allusion is to the legend of Tuccia, a Vestal Virgin in ancient Rome. When her chastity was impugned, she offered, with self-evident symbolism, to prove her innocence intact by carrying water from the Tiber to the Temple of Vesta in a sieve. Around 1580, in the context of the controversial negotiations for Queen Elizabeth to wed the Duke of Anjou, praising her virginity became a subtle way of discouraging her from marrying, and the Sieve Portraits were a reflection of this.

After the rebellion of 1569 and the papal bull of 1570, things got steadily worse for the Catholics of England and Wales. They were lucky to avoid widespread persecution from this time. The House of Commons rang with vengeful demands for draconian legislation against them, and many proposals were only kept from becoming law by Elizabeth's veto. England's Catholics moved into survival mode. They had been adjusting to their new situation since the 1560s. While it would be too much to credit them with planning for a future as a persecuted minority, the steps taken by leading refugees in the 1560s made the long-term survival of English Catholicism possible. Early on, many of them had gathered at the university town of Louvain (Leuven, in modern Belgium), from where they had launched a systematic print campaign against the Protestant Church of England. Philip II's years as King of England left him with a lasting sense of responsibility for English Catholicism there, and the refugees benefited from his patronage. One of them, the much published Dr Richard Smyth, was made first a professor and then vice-chancellor of Philip's new university at Douai. A few years later, the community that had gathered around him there inaugurated an English College under the leadership of William Allen, who was himself a salaried professor at Douai from 1570. From the start this institution saw its role as the training of priests to return to England to serve the Catholics there, and before long it was conceiving itself as a 'seminary' in accordance with the model for priestly education and formation first set out by the Council of Trent in 1563.

The first of the 'seminary priests' were sent to England in 1574, and a steady stream of them followed over the next three decades and beyond. This prospect of the replenishment of the thinning ranks of England's Catholic clergy caused the government to intensify its efforts at repression. The first of the seminary priests to be executed was Cuthbert Mayne, who was captured in Cornwall in 1577 and convicted of treason at the Launceston Assizes in October. His 'treason' consisted principally in possessing a copy of a papal bull and a devotional object known as an 'Agnus Dei' (which had been categorised as treasonous in a statute passed in 1571). The conversion of the ancient English pilgrims' hostel in Rome into another seminary, the English College, in 1579 increased the supply of new, highly trained seminary priests. By this time, also, the liveliest of the new Catholic religious orders of the Counter-Reformation, the Society of Jesus (aka the Jesuits) was beginning to attract English recruits. It was a pair of English Jesuits, Edmund Campion and Robert Parsons, whose 'mission' to England in 1580–81 changed everything and nothing for England's Catholics. Campion and Parsons crossed from France in June 1580 to embark on a clandestine tour of England which was a paradoxically public secret, thanks to Campion's indiscretion in allowing a couple of his writings to be circulated. Their whistle-stop tours in the Midlands and the north heartened England's Catholics and impressed upon them the hard line of the Counter-Reformation against any level of participation in heretical rites. And their success in evading capture for just over a year made them famous. Campion was finally taken at Lyford (Berkshire) in July 1581, with several other priests, which caused Parsons to flee the country. Campion (who was repeatedly tortured) and his fellow defendants were brought to trial in November under the ancient treason act. The prosecution therefore brought forward witnesses of doubtful repute who testified to allegedly treasonous past conversations which it is difficult to credit. But it was enough for the jury, which dutifully found them guilty. They were executed on 1 December, and were soon being celebrated as martyrs by their co-religionists abroad.

The 'Jesuit Mission' led to fresh legislation against Catholics. The scope of treason was extended to being ordained a Catholic priest abroad and to converting people to Catholicism. Saying and attending Mass were punishable by fines and imprisonment, and refusing to attend Church of England services ('recusancy') rendered the culprit liable to a fine of £20 a month. The actual enforcement of these draconian laws, of course, varied considerably by time, place and circumstance. But henceforth it was in principle extremely dangerous to be a Catholic. William Cecil's attempt to maintain that Catholics were troubled only for political reasons and not for their religion as such was an increasingly threadbare pretence, though it is important to note that it was almost always the political context that determined the intensity with which the laws against Catholicism were implemented. One thing these laws did achieve was to drive a little more of a wedge into the Catholic community by increasing the incentive to occasional conformity with Church of England worship in order to escape financial ruin. Hard-line 'recusants' were the core of the Catholic community, but by no means all Catholics had the courage or the means to live up to the costly ideals put before them by the seminary priests. The 'church papists' (as they were known) clustered around that recusant core are impossible to count or even estimate, which made them if anything more of a worry to the regime than the essentially countable recusants. From the point of view of the seminary priests, though, occasional conformity was a slippery slope to apostasy, and 'church papists' were more likely to inch away from their

Catholicism under the continued social pressure set up by preaching, propaganda, and, in time, the state of war with Catholic Spain.

The extraordinary length of time it took to catch Campion, and the complete failure to capture Parsons, may help explain the precocious development of espionage and intelligence activity in English government in the 1580s. It was also around this time that the regime became aware that Mary Queen of Scots was in contact with supporters in France and Scotland. Kings and their councillors had always used spies, of course, but under Elizabeth, largely through the work of Francis Walsingham, spying became almost a professional business. The fear of assassination plots that was started by the publication of the papal bull deposing the queen became more real once it was clear that Jesuits and other foreign-trained Catholic priests were crossing the Channel and finding shelter in networks of well-connected Catholic gentry. Although no solid evidence of actual treason was offered against Campion and his companions, the regime may indeed have believed that their intentions were treasonous. It was therefore essential for Elizabeth's chief councillors to secure the best intelligence they could about their enemies' hopes and plans. They even coined a word for it: 'intelligencer'. And Walsingham earned a reputation for his skill in managing and turning agents. Modern fascination with intelligence services and operations has given rise to the romantic myth that he 'founded the secret service'. But he was systematic in the gathering of intelligence from Europe's major Courts and cities, and in infiltrating the Catholic seminaries and colleges abroad with plausible would-be priests, or occasionally with captured priests whom he had turned by intimidation or bribery, such as Anthony Tyrrell and George Gifford. He employed an expert codebreaker and forger, Thomas Phelippes, to co-ordinate his legion of sources and agents. These men, especially Phelippes, would play crucial roles in uncovering a series of major plots against Elizabeth, culminating in the Babington Plot, which brought about the destruction of Mary Queen of Scots.

The role in these plots of agents and informers whose primary motivation was financial, however, leaves the historian with serious and entirely unresolvable doubts as to how far these intelligence coups were the result of entrapment or of detection. Certainly, many of the rather hapless victims were indeed driven by dreams of romantic or crusading zeal to free a captive queen or kill a tyrant. But there remains a soupçon of concern about the way some of these plots advanced the political or personal objectives of Cecil, Leicester and Walsingham. Thus when the deranged John Somerville was arrested for his declared intention of shooting the queen dead, a plan he shared with anyone and everyone while he made his way from Warwickshire to London, his interrogators built this up into a Catholic conspiracy that took in his father-in-law, Edward Arden.[16] Contemporaries noted wryly that Arden, who protested his complete innocence but was executed on 20 December 1583, was a bitter enemy of the Earl of Leicester.

If Catholicism was, for the regime, a running sore in Elizabethan England, in Ireland it was a gaping wound. The English Reformation had simply never taken root there at all, and the self-serving maladministration of the landless freebooters who were practically the only Englishmen the Crown could induce to undertake the government of the second kingdom alienated not just the Irish but also the so-called Old English (descendants of the Norman invaders). The fact that before Henry proclaimed it a kingdom, Ireland had previously been a lordship, granted to the English crown by the papacy (in point of fact, by the only English Pope, Adrian IV) in 1155, and that 400 years later Pope Paul IV had re-granted it, now constituted as a kingdom, to Philip and Mary, encouraged Pope Gregory XIII to make it a test case for the papacy's languishing claims to temporal as well as spiritual primacy. His predecessor's excommunication and deposition of Elizabeth left its throne theoretically vacant, and Gregory commissioned a freebooter of his own, Sir Thomas Stucley (rumoured to have been fathered by Henry VIII), to sail a shipload of mercenaries and exiles to foment a rebellion in Ireland. En route from Rome, Stucley was waylaid at Lisbon and persuaded by King Sebastian to join the ill-fated Portuguese crusade against the Sultan of Morocco in 1578.[17] They died together at the Battle of Alcazar (Alcacer Quibir), but the Irish plan lived on. Nicholas Sander, who had been tangentially connected with Stucley's enterprise, sailed on a similar expedition with James Fitzmaurice Fitzgerald the following year. They landed on the Dingle Peninsula, and despite Fitzmaurice's early death in battle, the rebellion he had provoked left Munster in turmoil for four years (1579–83). A ruthless and uncompromising Lord Deputy, Arthur Grey (Lord Grey of Wilton), was despatched to pacify the island. He showed his mettle by massacring almost the entire garrison of Smerwick when it surrendered after a two-day siege in November 1580. His brutality still finds occasional apologists, but this devout Puritan, haunted by the memory of the horrific Massacre of St Bartholomew, was personally responsible for massacres and slaughter at least as profligate and indiscriminate through his scorched earth policy. And Queen Elizabeth was no more concerned for her rebellious Irish subjects than she had been for the rebels of Yorkshire and Durham in 1570.

The theologically driven Puritan politics that motivated Lord Grey's savagery were very different from the 'republicanism' that has often been attributed to English Puritans by historians, largely as a result of 'reading history backwards' from the Civil Wars of the 1640s, in which the Puritans mostly took the field against their king. Thus William Fulke, in a sermon of 1581, rebuked the common people of his time, 'who were never so curious to enquire of princes causes and matters of the state', nevertheless went on to warn that 'if pride possess the heart of a King, he will either neglect religion altogether, or else think that he may do and decree in religion what he list', and that this showed 'how dangerous to the state of religion, is the sin of pride and presumption in the heart of a Prince'.[18] The resonance of these comments was in the context. Parliament had opened in January in the midst of the furore over the mission to England of the Jesuits Campion and Parsons, and at the behest of Cecil was busy working out new ways to clamp down on Catholics. But Elizabeth was reluctant to go as far as her councillors, and was a scarcely veiled target of Fulke's admonition. Yet his comments are hardly 'republicanism'. In 1570, preaching likewise before the queen, Fulke had been at pains to conclude with the prayer that 'all subjects may continue in holy obedience, first to God, and then to their Prince'.[19] Nor does Patrick Collinson's mischievous notion of Elizabethan England as a 'monarchical republic' help much in understanding Elizabethan politics. It is an entertaining oxymoron but a deeply misleading idea. Those historians who have taken up his half-jest do not pay enough attention to the deep bifurcation in the political discourse of the English elite. Cecil and his cohorts, in speaking with and of each other, and with and of the queen, emphasised the politics of counsel. They were obliged to offer her their plain and unvarnished advice, as they saw it, and she, like any wise monarch, was obliged to 'take' counsel (there is a world of ambiguity in the word 'take'). Nevertheless, when they spoke to the people, they were relentless in their emphasis on the duty of unquestioning and wholehearted obedience to the commands of a sovereign set over them by divine authority. Managing downwards and managing upwards were two very different operations for Elizabeth's councillors, and they used two very different languages for those tasks.

It remains an intriguing question, however, whether there was not some 'Puritan paradigm of politics', as one historian has recently put it.[20] Certainly the enemies of the Puritans, such as Elizabeth herself, thought or wished it so. The charge of 'popularity' – meaning the crime of seeking authority and approval from the people – was a routine recourse of anti-Puritan polemic. Puritans themselves, though, anxiously fended off this imputation, as likewise the claims that they shared the beliefs of the Anabaptists or disdained set forms of prayer in favour of improvised worship in the Spirit. Thus Matthew Sutcliffe accused the doyen of Puritanism, Thomas Cartwright, of asserting the authority of 'inferior magistrates' to undertake the correction, where necessary, of their own political superiors. This was an argument in vogue among French Protestants as a justification for their armed resistance to the Catholic kings of France in the 1570s and 1580s, so it was a dangerous thesis with which to be tarnished. Cartwright protested that nothing could be further from his mind, though he implied that such a power was entirely proper in a polity in which it was constitutionally established.[21]

Teasing out the political leanings of the Puritans is a delicate business. The nature of Elizabethan politics was such that no English subject could safely state or imply that political authority emanated anywhere other than from God, flowing downwards through his appointed deputy, the queen. The Act of Supremacy itself, in establishing complete royal jurisdiction over the Church, did so by asserting that this jurisdiction was as total in spiritual as in temporal affairs. So when Cartwright emphasised his political orthodoxy by reminding Sutcliffe that he had taken the oath to the supremacy 'five or six times', he was not engaging in empty rhetoric. English public doctrine, from 1559, recognised the monarch as the 'Supreme Governor' in spiritual and temporal domains, without exception or caveat. No Elizabethan Puritan ever said anything that could call that into doubt. George Gifford's sermon at Paul's Cross in 1591 lays down the law on obedience in no uncertain terms.[22]

There may or may not have been a 'Puritan paradigm of politics', but there was certainly a Protestant paradigm in foreign policy to which Puritans were strongly attached. A deep-seated loathing of 'popery' led Puritans to lobby for intervention in both the civil war in France and the rebellion against Spanish rule in the Netherlands. When Leicester led the expeditionary force to the Netherlands in 1585, he was accompanied by Puritan chaplains such as John Knewstub and Humphrey Fenn, and as long as Mary Stewart was still alive, Puritan MPs were loudest in calling for her execution. Elizabeth's foreign policy did not entirely live up to Puritan expectations, but there was a consistent anti-Spanish undercurrent from 1569 onwards. England had given harbour to rebel Dutch privateers and had helped them prepare for their dramatic seizure of Brill in 1572, a key strategic moment in the conflict in the Netherlands. English volunteers were tacitly allowed to fight against

Spain in the Dutch rebel forces. And English commanders such as John Hawkins, Humphrey Gilbert and Francis Drake were permitted and even encouraged to prey upon Spanish shipping and colonies throughout the 1570s and beyond.

These provocations or precautions (depending on the point of view) culminated in Drake's famous circumnavigation of the globe (1577–80), during which he harassed and plundered Spain's Pacific Rim settlements. When Philip II seized the kingdom of Portugal for himself in 1580, after the expiry of the legitimate line of Portuguese rulers, Elizabeth initially supported and then gave safe haven to the strongest Portuguese claimant, Don Antonio, a grandson of Manuel I, but of illegitimate birth. The anti-Spanish policy was entirely understandable but also fraught with risk. It is equally understandable that Philip II, whose fortunes were at their zenith in the early 1580s after the inclusion of the wealth of the Portuguese Empire in his already vast domains, started to contemplate countermeasures.

In collaboration with the ultra-Catholic Guise faction in France, Philip was happy to offer financial support to the Guises in their plans to further the cause of their cousin Mary through an invasion of England. Both England and France were interfering in the Netherlands, so Philip was keen to distract them with other problems. An English Catholic gentleman named Francis Throckmorton was drawn into the plot as a linkman with Mary and Catholic malcontents in England. There is no doubt that he was in the counsels of Spain and the Guises. Unfortunately for them all, he had been under surveillance for several months when he was arrested in November 1583, and incriminating papers were found in his residence. His initial denials of knowing anything about the papers were reversed in later interrogations, but only after torture. So the full details of his confessions, subsequently summarised in print, cannot be entirely trusted. At his execution he maintained not the absurd pretence of innocence but, credibly enough, that some of his admissions were made solely to escape the pain of the rack. The episode heightened the tension between England and Spain still further.

Throckmorton was executed on 10 July 1584. By a strange coincidence, that very same day saw the assassination at Delft of the Protestant warlord of the Netherlands, William of Orange. This awful instance of the threat that also menaced Elizabeth spurred the Privy Council into action, not least because there were immediate rumours that the assassins would be dealing with her next. Exhaustive searches of the premises of known Catholics were undertaken in August. In September Mary Queen of Scots was removed from the custody of the Earl of Shrewsbury and entrusted to a reliable old Tudor administrator, Sir Ralph Sadler. In the midst of this panic, the Privy Council started work on a spontaneous manifestation of national unity, drawing up a formal legal instrument that was to be circulated throughout the realm for signature by the gentry of every county.[23] The Bond of Association, as it was called, is a startling document, testimony to the pitch of tension running through English politics in the 1580s. Initially devised by the Council as part of its emergency plan to resolve the open question of the succession in the event of the assassination of the queen, it became a nationwide manifesto of fanatical loyalism. Despite its bloodthirsty promises, one of the earliest copies is a manuscript signed and sealed by the bishops and clergy in or near Hampton Court on 19 October. The gentry of Lancashire, led by the Earl of Derby, swore to it in a church in the presence of their bishop. Like monarchy itself, the Bond was hedged about with holiness. It serves as an incontrovertible reminder of the impossibility of separating politics from religion in sixteenth-century Europe.

The Bond is remarkable not least for the delicacy with which it skirts around the nub of the issue – the queen's death. Under English law, 'imagining the death' of the sovereign was, in itself, a treasonable offence, punishable by death. The Bond therefore has to tread a delicate path, planning for action in the event of the assassination of the queen without actually imagining it. So while it sets the scene by lamenting that the queen's life has been 'most traitorously and devilishly sought ... to the peril of her person', it presents itself as a voluntary society sworn to the task of preserving the queen's safety. The 'untimely death of Her Majesty' (which the document prays 'God for his mercy's sake forbid') is mentioned – but only as the intermediate objective of wicked plots to place on the throne some 'pretended successor' – easily identifiable as Mary Stewart. Thus the Bond tightens around its intended victim, as the signatories bind themselves by a sacred oath to pursue 'as well by force of arms as by all other means of revenge' the 'uttermost extermination' of anyone who should 'attempt by any act, counsel or consent to anything that shall tend to the harm of Her Majesty's royal person'.[24] The Bond of Association is nothing less than a solemn oath to lynch Mary Queen of Scots in the event of Queen Elizabeth's assassination or mysterious death.

It is astonishing that such a document, which today would constitute a criminal conspiracy, should have been drafted and signed by the queen's Privy Council and her leading bishops. Still more astonishing is that it was then rolled out across the country, via the Council's channels of communication to Lords Lieutenant, sheriffs and justices of the peace in the counties, so that it could be signed by the local authorities and the gentry. It was an attempt to bind the entire 'political nation' to the enterprise, and it was circulated in print for people literally to sign up to. Subscribing became such a test of loyalty that sometimes even Catholics put their names to it. And in some areas the charmed circle was extended beyond the elites, allowing humble yeomen and freeholders to add their names as well.

The Bond of Association demonstrated the latent power of the new force that had been conjured up in English politics over the previous twenty years: anti-popery, the fear and hatred of Catholicism. This hatred of popery was common coin among Elizabeth's bishops and the preachers and polemicists of her Church. There is no evidence at all to suggest that this ideology, or theology, had any purchase on the queen herself, nor that she herself ever did anything to foster or exploit it. She, after all, would have remembered the England of her childhood, with its daily celebration of Mass (which she had attended throughout Mary's reign), so she perhaps found that ritual less horrifically demonic than her bishops did. But many of her closest advisers were touched with anti-popery, and Francis Walsingham was plainly obsessed by it.

As Neil Younger has argued, the crisis of anxiety over the possible assassination of the queen provoked not only the Bond of Association and the subsequent statutory modification and mitigation of it, but also the revival – in strategically important English counties – of the office of Lord Lieutenant. The Lord Lieutenancy had appeared in the crisis of Edward's reign, and had resurfaced periodically under Mary and Elizabeth, most recently in response to the rising of the Northern Earls in 1569–70. Lieutenancies had lapsed during the years of peace and stability. Their reappearance in 1585, as Younger has shown, was concentrated in the counties of the south coast, obviously because of their vulnerability to invasion, and also in the two counties in which Mary was mostly held (Derbyshire and Staffordshire) as well as in Cheshire and Lancashire, probably because of the considerable strength of Catholicism there. Over the following years, as the war with Spain intensified and fears of invasion grew, the lieutenancy system was gradually extended over the entire country. While there was still a preference (probably more Elizabeth's than her Council's) for choosing locally rooted peers as Lords Lieutenant, this was problematised by the fact that so much of the peerage remained Catholic: Catholics were almost never appointed to such offices after 1585. Cecil himself seems to have contemplated a systematic selection of committed Protestant loyalists in preference to local peers, but the queen's conservative instincts quashed this radicalism.[25] Nevertheless, undoubtedly loyal but unflinchingly Catholic peers (such as Viscount Montague in Sussex) finally had any remaining grip on the levers of local power prised loose during the crisis of the 1580s.

The consequences of the assassination of the Prince of Orange were as significant in foreign policy as in domestic policy. On 10 October 1584 Cecil penned one of his characteristic policy papers.[26] This one was designed to persuade the queen to intervene in the Netherlands to ensure her own security. The assassination of William of Orange, following so soon after the death of the Duke of Alençon, gave Cecil and his Privy Council colleagues serious reason for alarm about the prospects for the rebel provinces in the Netherlands. Spanish forces led by the gifted general Alessandro Farnese, Prince of Parma, had already been regaining lost ground. It was now clear to the English regime that direct intervention would have to replace indirect aid. Negotiations with the United Provinces concluded in the Treaty of Nonsuch (10 August 1585), by which Elizabeth undertook to send a substantial force to aid the rebels directly. The English army was led, incompetently, by the Earl of Leicester, who was no match for Farnese in the field and lacked the political skills to manage his Dutch allies. When in January 1586 he unwisely accepted their offer of the position of Governor-General of the Netherlands, he also managed to sour his relationship with the queen, whom he had not consulted, and who was enraged by his temerity. Leicester's expedition achieved nothing in military terms. Politically it was a commitment to open war with Spain that was bound to elicit a direct military response.

Rising political tensions made the English regime ever more anxious about Catholic plots, and some Catholics more willing to engage in them. Walsingham's *agents provocateurs* were busy, and sometimes fell over each other's feet. In autumn 1585 one of them, Edward Neville, managed to betray another of them, William Parry, before Parry could betray him. The tragic farce of the 'Parry Plot', however, was succeeded by what might have been the most threatening of the Marian plots had it not been penetrated by Walsingham's spies from the very start. It bears the name of Anthony Babington, a young Derbyshire gentleman who was induced by a couple of Catholic clergymen (at least one of whom, Gilbert Gifford, worked for Walsingham) to conspire on behalf of Mary Queen of Scots. Babington recruited a number of fellow Catholic gentlemen, young and hot-headed, for an enterprise not unlike some of the more hare-brained terrorist enterprises of the early twenty-first century (he even delayed the plot so that the conspirators could memorialise themselves with an official portrait). A handful of men would carry out the assassination (in effect a suicide mission) while a troop of 100 or so others broke Mary out of captivity in expectation of military assistance from Spain. This airy grand strategy would have had little enough chance of success even if Walsingham had not followed it closely from conception to denouement. As it was, the plotters were allowed to communicate with Mary via coded messages smuggled to her in beer barrels, and the correspondence went via Gifford through Walsingham's office in both directions. There it was carefully transcribed and edited by Walsingham's codebreaker, Thomas Phelippes, until enough had been written to implicate the helpless Scottish queen inextricably in the hapless escapade. By mid-July Mary seems to have consented to the plan, and the conspirators were rounded up in the middle of August The evidence of the letters was enough to secure convictions at law, and subsequent confessions, some obtained under torture or the threat of it, showed that those involved had indeed plotted to kill their sovereign. After lengthy interrogations, they were briskly tried, convicted and executed in September 1586.

Much ink has been spilled over the allocation of blame in the Babington Plot, formerly in an often partisan spirit, though more recent assessments acknowledge the difficulty of ascertaining precisely what was going on behind the smoke and mirrors of surviving sources.[27] There can be no doubt that Babington and his followers thought they were going to kill a false queen and set a true one free, nor that powerful Catholic political interests in France, Spain and Rome thought likewise. Yet it is equally evident that the whole affair was entrapment of the highest order, and the plainest evidence for this is in the correspondence that flowed through Walsingham's office to the chambers of the Queen of Scots. The evidence is not what was written, but the fact that the correspondence exists at all, which shows that what was afoot was not so much a plot to kill Elizabeth as a plan to kill Mary, a plan in which the plotters played an unwitting part. There was never, in the 1580s, anything that Mary herself could usefully do to advance any plot in her own interests, which to any half-competent plotter would self-evidently have been best served by insulating her totally from any involvement. The bungling conspirators who were haplessly lured to their dreadful deaths were pawns on the board of a much more skilful and practised player. Francis Walsingham thoughtfully provided them with the means to incriminate themselves and the Scottish queen.

It was evidently important to the Elizabethan regime to create a political atmosphere in which the trial and execution of a queen could be seen as morally justified. This policy had been pursued spasmodically since 1570, but with the arrest of the Babington plotters it was taken up with renewed vigour. An immense sermon of undiluted anti-Catholic polemic was delivered in the Tower of London and published almost at once, with a dedication to Sir Francis Walsingham. It encouraged 'English Israel' against 'our English Italianated Papists' the 'Romish runagates at Rheims', and their 'treacherous attempts against Her Majesty' and 'this church and kingdom'.[28] At the end of August, a client of Walsingham's in Oxford, Dr John Reynolds, preached there a pithier sermon of thanksgiving, recapitulating Elizabeth's deliverance from popish threats and plots from the papal bull of 1570 to this last desperate attempt ('I beseech God it be the last') – of which he evidently knew no details whatsoever.[29]

In the wake of the Babington Plot, an emergency Parliament was summoned. The writs went out on the day the trials ended (15 September). Parliament had been due to reconvene in November, but the urgency of the situation and the niceties of an already highly developed parliamentary procedure were such that it was easier to dissolve Parliament and summon a new one, to convene in mid-October – though this was made to look pointless when it was promptly adjourned. In the meantime, a tribunal was authorised under the terms of the Act for the Queen's Safety, and Mary herself was put on trial at Fotheringhay Castle on 14 and 15 October. After the evidence had been heard, though, the hearing was referred back to Star Chamber in Westminster for the solemnity of a verdict. There, on 25 October, the peers and councillors found her guilty of conspiracy to bring about the 'death and destruction' of the queen. With that formality completed, the emergency Parliament got down to business on 29 October. A series of Privy Councillors rose in each house to call for the execution of the Queen of Scots, and a delegation of both houses took this message to Elizabeth on 12 November. Hesitating, understandably, to take such a momentous decision, Elizabeth had to be coaxed and bullied all the way. The two houses sent another delegation on 24 November, and she seems to have been persuaded.

Its work done, Parliament was adjourned on 2 December, and two days later a lengthy proclamation announced and explained Mary's condemnation. Most proclamations took up only a page, but this one occupied three. Interestingly, it shifted full responsibility for the execution onto Parliament, which, 'representing the State of all our Realm', had pressed the queen urgently to confirm and execute the sentence of the tribunal.[30] The proclamation was systematically published, starting in

London, where it was read aloud by the town clerk in the presence of the Lord Mayor and Aldermen, accompanied by numerous lords, courtiers, leading citizens and gentlemen. It was greeted with universal rejoicing amid bonfires and bells. Outside London, sheriffs and JPs held similar ceremonies. Even now, though, Elizabeth hesitated to authorise the deed, beset by political and religious scruples. It was not until 1 February 1587 that she at last set her hand to the death warrant, and even then wavered about despatching it. After it had been sent, she told anyone who would listen that her Principal Secretary, William Davison, had done it without her knowledge or approval. It was the hardest decision she ever had to take, and she did everything she could to persuade herself she hadn't taken it.

6

THE WAR WITH SPAIN AND THE SUCCESSION, 1587–1603

At eight o'clock in the morning on 8 February 1587, Mary Stewart, Queen of Scotland and France, was summoned from her chambers in the castle of Fotheringhay by the Sheriff of Northamptonshire, accompanied by the earls of Shrewsbury and Kent. She had already been assigned a royal chaplain, Richard Fletcher, Dean of Peterborough Cathedral, to help her prepare for death, but as a Catholic she had predictably spurned his pastoral attentions. When she was led between the earls into the Great Hall, Fletcher embarked on some edifying remarks which the queen at once requested him to desist. Giving her blessing to her servants, whom she recommended to the kindness of the lords gathered there to witness her death, she prayed a while, and then asked her attendants to remove her veil, cloak and doublet. Kneeling down, she prayed a little more, briefly raising aloft a small crucifix that she kept with her until the end. Once her maids had blindfolded her, she raised her head erect, expecting to be despatched in the French fashion by a whirling sword. It was explained to her that she had to bend forwards onto the block, which she did. Her physician reported with evident disgust that the job was to be done with the sort of axe used for chopping wood. Given that the headsman took three blows to finish his job, this may indeed have been the case. Mary waited, repeating in a clear voice the words 'Domine, in manus tuas commendo animam meam' ('Lord, into your hands I commend my spirit'), until the first blow fell.[1] Thus William Cecil achieved the goal he had sought for fifteen or perhaps twenty years, the final destruction of the most dangerous rival to Elizabeth's throne (Figure 6.1).

If one threat had been averted, however, another was looming. Philip II's planned Armada was the worst kept secret in Europe. Ships

Sketch of the Execution of Mary Queen of Scots
This contemporary sketch of the Great Hall at Fotheringhay Castle on the morning of 8 February 1587 shows three successive moments: the queen's entry into the chamber (left), the removal of her outer garments (stage, front central – note her crucifix on the little table), and the headsman swinging the axe (stage, back right).

were being laid down or docked for refurbishment. Vast quantities of stores and arms were being ordered and amassed. Troops were being raised or despatched from other theatres for an amphibious operation on an unprecedented scale. The invasion of England was on. From the perspective of Elizabeth's Court, it was a struggle for personal as well as national survival. Elizabeth was already a relapsed and excommunicated heretic. Now she was also responsible for the execution of an anointed Catholic queen, an act of questionable legality. Moreover, the victim was readily presented to Catholic audiences in Europe as a martyr. If Elizabeth fell into the hands of a Spanish invasion force, her own execution was inevitable, while Cecil and her other close advisers could scarcely expect any more mercy than their sovereign. Mary's death may have stiffened Philip's resolve to press on with the invasion. It certainly handed him a propaganda coup that his supporters exploited to the full.

English attempts to parry this threat included not only frenetic though for the most part fruitless diplomacy but also a pre-emptive strike. Sir Francis Drake was appointed to lead the expedition that he would later famously label 'the singeing of the King of Spain's beard', his raid on Cadiz and subsequent harrying of the Iberian Atlantic coast in spring 1587. The high point of this piratical campaign came on 19 April, when he surprised a merchant fleet in harbour at Cadiz. The Spanish ships were caught unprepared by Drake's characteristic impetuosity and the pickings were rich and easy. His ships sailed away fully revictualled and loaded with plunder. The episode was one of the most profitable of the many joint-stock piracy ventures in which early capitalist London excelled. It was formally repudiated in due course by the virtuous queen, but Drake remained high in royal favour and popular esteem. The intelligence he had acquired along the Iberian coastline was invaluable and his coup seriously disrupted Spanish preparations. The time thus won was put to good use in England over the next year and a half as troops were equipped and trained.

Drake's raid may well have prevented the Armada sailing in 1587, though perhaps the plan was so vast that it could never have set off so soon. That Drake himself, who was regarded in England and Spain alike as England's premier naval commander, was not put in charge of the English fleet in 1588 might seem odd to modern eyes. But in the hierarchical world of Tudor England, the other gentleman pirates or honest gentlemen who commanded vessels or squadrons in the Elizabethan navy would never have been able to subordinate their rivalries and resentments to a man they thought no better than themselves. It was a pragmatic necessity that a nobleman should command any sizeable military or naval force. Charles Howard, Baron Howard of Effingham (a nephew of the third Duke of Norfolk), had the social rank and, fortunately, enough genuine nautical experience to impose a measure of discipline and strategy on the fleet that made its rendezvous at Plymouth that spring. He also had the nous to take advice from his captains. This wisdom, with a deal of luck, saw him and his fleet through. Bad weather had kept his fleet in harbour through June and July, which may well have saved them from missing the Armada in open seas, as they had hoped to sail to intercept it.

When the Armada was sighted in the Channel, luck stepped in once more. The Duke of Medina Sidonia, its nautically inexperienced leader, who was without anyone of Drake's acumen or panache to advise him, was not the man to seize the tactical initiative by trapping the English fleet in harbour, which might have left him in complete command of the Channel. This was the only situation which would have allowed him to make his rendezvous with the Prince of Parma at Dunkirk in such a way that Parma's shallow-draught troopships could be safely escorted across to Kent. As it was, the English fleet was allowed to leave port in difficult conditions and make its dispositions. The English harried the Armada all the way up the Channel, though to little enough effect until it moored off Gravelines, between Calais and Dunkirk. At this point, the superior gunnery of the nimbler English ships put the Spanish amphibian force at enormous disadvantage, especially once fireships were sent among the clumsier Spanish vessels, inducing a panic in which they cut anchors and broke defensive formation. With that, the English strategic victory was complete. The unceasing winds dispersed the Spanish fleet to the north, chased by the English more in triumph than intent. What was at the time the largest sea-fight in history saw relatively few ships lost in direct combat, though most of those were Spanish. From the Spanish viewpoint, a massive invasion force first embarked on an ill-conceived strategy, then threw away its greatest tactical opportunity, and was ultimately unable to respond effectively to English tactics at anchor off the coast of the Netherlands. From the English viewpoint, the Spanish strategic goal of a landing on English shores was frustrated, Parma's battle-hardened veterans never put to sea from Dunkirk, and the Armada itself was shattered by superior tactics and subsequently destroyed by terrible weather at sea.[2]

In the meantime, the main English army was camped at Tilbury on the north bank of the Thames, under the command of the Earl of Leicester. Famously, Elizabeth came to the camp to review her troops on 8 August and next day made a stirring speech to them, exhorting them to courage in battle, and boasting 'I have the body but of a weak and feeble woman, but I have the heart and stomach of a king and of a king of England too' – an invocation of her father, that most kingly Henry VIII. This event did not take place, however, under quite such perilous circumstances as has often been thought. The chronology of the Armada campaign is made dreadfully complicated for historians and modern readers by the fact that Spain, in common with Catholic Europe, was operating on a revised calendar which had been introduced by Pope Gregory XIII in October 1582 to correct the long-term drift of the traditional Christian calendar (the Julian calendar of imperial Rome) from the solar year. England, along with several other Protestant states, refused to adopt this reformed calendar because it was the work of the papacy, which they viewed as the Antichrist. As a result, the date of any given day in England was less by ten days than the date of the same day in Spain, France, or the Spanish Netherlands. So while the Spanish reported that their fleet was attacked at Gravelines on the night of 7–8 August, that was not the eve of the queen's appearance at Tilbury on 8 August. It was ten days earlier – in English terms the Armada had been attacked on 28–29 July. By the time Elizabeth spoke at Tilbury, the Spanish fleet was scattered far across the North Sea and her government knew it, which is why orders were given to break the camp just a couple of days later.

Culturally and psychologically decisive as it was, the defeat of the Armada was not militarily as conclusive as it has come to seem. The Anglo–Spanish war alternately blazed and smouldered on for another fifteen years, from the North Sea coast of Europe to the West Indies. But Spain's best chance of a knockout victory was gone, and the gargantuan investment in that single failed operation had a lasting impact on Spain's capacity to wage war, as well as upon the nation's morale, hitherto buoyed by a string of victories marred only by setbacks – not, as now, by utter disaster.

Given the nature of the fight at sea, news of final victory was slow to dawn. But the presses of London were soon stamping out celebratory texts – simple poems and prayers, broadsheet ballads that served something of the purposes of newspapers, longer pamphlets and sermons. The official victory sermon was preached at Paul's Cross on Sunday 20 August by the Dean of St Paul's, the aged Alexander Nowell, and several others followed. A grand State service of thanksgiving was arranged there for Sunday 24 November, and reports of the scenes in London on that occasion remind the modern reader of those on Victory in Europe Day in

1945. Queen Elizabeth progressed in pomp from Somerset House to St Paul's Cathedral, besieged by joyous surging crowds, her route studded with bands playing lively music. After brief prayers in the cathedral, she was escorted to a specially made stall outside, from which she could overlook the huge audience gathered for a Paul's Cross sermon by her Almoner, John Piers, Bishop of Salisbury. The last royal visitor to the Cross for a sermon had been her antagonist, Philip II himself, back in 1554, to hear a sermon on England's reconciliation with Rome. Her own decision looks like a reply across those three decades, and her personal identification with the crowds and with the triumph over Spain was voiced in a verse prayer or anthem she wrote herself, which was set to music for performance in the Chapel Royal.[3]

It did not go well for Catholics in the aftermath of the Armada. Eight Catholics, some of them priests who had been in prison for months or even years, were executed at gallows around London on 28 August. Among them was Thomas Felton, son of the man who had nailed Pius V's bull to the Bishop of London's door. A handful more were hanged at Tyburn two days later.[4] Others followed through the autumn. John Hewitt (alias Weldon), a priest who had been in Newgate for a year and a half, was abruptly tried on Friday 4 October with two others. The trio were marched to and fro across London next day for their various executions: Hewitt out at Mile End Green; another seminary priest called William Hartley near the theatre in Shoreditch; and the third, a layman called Robert Sutton, at Clerkenwell. The same preacher pestered each of them at the last, seeking to win their conversions, particularly that of Sutton, who had been forced to watch his two fellow victims hanged on that little odyssey around east London.[5]

The association of popery with treason was reiterated ever more insistently, with the popes (aka 'the Romish Antichrist') blamed for everything from the Pilgrimage of Grace onwards. Other spectacles, equally edifying but less bloody, were also staged. On the first Sunday of Advent, a Catholic priest called William Tedder appeared at Paul's Cross to make a formal recantation of the faith he had held from childhood, followed the week after by an almost identical performance from Anthony Tyrrell. For Tyrrell this was but one episode in a picaresque career that saw him shuttle between Catholicism and Protestantism and eventually die, once again a Catholic, an exile in Naples. It is difficult to judge the psychological impact of the complex events of 1588 on England's Catholics, whose numbers were already much diminished since the time of Elizabeth's accession. But the feeling of the moment was summed up in *Elizabetha Triumphans*, an heroic poem written in celebration of the great victory. After recounting the frustration of papal machinations against the queen and the defeat of the Armada, it ended with an appeal to English recusants to 'turn your hearts unto your sacred queen'.[6] The open support for the invasion voiced by the papacy and by many Catholic refugees, popular revulsion at the horrors this would have unleashed upon the land, a surge of patriotic royalism in the wake of victory, and the renewed financial and judicial assault upon recusants and seminary priests, all played their part in swaying large numbers of waverers. The defeat of the Spanish Armada was the epitaph of Catholic England.

In the history of the Church of England, however, the turning point of Elizabeth's reign had come a little earlier, with the enthronement of John Whitgift as Archbishop of Canterbury in October 1583. Whitgift had set out his stall in the 1570s, during his tedious exchange with Thomas Cartwright, and Elizabeth looked to him to bring the Puritan movement to heel. Within a week of taking up his office, he had promulgated a set of articles which, among other things, required all clergymen to subscribe formally to the royal supremacy and to the Thirty-Nine Articles, and to affirm that the Book of Common Prayer contained nothing contrary to the Word of God. This particular requirement was designed to flush out Puritans who could cope with the book by swallowing hard and, as often as they could, leaving out what they didn't like. Those with especially tender consciences, if cornered, were forced out of their parishes, but there was a good deal of intransigence, and implementation was patchy. The Puritans fought back with the aid of their lay friends and patrons. Powerful supporters lobbied hard for a mitigation of Whitgift's harsh strategy. Thus Sir Francis Knollys wrote to Cecil in June 1584 protesting about Whitgift's campaign, and Cecil took this up with the archbishop, likening his campaign to the Spanish Inquisition.[7] By autumn 1584 Whitgift found almost the whole Privy Council against him, and he had to back down.

The Puritans were anything but broken by Whitgift's campaign, and in many places they were encouraged by the support they received to work for further reformation. Puritan MPs were vocal in the Parliament of 1584, advancing a bill to replace the Book of Common Prayer with the church service used in Geneva. Such endeavours were doomed to fail, but others made more progress at the grass roots. The more committed Presbyterians among the Puritans, realising that the prospects of seeing their ideal form of Church government introduced officially were extremely dim, instead set about trying to establish the substance of the

Presbyterian 'discipline' (as they called it) on a local and voluntary basis. The best known of these is the 'Dedham Conference', established by the godly ministers of Essex in 1582, which lasted until 1589. Unusually, its records have survived, but other such groups are known to have sprung up in such Puritan regions as Suffolk and Northamptonshire.[8] The movement was so widespread that something like a national Presbyterian synod was held at Cambridge in 1589, in St John's College.

At the same time, however, the Church of England was becoming steadily more English. In the early years of Elizabeth's reign, the Protestant religion was for many still an exotic import, something German or 'Dutch'. And the restoration of Protestantism was driven on the ground by a generation of fiercely devout men who had fled their country rather than conform to what they saw as pernicious idolatry. They had seen the true faith and pure discipline of Reformed religion at first hand, in Strasbourg, Zurich and Geneva. On their return to England, they remained in touch with their European brethren via networks of correspondence which themselves testify to their sense of oneness with the wider Reformed Church. Bishops such as Grindal, Horne, Jewel and Parkhurst were among the many prelates who cultivated these more Presbyterian connections. By the 1590s, that generation had passed, and so, too, had the dreams of those committed Protestants who hoped to see the English Church more closely aligned in its worship and practice with those of Switzerland, France, the Rhineland and the Netherlands.

Whitgift did not exchange letters with Zurich or Geneva, and neither did such episcopal allies as Richard Bancroft. They were no less hostile to popery in all its forms, and no less Protestant in their theology, but they simply had less interest in seeking the religious sanction of patriarchal authorities beyond the Channel. This new generation of clergy lacked direct experience of the Reformed tradition in Europe, as few had ever left the country. The Church of England itself, with the passing of time, was beginning to take on a patina of antiquity. The Book of Common Prayer and the Thirty-Nine Articles were acquiring the character of sacred texts. The first learned commentary on the articles was published by Thomas Rogers in 1585, under the revealing title *The English Creed*, even though he was still at pains to emphasise that the Church of England was in doctrinal harmony with reformed churches abroad. His personal history, however, reflects the drift away from dependency on European Reformed religion. In his youth he translated several works by European Protestants into English, and moved in the godly circles of Suffolk Puritanism that looked across the Channel for inspiration. But he was excluded from the Bury St Edmunds 'exercise' in 1589, after a sermon attacking Calvin's notion that his fourfold ministry was mandated in the New Testament. Subsequently he attached himself to Sir Christopher Hatton and then Richard Bancroft, two pillars of anti-Puritanism, and went on to attack Puritan Sabbatarianism. He translated no more from European Protestant sources.[9]

Even more influential, if rather more subtle, was the polemic against Calvin and Geneva framed by Richard Hooker in his monumental *Laws of Ecclesiastical Polity*, the first half of which appeared in 1593. Hooker was a client of Whitgift's who had first come to prominence in 1584 when the archbishop imposed him as Master of the Temple Church in London against the Temple lawyers' preferred candidate, the Puritan Walter Travers. Hooker aimed to overwhelm with sheer weight of argument the fiercer Puritans who insisted on Calvin's version of Church government and judged that the Church of England fell short of the standards set by the 'best reformed churches' of Europe. On the contrary, Hooker maintained, the Church of England was itself ideal, at least for England. Episcopacy was a tried and trusted form of Church government, with roots deep in the early Church. But what was most remarkable about his *magnum opus* was its preface, a lengthy relativisation of Calvin and Geneva, a verbally gentle but intellectually brutal dismantling of the tendency of Calvin's English followers to idolise him and fetishise his system. Calvin was, it transpired, just a man, while Geneva was simply a small city, far away. There was no intrinsic reason to conclude that what worked for a remote city-state would work for a populous and disparate kingdom such as England, and Calvin's pretensions to scriptural warrant for his elaborate ecclesiastical prescriptions were deftly brushed aside. For Hooker, the survival and flourishing of the Church of England as by law established under Elizabeth were evidence of God's miraculous favour:

> What can we less thereupon conclude, than that God would at leastwise by tract of time teach the world, that the thing which he blesseth, defendeth, keepeth so strangely, cannot choose but be of him? Wherefore, if any refuse to believe us disputing for the verity of religion established, let them believe God himself thus miraculously working for it, and wish life even for ever and ever unto that glorious and sacred instrument whereby he worketh.[10]

Hooker's work, however, still testifies to the force of Puritanism and Presbyterianism in English religious culture. The Church of England may have been becoming more English, but the Puritans were more numerous than ever before, and as determined as ever to bring it into line with those 'best reformed churches'. The specific cause of Presbyterianism, though, suffered in the latter years of Elizabeth. There were several reasons for this. First and foremost was the rising tide of anti-Puritanism, in which Bancroft became ever more prominent.[11] Bancroft had been Whitgift's lieutenant in repressing Puritan activism through the 1580s, but what brought him to the fore was the publishing *succès de scandale* of the Armada years, the so-called 'Marprelate Tracts' (1588–89), a series of scurrilous pamphlets poking bawdy fun at the bishops and their minions.

Among the funniest things written in Tudor England, these pamphlets aimed to promote Presbyterian ideas by discrediting the English bishops. Bancroft led the counter-offensive with a vigorous defence of episcopacy in a sermon at Paul's Cross on Sunday 9 February 1589, plainly timed to coincide with the opening of Parliament (4 February). By the end of August, police work masterminded by Bancroft had run to earth the peripatetic press that printed the Tracts. Martin Marprelate, wickedly amusing though he was, probably went too far for many of the solid and substantial men who formed the backbone of Puritanism. The extremism of Marprelate, coinciding with a crisis of national security, enabled the ecclesiastical authorities to clamp down effectively on the practical Presbyterianism of conferences, exercises and national synods, which disappeared completely in the 1590s.

It was easy for the establishment to draw a plausible but logically insecure connection between Marprelate's libellous rodomontade and the bizarre episode of the self-styled prophet and condemned traitor, William Hacket. After some years criss-crossing England with his eccentric itinerant preaching, during which time he was charitably regarded and uncharitably whipped as a harmless lunatic, this Hacket made his way in 1591 to London where, with the support of two Presbyterian gentlemen who should have known better, he advanced himself rapidly up the great chain of being, progressing in his final few days from the prophet of Christ's second coming to the Lord's Anointed in person. His acolytes proclaimed him Messiah and King of Europe at Cheapside Cross on 16 July 1591. He was executed on the same spot before the month was done, proclaiming himself the mighty Jehovah even as he squirmed to keep his head out of the noose. Hacket's delusions, however, had an undeniably Puritan and Presbyterian flavour. His aims included the abolition of episcopacy and the implementation of 'the discipline', and his turn of phrase was ostentatiously biblical in the manner that non-Puritans found so tiresome. The detailed official account of the case, penned by a close associate of Whitgift's called Richard Cosin, concluded with a fine peroration linking the errors of Presbyterianism to the notorious excesses of the 'Anabaptists' at Münster in the mid-1530s.[12] However, the taint of sedition was not quite so tangible as that imparted to Catholicism by Pius V's untimely bull in 1570, and English Puritans were exemplary in their refusal to dabble in the dangerous waters of resistance theory. They were eager translators and readers of the writings of the Huguenots (French Calvinists), but they avoided those texts in which the Huguenots justified their various acts of rebellion against their anointed Catholic monarchs. Once it was France's Catholics, rather than Protestants, who were rebelling against the king (Henry IV, a Huguenot until 1593), then Huguenot political pamphlets became acceptably royalist and were readily published in England.[13]

If English Presbyterianism did not go away, it certainly went very quiet. Between them, Marprelate and Hacket had played into Whitgift's hands. The executions in spring 1593 of three notorious separatists, Henry Barrow, John Greenwood and John Penry, were followed by a period of relative religious calm, without overt Presbyterian agitation in Parliament or elsewhere. Oxford's leading Puritan, Dr John Reynolds, was induced at this time to accept promotion, becoming Dean of Lincoln Cathedral. The Presbyterian firebrand of the 1580s, Walter Travers, was sent out to the new Protestant foundation of Trinity College in Dublin in the 1590s, and became its Master in 1594. He was careful in this 'establishment' role not to rock the boat, while nevertheless embedding the new college firmly in the Calvinist tradition. The works of the moderate Cambridge Puritan, William Perkins, poured from the London presses throughout the decade, for it was devotional writings, not ecclesiastical polemics, that typified late Elizabethan Puritanism. Puritan endeavours in parishes and towns aimed at the formation of godly individuals and groups. Discreet disregard of the ceremonial aspects of the Book of Common Prayer was winked at by many bishops in exchange for zealous preaching and devotion to pastoral care in the parishes. So Puritans such as John Dod at Hanwell (Oxfordshire), Ezekiel Culverwell at Great Stambridge (Essex) and John Knewstub at Cockfield (Suffolk) remained in their pulpits through the 1590s and sometimes well beyond.

The need for national solidarity in the face of war also played its part in the disappearance of Presbyterian agitation after the clampdown of the early 1590s. And if that was not enough, the Puritans were now facing open challenges in both the doctrinal and the public sphere. The doctrinal challenge was not too threatening. Some theologians were starting to question the harsh notion of 'double predestination' which was one of the distinguishing features of the high Calvinist theology that had held sway in the Church of England since the 1560s. The thesis that God unconditionally predestines some people, perhaps most of them, to everlasting torment was formulated for the first time by Martin Bucer and John Calvin, earlier in the sixteenth century, as a logical corollary of the older and more widely held doctrine that God unconditionally predestines the elect to salvation (hence 'double' predestination). Logically compelling or not, the notion of divine predestination to hell has always provoked disquiet. The Puritan Walter Travers thought Richard Hooker shaky on the doctrine when they were both preaching in the Temple in the mid-1580s.

More insistent doubts were voiced in the 1590s by figures such as Peter Baro and William Barrett in Cambridge. Calvinist theology remained dominant, however, and both men were hounded out of the university. Even Whitgift leaned more towards Calvin than towards Baro, and this essentially academic controversy was brought to some kind of closure in 1595 with the Lambeth Articles, a set of propositions drafted by the doyen of Cambridge Puritanism, William Whitaker (Master of St John's College), and approved by Archbishop Whitgift himself.[14] The Lambeth Articles upheld a Calvinist view of predestination. But the fact that they had to be drawn up at all, and the equally significant fact that they never gained the royal backing they needed to make them truly binding, were both ill omens for the long-term security of the Calvinist theology that was the foundation for Puritanism (though not its exclusive possession – it cannot be emphasised too strongly that the doctrinal position of the Church of England at this time remained broadly Calvinist).

More damaging to Puritan interests was the emerging phenomenon of anti-Puritanism. This was originally driven from the top, by sermons from chaplains and clients of Whitgift, Bancroft and others. But solemn moralising was no way to deal with Marprelate, so racier replies were commissioned from the sharper pens of wits such as Robert Greene and Thomas Nashe.[15] Their efforts set a trend, and the hypocritical Puritan became a stock character on stage in such roles as Malvolio and Zeal-of-the-Land Busy (Puritan naming habits were wide open to satire). Yet for all this, Puritan works of doctrine and devotion still found their way into print, and colleges such as Emmanuel and St John's in Cambridge, and Brasenose and Exeter in Oxford continued to send out godly ministers to serve ever larger numbers of England's parishes.[16] Thus William Burton, a moderate Puritan, served at St Giles in Reading from 1591 until 1614, publishing reams of Puritan devotion, but steering clear of controversial matters of Church government. The authorities, in any case, remained ambivalent about Puritan ministers. John Allenson, a protégé of William Whitaker, was harassed for non-conformity in the 1580s, yet served from 1611 until his death in 1619 as the rector of Whickham (Northumberland), to which he was presented by the Bishop of Durham. Committed Puritan patrons such as Sir Robert Jermyn of Rushbrooke (Suffolk) continued to advance like-minded clergymen in the parishes within their gift. Thomas Carew was presented by him to the rectory of Bildeston (Suffolk) in 1591, and served there until his death in 1616.

Richard Bancroft, who probably missed his true vocation by becoming a clergyman, was equally successful in dealing with the regime's Catholic opponents. Having quashed the Presbyterians, he turned to the papists, whom he undermined by fomenting dissension in their ranks. As in Europe, so too in England there were tensions between the most successful new religious movement of the century within Catholicism, the Jesuits (members of the Society of Jesus, founded by Ignatius Loyola), and the 'secular' priests (that is, priests who were not members of religious orders). The Jesuits, highly educated, highly trained and highly motivated, were at the forefront of Catholic revival everywhere, and their publicity was as effective as their ministry. They tended to treat Catholic doubters or rivals as at best jealous and at worst a fifth column. Many Catholics, in return, saw the Jesuits as excessive in their papalism and as driven by worldly and political ambition. Jesuits were indeed busy at princely Courts, where they were often to be found as confessors or spiritual directors to kings and were thus well placed to dabble in politics. In the English context, secular priests thought the Jesuits (especially Robert Parsons) far too ready to meddle in politics and in perilous debates over the succession, and liked to blame on them all the real and alleged plots and practices that brought opprobrium upon Catholics in general, in the hope of securing better treatment from the regime. When an 'Archpriest' (named George Blackwell) was appointed by Rome as head of the English secular clergy in 1598 in an effort to calm the situation, many of them resented the fact that his orders required him to work closely with the leader of the English Jesuits, Henry Garnett. Bancroft nurtured their sense of grievance and made it possible for them to publish their complaints and accusations in print, with a view to dividing and weakening the recusant movement – which it did. The resulting controversy raged until the end of the reign.

The politics of the 1590s were somewhat disrupted by the rise and fall of Robert Devereux, Earl of Essex, who was the political heir of Leicester as the figurehead of the militantly Protestant nexus and as a royal favourite. Essex was a figure very much of his own time, yet imagined himself the heir to ancient aristocratic pre-eminence. He was hardly a magnate in the medieval mould. Though Devereux was a noble lineage, the earldom had been attained only by his father, Walter. Robert's ambitions were focused on success at Court and victory in war, and his income depended on office, not on hereditary estates. The chivalric imagery with which he loved to bedeck himself was little more than a fantasy in the 1590s, as is made evident in the *Faerie Queene*, the late chivalric romance penned by Edmund Spenser, of whose later years Essex was something of a patron and protector. Accession Day 'tilts' still pitted armoured knights against each other for sport, but this ritualised combat no longer had any relevance to the battlefield. Devereux was a young man in a hurry. Determined efforts have been made to rehabilitate him as a political heavyweight, a man of vision, talent and accomplishment,[17] but on balance it still seems as though his glamour dazzled not only his contemporaries but also himself. His attempt at the simultaneous pursuit of serious influence at the Council table through assiduous attendance at Court and of aristocratic greatness through military campaigning overseas was fundamentally inconsistent. One might realistically aim for one or the other, or even for first one and then the other, but not for both. As it was, Essex fell between two stools, now fawning or scheming at Court, now embarking on military adventures for which he was not as well qualified as he liked to think.

Essex had first been noted as a rising favourite of the aging queen in 1587, after returning from service with Leicester's campaign in the Netherlands (1585–86), and he replaced Leicester as Master of the Horse in April that year. His impulsive unguardedness was immediately revealed when he had an ill-tempered exchange with the queen that summer because of the favour she was also showing to Walter Raleigh. Leicester had always known better than that. But Essex's adolescent temperament remained with him through his brief adulthood. The man who challenged Raleigh and then Charles Blount to duels in 1588 carried on losing friends and alienating people throughout the 1590s. Essex was keen to situate himself as England's Protestant champion in succession to Leicester. It helped that he married the widow of Sir Philip Sidney, the peerless knight of English Protestantism, in 1590 – though of course, like so many of Elizabeth's courtiers, he married secretly for fear of her displeasure. But while Essex had a distinct political vision, it was more ideological and less pragmatic than that of William Cecil, and he lacked both the wisdom to pick his battles and the robustness to pursue a steady purpose in the face of setbacks. It had taken Cecil ten years to establish himself securely at the head of the Queen's Council, and Elizabeth owed him a great deal. She owed Essex nothing, yet he expected instant pre-eminence.

For all his bright prospects at Court, Essex hankered after martial glory, and in the aftermath of the Armada he was a fervent supporter of the idea of a counterstrike against Spain which was mooted over the winter of 1588–89. Astonishingly, an expedition was indeed planned and launched. Less surprisingly, it proved to be a complete waste of effort. Its chief claim to fame is that Essex, defying Elizabeth's prohibition, sneaked away from Court to join it. The expedition set off for Lisbon in April 1589 in the hope of stirring the Portuguese to rise up against their Spanish overlords. But a decision to attack Coruña on the way wasted time and men, and threw away the element of surprise. English troops successfully completed a fiercely opposed landing north of Lisbon, but the expected rising never materialised, and the expeditionary force was not up to the task of besieging the great Portuguese capital. A contingency plan for an assault on the Azores was frustrated by the weather, and the fleet was back in England by midsummer with nothing to show but prodigious losses. It was said at the time that 11,000 of a notional 23,000 effectives died on the voyage – mostly of disease, the chief cause of death in early modern warfare. No army of that era was ever as large as its official rollcall suggested, but thousands of men were indeed lost on this ill-planned, ill-executed and ill-fated enterprise.

English attempts to bloody the Spanish nose continued in other spheres, most immediately in France, where yet another unpredictable turn of events threatened to shift the balance against Spain. Having freed himself from Guise tutelage through the assassination of the Duke of Guise and the Cardinal of Lorraine just before Christmas 1588, Henry III of France was in his turn assassinated by a Catholic fanatic on 22 July 1589. This left the leader of France's massive Huguenot community, Henry of Navarre, with the strongest claim to the throne, offering the prospect of toleration, and perhaps even more, for Protestantism in France. But the bitterness left by decades of civil war meant that France's Catholic majority was by no means prepared to accept a Protestant succession without a fight. The forces of popular Catholic activism (the self-styled 'Holy League') that the Guises had unleashed ensured that Paris and several other major cities refused Henry's claims, while other Guise dynasts were still able to put powerful forces into the field against him. Elizabeth was persuaded to send 4,000 men across to assist in Henry's first siege of Paris in autumn, and they served with some distinction until recalled home early next year. Paris did not fall, but the League was only able to hold out there and elsewhere because Spanish troops were sent south from the Netherlands to relieve the capital and to support Catholic resistance in Normandy and Brittany.

From the English viewpoint this was at least a strategic gain: the diversion of Spanish troops into France took pressure off the Protestants of the northern Netherlands. English interventions in France and the Netherlands continued through the early 1590s, never enough to achieve victory, but always helping to keep Protestant allies in the field and thus to consume Spanish resources that might otherwise have been used directly against England. Thus another English expedition crossed the Channel in 1591, under the leadership of the irrepressible Earl of Essex, to assist Henry in the siege of Rouen. That campaign was equally inconclusive, though Henry and Essex revelled in the action. Yet Rouen, like Paris before, held out, thanks to yet another Spanish relief expedition in spring 1592. About 20,000 Englishmen saw action in France in these years, with very little to show for it. These campaigns did nothing to make Elizabeth any less sceptical about deploying English troops beyond the sea. The Rouen campaign did at least secure significant political advancement for Essex himself. In February 1593 he was recruited to the Privy Council and for a while was assiduous in attendance. But his spectacular misjudgement in his unremitting and doomed advocacy of Francis Bacon for the vacant positions first of Attorney General and then of Solicitor General (in 1594 and 1595) soured his relationship with the Cecils (what was left of it) and even with the queen.

English military engagement took a different direction from 1593, largely because Henry of Navarre realised that, as a Protestant, he would always struggle to vindicate his claim to the throne, let alone to win the loyalty of his Catholic subjects. Bowing to the inevitable, and after having put out diplomatic feelers in this direction for a year or two, Henry first agreed to 'take instruction' in Catholicism and then, in July 1593, formally abjured his Protestant beliefs. It took some time for all the dominoes to fall, but Henry was welcomed into Paris within a year and had mopped up the resistance by 1596. France's Catholics were war-weary and keen not to enquire too closely into the case of a king who, cynics suggested, had changed his religion seven times. It was enough for them that the ball had finally come to rest on black. French Protestants were mostly and rightly confident of toleration from their own former leader. With France increasingly united under a Catholic ruler, there was little reason to keep English troops there, and they were soon withdrawn. There was one more serious English intervention in France, in 1594. A fleet landed a force in Brittany in order to overthrow a base that the Spanish had established there. But that was all about England's ongoing struggle with Spain.[18]

Any hope of a peace dividend out of disengagement from France was rapidly dispelled by developments in Ireland. As early as 1593, the English regime in Ireland was responding to raids and risings from the subjects they oppressed. In 1595 this disruption moved onto another level under the leadership of Hugh O'Neill, Earl of Tyrone. O'Neill had successfully vindicated his claim to the lands of his father and grandfather by lobbying at Elizabeth's Court in the later 1580s. But his ambitions to hold sway throughout Ulster with royal backing were undermined by his rivalry with Sir Henry Bagenal, a leading figure in the new English colonial administration in Ireland, who had ambitions of his own on the province. The fact that a thief once made away with £200 in cash hidden in Bagenal's chamber at Court in 1596 is evidence of the extent to which he profited personally from his role.[19] His vendetta against O'Neill mired Ireland in civil conflict and was to lead to his own death. O'Neill managed to outmanoeuvre a punitive expedition under Bagenal's command in 1595, driving him to the coast in ignominious retreat. After that, he waged a guerrilla war against the English garrisons for the next few years, and reached out for Spanish aid. Ireland thus also became part of England's great war with Spain.

By this time, Essex was ready for fresh adventures, after a few years of largely fruitless endeavour on the Privy Council, during which the nearest he came to solid achievement was the execution for treason in 1594 of the unfortunate Portuguese Jewish physician, Ruy Lopes, on the flimsy grounds of a conspiracy to poison the queen, the evidence for which was obtained exclusively from the torturing of two other Portuguese expatriates. Essex's own manoeuvres to promote Francis Bacon had failed, and he had failed in his frankly spiteful attempt to block the appointment of Robert Cecil (William's second son) as Secretary of State in 1595. He ascribed his lack of success to the malice of the Cecils rather than to his own misjudgement or incompetence and had managed by the middle of the decade to bring a needless dimension of factiousness to the heart of government. However, his itch to return to action offered everyone a way out. He had been lobbying consistently for an attack on Spanish power, and was given command of an amphibious force to attack Cadiz in 1596. Planned on the mistaken notion that the Spanish were meditating another Armada, this was an attempt to reprise Drake's coup of 1587. Tactically it was a triumph, and Cadiz was plundered and razed. Essex was typically dashing in action, and the exploit won him huge acclaim back home. Strategically, however, the expedition was a disaster. It provoked the very thing it had been designed to frustrate. Until attacked, the Spanish had no intention of launching yet another armada against England, but they swiftly rustled one up for a revenge mission later that year. It was dispersed by storms long before it got anywhere near English shores. Having thus managed to reignite all-out war with Spain, Essex was once more given a major command in 1597, this time with a view to disrupting yet another Spanish revenge fleet before it could sail from its rendezvous harbour at Ferrol, a natural haven across the bay from Coruña on the Galician coast. Finding that he could not get at the fleet, Essex pivoted, without authorisation, into an attempt to capture the annual Spanish treasure fleet on its transatlantic voyage. This too failed, perhaps unluckily.

The Spanish fleet at Ferrol, meanwhile, had set off. This time, its projected destination was Ireland, where it was headed in the hope of bolstering Hugh O'Neill's cause and making Ireland as problematic for Elizabeth as the Netherlands were for Spain. Effective Spanish intervention might indeed have transformed that conflict from regional rebellion to national resistance. But, as usual, the armada was dispersed by storms before it made its objective. Despite this disappointment, when a substantial English force was sent north from Dublin under Henry Bagenal in 1598, O'Neill inflicted a crushing defeat on it at the Battle of the Yellow Ford, just to the north of Armagh. Bagenal himself was killed, with hundreds of his men, and the English grip on the island was shaken. O'Neill and his allies held most of it outside Dublin and the Pale, and O'Neill's own ambitions now seem to have embraced the Irish crown.

A challenge on this scale demanded an overwhelming response. Elizabeth was persuaded of the need for action, and in April 1599 the Earl of Essex was despatched with over 17,000 men to reduce Ireland and O'Neill to obedience. But Essex dawdled once he reached Dublin, and allowed himself to be distracted from his core mission, which was to confront Tyrone in Ulster, instead mopping up less important points of resistance in the south. Leaving active campaigning in the north until too late in the year, and lacking confidence that even his substantial force was adequate to the task of pacifying Ireland, Essex was obliged to parley with O'Neill at Dundalk. He was by now, rightly, more anxious about what rivals at the Court might be saying behind his back than about the situation confronting him in Ireland. By abandoning his post and hastening back to Westminster in September 1599, he signed his own political death warrant and left the opportunity of triumph in Ireland to others. Charles Blount, Lord Mountjoy, succeeded to Essex's command in 1600 and gradually ground down Irish resistance with the kind of gritty, bloody and methodical campaign for which the flashy Essex would never have had the patience. O'Neill's continual pleas for aid from Spain brought a Spanish force to the island in 1601, but Mountjoy disrupted his enemies' attempt to rendezvous at Kinsale and shattered their forces in a decisive battle on Christmas Eve. It took him another two years to bring Tyrone to heel although, amazingly, O'Neill was still allowed to submit on easy terms and retain his earldom, notwithstanding the years of costly trouble he had caused.

Essex's desertion of his command in 1599 squandered what little political capital he still possessed. The death of Philip II in 1598 considerably reduced the threat from Spain, and France was now at peace, with the Edict of Nantes guaranteeing, it seemed, a peaceful future for French Protestants. There was not much room in English politics for a successful military leader, and Essex was not even that. His bedraggled return to Court that autumn led only to arrest, imprisonment and then, in June 1600, a Star Chamber inquiry into his mishandling of the Irish campaign. This resulted in his being stripped of all his offices and barred from Court. Despair now overwhelmed him, and with the sorry remnants of his once powerful faction, padded out with a ragbag of malcontents (including some of the future Gunpowder Plotters), Essex meditated some kind of coup that was perhaps modelled on the successful seizure of power by the Catholic military hero, Francis Duke of Guise, at Paris in 1585. Like Guise, Essex led his armed entourage into the capital city, but London's Protestant mob was not as easily aroused against the popular Elizabeth as the Parisian Catholic mob had been against the widely hated Henry III. The coup sputtered out on 3 February 1601, and Essex was consigned to the Tower. He was beheaded before the month was out. For once, Elizabeth did not hesitate.

The inevitable social costs of prolonged naval and military commitments from 1585 were sorely exacerbated in the 1590s by natural disasters of two kinds, epidemic disease and harvest failure. In an age when the attentions of physicians and surgeons were the dubious privilege of the rich, epidemics caused deaths on a scale almost unimaginable to modern Western societies. While the 1590s did not equal the horrors of 1557–59, the death toll was terrible. Alongside epidemic disease, the general failure of four successive harvests in the years 1594–97 put English society under enormous strain. As a result, the decade saw what the best history of England's population in this era defines as 'crisis mortality' (a death rate in any given year at least 10 per cent higher than a 25-year moving average) in 1590–91, 1592–93, 1596–97 and 1597–98 (counting years from 1 July to 30 June). The year 1592–93 was the worst, with mortality nearly 30 per cent above average.[20] In the calendar year 1593, the London authorities were able to keep some track of it, and it was noted that in the city and suburbs there were nearly 18,000 deaths, over 10,000 of them attributed to 'the plague' (at that time a catch-all term for any epidemic, rather than a specific reference to what is now known as bubonic plague). But 1596–97 and 1597–98 saw death rates respectively 20 per cent and 25 per cent above average. The extreme circumstances of the 1590s, however, generated a new governmental response, or at least a response on a new scale. The authorities in England's towns and cities imported grain from overseas in an attempt to meet basic needs for food. The Lord Mayor and Aldermen of London were particularly busy and effective in managing the challenges of disease and potential famine. Moreover, the Privy Council, notwithstanding the pressures of war, devoted considerable time to ordering and co-ordinating local interventions, as well as to establishing martial law under officers known as Provosts Marshal where law and order seemed under threat. As a result, while the crises of the 1540s and 1550s had seen a number of significant popular rebellions and considerable unrest, the crisis of the 1590s is remarkable for the level of stability that was successfully maintained by the kingdom's governing authorities. There were occasional riots, but the absence of significant rebellions in the 1590s is an index of the growing sophistication of English government at all levels.

The crisis of the 1590s, and in particular the successive harvest failures, concentrated the minds of England's legislators wonderfully upon the problem of poverty, which had been gradually pressing itself upon their attention since the 1560s. Around the middle of the century, the Reformation had suppressed most of the institutional and cultural equipment with which medieval society had sought to cope with poverty. Gone were the monasteries and most of the 'hospitals' ('hospices' would be the more appropriate modern term for the limited aspirations of these institutions), as well as the confraternities, some of which could offer assistance to their members. Gone too were indulgences, which could be issued to encourage donations for the poor, along with the multitude of small temporary endowments which offered annual 'doles' to the needy. Culturally, the suppression of prayer for the dead had therefore removed the motivating force of much medieval almsgiving. The Edwardian invention of the 'poor box' had sought to replace the enlightened self-interest of purchasing the prayers of the poor with the pure disinterested altruism of true charity – with entirely predictable consequences. This does not mean that the destruction of medieval Catholicism put an end to a 'merry England' in which the poor were properly assisted, nor that the Reformation caused impoverishment. The problem of poverty worsened sharply from the mid-sixteenth century for a number of reasons, including a broad economic shift in favour of the rich and of larger landowners or traders over smaller, inflation, and increasing demographic pressure on food supply. But the abrupt and total change in society's strategy for coping with poverty through the apparatus of Catholicism made this worsening problem very much more visible and tangible.

Statutes passed in 1563 and 1572 grappled ineffectively with the problem, hampered by a punitive moralism that sought to distinguish deserving from undeserving poverty. The later 'Poor Laws' (a statute of 1598, somewhat amended in 1601) hoped to eliminate or at least curtail the practice of begging on the streets or door-to-door, but this was never a realistic goal. More constructively, they encouraged and facilitated the founding of almshouses and hospitals, of which a considerable number would indeed be founded in the ensuing century. But their real significance lay in pulling together experience gained in many of England's leading towns by envisaging poor relief as a function of local government, to be managed at the level of the parish. This was itself a development of medieval parish custom. While much of the expenditure on parish churches in the later Middle Ages was entirely voluntary, many of the grander projects, such as the addition of a steeple to the tower, or of a porch to the south wall, were financed on the basis of parish-wide contributions assessed by churchwardens – voluntary in a sense, but with non-payment leading to informal but potent community sanctions. Now, however, for the 'poor rate', there was a formal machinery for assessment, collection and distribution, with formal sanctions for non-compliance. The late Elizabethan legislation hardly had time to achieve significant change before Elizabeth died, but it proved to be of remarkable durability and even to have a modicum of efficacy. The Poor Laws, with occasional modifications, governed English poor relief for as long as England remained a Protestant Confessional State. They were not replaced until 1834, by which time religious and demographic change was making the parish a less relevant and effective unit of civil government.

The latter years of Elizabeth's reign were different, harsh. J. R. Seeley was perhaps the first to observe the sharp difference between the two phases, seeing the transition in 1585.

> Transition is observable throughout the reign of Elizabeth, but the moment of transition, abrupt, decisive, is in the year 1585, when open war began between England and Spain.[21]

The doyen of modern Tudor historians, John Guy, went so far as to suggest, tongue in cheek, that we might see the period after 1585 as her 'second reign', connecting the manifest difference in politics, the shift from decades of peace to years of war, with a more subtle change in the manner and tone of government, associated with the narrowing of the corps of councillors clustered around the aging queen.[22] The notion of the second reign is rhetorically alluring but not analytically compelling. The differences between the 'two reigns' come down to one brute reality: a protracted war for survival. The English decision to send an expeditionary force to bolster the rebels of the northern Netherlands in their struggle for independence from their sovereign, Philip II, turned the long cold war against Spain into open war. And the execution of Mary Queen of Scots in 1587 licensed Elizabeth's enemies to turn that war into a crusade. England – perhaps more precisely William Cecil? – had picked a fight with the most powerful nation in Europe, indeed, with one of the most powerful in the world. It was a gamble. But when political gambles pay off they are statesmanship. This one paid off.

Central government did work somewhat differently in the 1590s. Sessions of the Privy Council were often down to a hard core of four or five men, though that was mostly when it was on progress with the queen. When the Council was nearer London, for example at Hampton Court, attendance would easily reach eight or nine, much the same levels as in the 1560s. And formally recorded council meetings, it must be emphasised, were more executive than deliberative or advisory. Privy Council business remained relentlessly administrative, though it was vastly heavier in the 1590s than it had been in the 1560s. Amid the demands of war every day brought fresh problems: raising troops for service in Ireland and organising their transport; levying ship money from coastal towns; managing the 'posts' (official communications);

investigating reports of seditious speech and suspicious persons; ensuring supplies of grain to areas stricken by harvest failure; repressing riot, piracy and vagabondage; and disciplining feuding among the gentry and individual delinquency of sundry kinds. There was more than ever to do, yet most of it was routine stuff which did not call for an elaborate weighing of pros and cons. War, especially defensive war, makes some aspects of politics simpler. There is no need to debate the overall direction of policy. There were still strategic choices – whether to send more troops to France or the Netherlands, how many troops to send to Ireland, whether to engage the Spanish in their homeland by seeking to raise Portugal in revolt. But the objectives were straightforward. There was certainly no crisis of governance in Elizabeth's last years.

Indeed, the pressures of war, as so often, drove important governmental developments. As Neil Younger has shown, the decision to go to war with Spain in 1585 led to a revival of the lieutenancy system that had been introduced under Edward VI to deal with the crisis of 1549.[23] Across much of England now, lieutenants (usually peers, and thus 'Lords Lieutenant') were appointed to coordinate the military aspects of local government, such as the raising of troops for overseas service and the mustering of men for training in defensive operations. The 'bastard feudalism' by which landowners mustered and led their own tenants for war at royal command, which had provided English armies under Henry VIII and his son, had eroded through disuse in the long Elizabethan peace. And the English tradition of the longbow, which had still played a valuable part in Henry's splendid Tournai campaign in 1513, was all but dead. Archery practice, where it survived, was by this time more sport than war. The bow was being put out of business by firearms, even if the cumbersome arquebus and its successor the musket lacked as yet the range and rate of fire of the longbow. Troops for service overseas were a motley assortment of professionals (though 'mercenaries' might be a better word), gentry volunteers in search of experience or excitement, and other ranks drawn from the marginalised – vagrants, beggars, fugitives, misfits, fanatics and dissenters. The county musters invented by Henry VIII around 1540 amid the first fears of a papal crusade against England had been an attempt to establish a trained militia along the lines urged by humanist scholars in imitation of ancient republican Rome. But this amateurish force, untried in serious action, was not remotely comparable to the county militias and regiments that would make the British Army fearsome through the eighteenth and nineteenth centuries. Nevertheless, the Lords Lieutenant were responsible for recruiting, equipping and commanding these county forces, in collaboration with the local officials and gentry. And this role, crucial throughout the years of war, made them the natural point men when the Privy Council had orders or business of any kind for the localities. Not every county had its own lieutenant as yet, but where they existed they became the crucial addressees for the growing mass of official correspondence from Westminster.

War has also often driven significant developments in State finance. Unfortunately for Elizabeth and her successors, this was not the case in the 1590s. Her wars were fought on the basis of a broken fiscal system, and the ingenious pursuit of desperate expedients took the place of badly needed reform. Lurking behind the fiscal challenge was the barely understood problem of inflation. Steady price inflation through the reign reduced the real value of taxes which were usually levied either on the basis of fixed valuations or on the basis of quantities traded (rather than price). The revenue from customs duties did at least rise in cash terms, as trade itself grew, though that increasing yield fell far behind traded values. But the yield from the main form of direct taxation, the 'subsidy' (a wealth tax levied mainly on land) fell through Elizabeth's reign not only in real terms but even in cash. This was because the subsidy was collected by commissioners recruited from the landed elite. The temptation to wink at inadequate valuations was just too strong under Elizabeth. Under Henry VIII, this tendency had been far less marked, doubtless out of fear of the king's wrath. Unlike the problem of inflation, that of systematic mutual underassessment was well understood at the time and was often lamented in papers written by and for members of the Privy Council. But those at the top of the social hierarchy were also landowners, and the fact that William Cecil was assessed at the end of his life at the same level as at the start of the reign shows how far the corruption reached. Cecil, at least, did not assess himself any lower. Yet a man who had built a couple of princely palaces during the queen's reign was evidently not contributing according to his means.

What royal finance needed in the 1590s was a realistic revaluation of landed wealth and of traded goods. That, however, would have required wholehearted commitment from Parliament, together with a realisation that the rich, having most to lose from military defeat, ought to contribute the most to avert it. For all the high-flown rhetoric of loyalty and the 'common weal' bandied about in the House of Commons, England's MPs were to a man devoid of any sense of realism about the military or fiscal situation. Thus in 1589, flushed with success after the defeat of the Armada, the Commons called for a counterstrike against Spain and at the same time modified the subsidy bill so as to slow down the collection of the tax. Looking back at the reign of Henry VIII, they were impressed with the fact that they were often voting multiple subsidies where earlier Parliaments had financed wars with but one or two subsidies. They had no idea that the taxes they were voting on an apparently unprecedented scale were bringing in less cash, nor that the cash collected was worth less. This absolute disconnection from fiscal reality was to plague English parliaments through to the 1620s. Only the inescapable pressures of civil war in the mid-seventeenth century provided the reality check needed to modernise England's broken fiscal machinery.

Unable to lay an appropriate tax burden on England's prosperous landowners (who spent the reign happily erecting the palatial country houses that would dominate the land for the next few centuries), the Crown had to resort to expedients old and new. The first recourse was selling off Crown lands, which of course secured viability in the present by exporting problems to the future. Another method was to treat the recusancy fines levied on Catholics as a revenue stream. Enforcement of the recusancy laws was always corrupt, spasmodic and arbitrary, but the pressure on Catholics intensified in the 1590s, mainly for fiscal reasons. The maritime character of much of the war, and the recurrent fear of a Spanish seaborne invasion, enabled the regime to revive the ancient levy of 'ship money' on ports and coastal districts, and to find some success in extending the levy inland towards wealthy towns whose prosperity also depended on maritime trade. Some military activity was organised in partnership with private enterprise, but profits from plundering enemy ships or ports could not be guaranteed, and disappointed investors were aggrieved, and when profits were made, the bulk went into private hands. As under Henry VII, ancient feudal liabilities and obligations, such as 'distraint of knighthood', were pursued with renewed energy. Purveyance, a traditional levy in kind designed to help supply the needs of the royal Court in an era of peripatetic kingship, was exploited to help supply fleets and armies.

An increasingly sophisticated commercial economy provided a somewhat easier fiscal target. By the 1590s London was for the first time a major European port, and a wider range of consumer goods and luxury products was available there than ever before. In the absence of a well-calibrated system of indirect taxation by value, and with customs duties frozen at the rates fixed under Mary I in 1557, the Crown exploited the traditional royal prerogative of regulating the market (medieval and early modern markets were not 'free' in the sense that some people like to imagine modern markets are – they were safe spaces, guaranteed by public law and power, in which merchants could trade with a vastly reduced risk of fraud or robbery). This was done by issuing licences that conferred on people the exclusive right to trade in particular products – in other words, monopolies. In return, the monopolists paid handsome regular fees, which they recouped with profit by subcontracting to merchants and traders further down the chain. Monopoly patents naturally raised prices and reduced margins, and therefore aroused enormous resentment among the people at large, and especially among the merchant classes and MPs. The monopoly system was in effect a tax, but it was not authorised and granted by Parliament, which was always sensitive, under any monarch, to the huge political risk inherent in accepting regular taxation without consent.

The Tudor age, and in particular the reign of Elizabeth I, witnessed a momentous change in the understanding of what England was. In 1500, England was a kingdom of three estates, very much the personal appanage of the monarch, who was understood to be the fount of power and justice within it. By 1600, a more sophisticated vision had come into being. England was still a kingdom, a monarchy, but power within it had come in certain limited ways to be abstracted from the person of the monarch in whom it was still theoretically vested. Without taking up the misleading oxymoron of the 'monarchical republic' (a phrase which nobody used at the time), one can detect this process of abstraction in the emergence and growing currency of the word 'State' in the sense we still attach to it when we speak of 'the State'. At the beginning of the century, the 'state' of something merely meant its condition, and the slightly more formal word 'estate' (from the same etymological root) might mean the same, but often bore the slightly more specialised connotation of social status or condition – hence the 'three estates', or the 'cloth of estate' beneath which a monarch sat on ceremonial occasions.

Yet a new sense began to emerge thanks to the intellectual currents of Renaissance humanism, which helped to bring to England the fifteenth-century Italian sense of 'stato', meaning a political entity capable of engaging in diplomacy or war. The Italian notion of 'ragione di stato' (*raison d'état*, reason of state) to describe the rationale for political action often carried negative associations with the 'politique' or Machiavellian approach to politics, but despite that it forced its way into usage, and as early as 1566 Elizabeth had remarked 'how dangerous it had proved to the state when second persons were appointed'.[24] One of the most notorious libels of the reign, *Leicester's Commonwealth*, illustrates the shift in meaning neatly. While the full original title, in describing the work as 'The copie of a letter ... about the present state...', may well mean simply the condition of the kingdom, the running title, 'A Letter of State of a Scholar of Cambridge', uses the term in a precisely political sense, as does the text itself at numerous points – for example in discussing people 'of a different religion from the state wherein they live' or 'great matters of state'.[25] The shift in meaning is equally marked in Elizabethan proclamations. For the first decade or so, the concept appears only in such phrases as 'the royal estate of Her Majesty', and this usage persisted. But starting in the 1570s, and with increasing frequency in the 1580s, the new concept appears alongside it, in such phrases as 'strangers to the state'. In the Armada year, a proclamation against papal bulls and books denounced the pope for seeking 'the utter ruin and overthrow of this state and commonweal'. The idea of the State had become part of the mental furniture of the English.

However familiar the concept of 'the State' may have been becoming to preachers, writers and officials, nobody in 1600 could envisage the English State in actual abstraction from the person of a ruling monarch. That monarch might be a boy, or might be a woman – each was seen as deficient in comparison with a grown man according to the understanding of the time – but there had to be someone there. So the question of the succession to the throne remained as vital in 1603 as it had been in 1485 or 1553. After the execution of Mary Queen of Scots, England's succession problem was once more a chronic condition rather than an acute crisis. But it was still a problem, because Elizabeth could no longer provide for the succession by marriage and childbearing, and was still adamant in her refusal to provide for it by any other means. It was therefore up to the personnel of the 'State' to cope with the situation, which they sought to do through the 1590s by opening up 'back channel' communications with the man who transparently had the best claim to the throne after Elizabeth: James VI of Scotland. The Earl of Essex had been looking northwards to the next regime since the early 1590s, but once he had destroyed himself in 1601, the task of negotiating James's succession fell to her as Secretary of State. When Elizabeth I died, on 24 March 1603, peacefully, in her bed at Richmond Palace, she still refused, to the very end, to settle the matter herself. So it was Robert Cecil who masterminded it with characteristic Cecilian competence. In 1485, the succession had been sorted in open battle. In 1553, it was decided in a bloodless coup. In 1603 it was resolved behind the scenes by the rudimentary machinery of the State, through negotiations and

Tomb of Queen Elizabeth I
Queen Elizabeth's magnificent tomb, like that of her grandfather Henry VII, stands in his chapel at Westminster Abbey. The lengthy Latin inscription (not shown) recapitulates the highlights of her reign, including the defeat of the Armada. But the tomb itself commemorates her achievement by its very existence. At the start of her reign, zealous Protestants began attacking even funeral monuments as displays of 'idolatry'. The queen intervened in 1560 with a proclamation specifically exempting funeral monuments from iconoclastic cleansing and explicitly permitting them still to be erected in churches.

letters, and James I was able to make a triumphant royal progress from Edinburgh to London to take possession of his second crown. Within the next century, England would see the monarchy first overthrown after a bloody civil war (1649) and then restored and transferred through two more bloodless coups (1660 and 1688). So the peaceful and untroubled transition of 1603 can hardly be said to mark an epoch. Yet it is a measure both of the pacification of the realm and of the domestication of its mettlesome elite that had been achieved by royal authority under the Tudors.

CONCLUSION

The long century of Tudor rule produced or at least witnessed crucial developments in English history. But it remains important not to overstate the extent of change. One might still wish to talk, with G. R. Elton, of a 'Tudor Revolution in Government'. But it could not be placed neatly in the 1530s, however crucial that decade was. Nor could one maintain that this 'revolution' turned England into a modern Nation State. The idea that personal, household monarchy was abruptly replaced by an impersonal governmental apparatus located outside the royal household is simply not true. Tudor England remained a personal monarchy, as did Stuart and indeed Hanoverian England after it. Access to the monarch was the highest political currency, and in its opening stages much of the driving force of the English Civil War (or the 'Great Rebellion') was provided by the feeling of exclusion that took possession of much of the political elite, the bitter sense of a 'Country' at odds with the Court. Unlike the Stuarts, the Tudors managed to keep most of the elite aligned with their dynastic interests most of the time.

It is just as misleading to see the sixteenth century, or the 1530s, as the cradle of English 'bureaucracy'. England was certainly not a bureaucratic State, and there was indeed hardly any bureaucracy at all in the sense of a body of salaried officials implementing government policy. There were men who held administrative or clerical offices under the Crown, but these positions were distributed on the basis of favour, nepotism or corruption, and were usually tenable for life, with little risk of dismissal for incompetence. Remuneration was at least as much a matter of fees and bribes as of wages. Enforcement of the law and the implementation of the royal will depended not on salaried officials but on amateurs, on the activity of gentlemen with sufficient private resources to serve as sheriffs, justices of the peace, or members of the innumerable commissions issued under the Great Seal to empower them to perform local tasks (such as raising troops or levying taxes), to investigate and resolve local problems (such as drainage), or to enforce laws and regulations. Most of the tasks that the gentry undertook for the Crown were entirely unpaid, though some carried fees and many offered the opportunity for peculation on a greater or lesser scale. But the chief motive for serving the Crown was the status it brought. Although the number of paid Crown offices increased steadily over time, it was not until the nineteenth century that the tradition of amateur governance gave way to a professional bureaucracy in the form of the civil service.

Even the widespread notion that Tudor England was a 'centralised' nation needs to be handled with care. England had long been a geographical curiosity, with but one metropolis, London, and no cities of the second rank such as characterise provincial France (e.g. Lyon, Rouen, Toulouse). In that sense, it had but one centre. Yet that did not make it 'centralised' as the term is now understood. English government under the Tudors remained, as it was for centuries both before and after, resolutely local. Laws were enforced by local powers and authorities. The Tudors, from Henry VII onwards, rendered those local powers and authorities far more accountable to the centre than they had ever been before, through their ordinary courts and also through the 'prerogative' jurisdictions, above all Star Chamber. The Tudor monarchs did not need to go to the outlying regions to impose their will on incompetent or recalcitrant subordinates: they simply summoned them to Court – and they came. But the laws had to be enforced, and orders had to be carried out, by local men on the ground, not simply by agents dispatched from the centre. More agents and officials were indeed being dispatched, but they too depended on local resources to achieve their goals. The achievement of the Tudors was to bring the large class of the landed gentry into line with the royal will. These who stepped out of line were briskly dealt with. Thus in November 1592 the Privy Council busted two Northamptonshire JPs, a knight and a gentleman, for brawling at the Quarter Sessions. Tudor rule was a successful and mutually beneficial collaboration between the Crown and the local elites – at least in England. Tudor Ireland here provides an instructive contrast. An ever more purposeful attempt to govern through agents despatched from the centre rather than in collaboration with local elites rendered Tudor rule there at best impotent, at worst anarchic, and in general disastrous.

It was more in the sphere of ideas than in political practice that the Tudor century saw a revolution. Most of this was driven one way or another by the Reformation, though not always in an obvious way. The Break with Rome accomplished by Henry VIII resulted in a grandiose conception of royal authority. Imperial, absolute, divine, it would later become known as the 'Divine Right of Kings'. It was accompanied by a domestication of the clergy that permanently diminished the political clout of the Church. The Church was henceforth an adjunct of the Crown or of the State – even under Mary I. This led to a default Erastianism neatly voiced by Sir Francis Walsingham, who told some zealous Protestants that he 'would have all reformations done by public authority'.[1] Yet Henry's changes needed some legitimation to challenge the massive and millennial legitimacy of medieval Catholicism, and this was supplied by parliamentary statute. Ironically, this mighty monarch's capacity to bend parliaments to his will over papal authority, ecclesiastical property and privilege, religious doctrine and practice, and the royal succession gave rise to the idea that the authority of Parliament was unbounded. There was, it seemed, nothing that statute could not regulate or change. Under Elizabeth in particular, MPs looked back on the work of their Henrician and Edwardian predecessors and marvelled at their power. Parliament might still have been, as Conrad Russell famously observed, 'an event and not an institution',[2] but in the minds of its members it was taking on a more institutional character. The supremacy of statute law had been vindicated in the most decisive way, and the idea that Parliament 'represented' the kingdom, an essentially mystical idea, took on a new reality.

Yet Elizabeth's long reign saw the ground shift once more beneath the English throne. The new politics of Henry VII had set up Henry VIII with unprecedented power, but the religious disruption of the mid-sixteenth century and the absence of a strong king from 1547 onwards prised the lid loose. It is far too much to talk, as some historians have done, of 'republicanism' among the Tudor gentry. They were far too hemmed in by the ideology of monarchy for that to have any meaning. One might do better to say that the Tudor gentry, rather than following the religion of the monarch, actually followed the religion of monarchy. Yet their self-interest and their family pride, their class-interest, their localism and their patriotism combined in a growing investment in the idea of Parliament, which would lead in the next century to the sense that England enjoyed a particular political constitution that set it apart from other nations. This made England simultaneously easier to govern and harder to change. The Tudor bequest to Stuart England included a bundle of ideas and attitudes that would coalesce into the powerful notion of the 'ancient constitution', which would be deployed to great effect against what its exponents denounced as 'popery and arbitrary government'. This bundle of ideas and attitudes combined in the middle of the Stuart century with the religious legacy of the Tudor Reformations (a confused blend of Protestant theological zeal with an Erastian hankering for an inclusive national Church) to generate a political crisis that brought down not the English monarchy (which proved stubbornly indelible), but the English King, Charles I. When in 1660 a weary people eventually opted to recognise the inevitable and put the monarch back into the system in the person of Charles II, the outcome was a monarchy that, while still real, was no longer the monarchy Henry VIII had nonchalantly wielded or Elizabeth I had wistfully invoked. It was a 'limited monarchy' – a monarchy limited by law, Parliament, religion and culture. It was not the monarchy of Tudor England. But it was shaped by the legacy of the Tudors.

Notes

INTRODUCTION

1 C. S. L. Davies, 'A rose by any other name: why we are wrong to talk about "the Tudors"', *The Times Literary Supplement*, issue 5489, 13 July 2008, pp. 14–15.
2 Rendering the Latin/Greek '*dynastia*', 'dynasty' was used primarily to denote the ruling houses of biblical and ancient times. Only later did it come to be used for the ruling houses of Europe.
3 Edward Hall, *The Union of the Two Noble and Illustrate Famelies of Lancastre and Yorke* (London, 1548. STC 12721 [STC refers to *A Short-Title Catalogue of Books Printed in England, Scotland, & Ireland and of English Books Printed Abroad, 1475–1640*; first compiled by A. W. Pollard and G. R. Redgrave; 2nd edn. rev. and enl., by W. A. Jackson, F. S. Ferguson and K. H. Pantzer (3 vols. London, 1976–1991)]). The quoted phrase is the conclusion of the book's lengthy title.
4 1 Mary I, c. 18, opening paragraph.

ESTABLISHING THE TUDOR REGIME, 1485–1515 1

1 *The Great Chronicle of London*, ed. A. H. Thomas and I. D. Thornley (Gloucester, 1983), p. 238.
2 *Our holy fadre the Pope Innocent the VIII* (no place or date. STC 14096). See also P. L. Hughes and J. F. Larkin (eds), *Tudor Royal Proclamations* (3 vols. New Haven, 1964–9), I, no. 6, pp. 6–7, at p. 6.
3 This act was never included in the printed acts of Parliament, perhaps because it was not in any useful sense a law (it did not seek to define any crimes or impose any punishments), and perhaps also because printing it among the

laws of the land would simply have laid bare the political embarrassment it was trying to cover up.

4 Paul Cavill, *The English Parliaments of Henry VII, 1485–1504* (Oxford, 2009), p. 42.

5 *Our holy fadre the Pope Innocent the VIII* (no place or date. STC 14096). See also Hughes and Larkin, *Tudor Royal Proclamations* I, no. 6, p. 6.

6 Cavill, *English Parliaments of Henry VII*, p. 176. The next proclamation to be printed did not appear until 1504.

7 John Fortescue, *The Governance of England*, ed. C. Plummer (Oxford, 1885), pp. 75–9.

8 See the excellent analysis offered by Emma Cavell, 'Henry VII, the North of England, and the First Provincial Progress of 1486', *Northern History* 39 (2002), 187–207.

9 Georges Duby, *The Three Orders*, trans. A. Goldhammer (Chicago, 1982).

10 There were two Convocations, one each for the ecclesiastical provinces of Canterbury and York. But the southern Convocation, for Canterbury, was far bigger, and the northern mostly followed its lead.

11 Virginia K. Henderson, 'Rethinking Henry VII: the man and his piety in the context of the Observant Franciscans', in Douglas L. Biggs, Sharon D. Michalove and A. Compton Reeves (eds), *Reputation and Representation in Fifteenth-century Europe* (Leiden, 2004), pp. 317–47.

12 Henry VII to Pope Pius II, 5 July 1487, in *Letters and Papers Illustrative of the Reigns of Richard III and Henry VII*, ed. J. Gairdner (2 vols. London, 1861–63), I, pp. 94–6, at p. 95.

13 Polydore Vergil, *The Anglica Historia of Polydore Vergil, A.D. 1485–1537*, ed. D. Hay (London, 1950), for his pilgrimage to Walsingham and a subsequent journey to Cambridge (p. 21), and thence to Coventry (p. 23); and for his votive offering (p. 27). Collating Vergil's account of his movements with the evidence of the location of his Chancellor furnished by the patent rolls, the pilgrimage was probably in April, because they were at Colchester on 2 April, Bury St Edmunds 7–8 April, Norwich 12–13 April and Cambridge 18–20 April. See *Calendar of the Patent Rolls . . . Henry VII. Vol. I. AD 1485–1494* (London, 1914), pp. 169–72.

14 Virginia K. Henderson, 'Constructing memory: the image of Henry VII in the stained glass window of the friary church at Greenwich', in A. Compton Reeves (ed.), *Personalities and Perspectives of Fifteenth-century England* (Tempe, AZ, 2012), pp. 109–40.

15 *Great Chronicle of London*, p. 286.

16 See Margaret Condon, 'God Save the King! Piety, propaganda and the perpetual memorial', in T. Tatton-Brown and R. Mortimer (eds), *Westminster Abbey: The Lady Chapel of Henry VII* (Woodbridge, 2003), pp. 59–97.

17 W. E. Wilkie, *The Cardinal Protectors of England: Rome and the Tudors before the Reformation* (Cambridge, 1974). See also Susan May, 'Establishing the Tudor regime: the role of Francesco Piccolomini in Rome as the first Cardinal Protector of England', *Royal Studies* 4 (2017), 103–40.

18 Margaret McGlynn, 'Ecclesiastical prisons and royal authority in the reign of Henry VII', *Journal of Ecclesiastical History* 70 (2019), 750–66.

19 Fortescue, *Governance of England*, pp. 127–30.

20 Steven Gunn, *Henry VII's New Men and the Making of Tudor England* (Oxford, 2016) furnishes a comprehensive study of this influential group.

21 Christine Carpenter, *Locality and Polity: A Study of Warwickshire Landed Society, 1401–1499* (Cambridge, 1992), ch. 15; S. G. Ellis, *Tudor Frontiers and Noble Power: The Making of the British State* (Oxford, 1995), chs 1–2.

22 C. J. Harrison, 'The Petition of Edmund Dudley', *English Historical Review* 87 (1972), 82–99, at 90. See James Ross, 'Contrary to the ryght and to the order of the lawe: new evidence of Edmund Dudley's activities on behalf of Henry VII in 1504', *English Historical Review* 127 (2012), 24–45, for further indications of how Dudley pushed the boundaries.

23 For the executions, see the *Great Chronicle of London*, pp. 244, 248, 250, 257–60, 278, 280 and 289–92. For Warbeck, see Ian Arthurson, *The Perkin Warbeck Conspiracy, 1491–1499* (Stroud, 1994).

24 William Blount to Erasmus, Greenwich, 27 May 1509, in P. S. Allen (ed.), *Opus Epistolarum Des. Erasmi Roterodami* I (Oxford, 1906), ep. 215, pp. 449–52.

25 Stephen Hawes, *A Joyfull Meditacyon to all Englonde of the Coronacyon* (London: Wynkyn de Worde, 1509. STC 12953), title page verso.

26 John Colet, *Oratio habita a D. Ioanne Colet* (London, 1511. STC 5545); Stephen Baron, *De regimine principum (1509)*, ed. P. J. Mroczkowski (New York, 1990).

27 The text of Julius's bull is included in the broadsheet print *Universis sancta matris ecclesie filiis* (London, 1512. STC 25947.7).

28 Wolsey to Richard Fox, Farnham, 26 August 1512, printed in Richard Fiddes, *The Life of Cardinal Wolsey* (London, 1724), *Collections*, p. 11.

29 G. W Bernard, *The Late Medieval English Church* (New Haven, 2012), pp. 1–16, offers the best brief survey of this *cause célèbre*.

30 The chief source for the crisis over ecclesiastical liberties ignited by the Hunne case is a summary in Law French of the proceedings at two sessions (one at Blackfriars, the other at Baynard's Castle) of a Great Council held late in 1515. It is found in Robert Keilway, *Relationes quorundam casuum selectorum* (London, 1602. STC 14901), fols 180v–85v.

FROM REFORM TO REFORMATION, 1515–1534 2

1 R. Fiddes, *The Life of Cardinal Wolsey* (London, 1724), 'Collections', pp. 251–2. The tale of the envoy's new clothes is from John Stow, *The Annales of England* (London, 1605. STC 23337), p. 840.

2 J. A. Guy, *The Cardinal's Court: The Impact of Thomas Wolsey in Star Chamber* (Hassocks, 1977).

3 Erasmus to Petrus Mosellanus, Louvain, 22 April 1519, in P. S. Allen (ed.), *Opus Epistolarum Des. Erasmi Roterodami* III (Oxford, 1915), ep. 948, pp. 541–8, at 547.

4 James P. Carley (ed.), *The Libraries of King Henry VIII* (London, 2000).

5 Paul's Cross was a public pulpit in the square outside St Paul's Cathedral in London, and as such the kingdom's premier preaching venue. Sermons were preached there to huge audiences most Sundays.

6 R. Rex (ed.), *Henry VIII and Martin Luther* (Woodbridge, 2021), p. 151.

7 Glenn Richardson, *The Field of Cloth of Gold* (New Haven, 2014).

8 G. W. Bernard, *War, Taxation and Rebellion in Early Modern England: Henry VIII, Wolsey and the Amicable Grant of 1525* (Brighton, 1986).

9 On Buckingham, see Barbara J. Harris, *Edward Stafford, Third Duke of Buckingham, 1478–1521* (Stanford, 1986).

10 The arguments regarding the date and legitimacy of her birth presented by Sally Varlow in the Oxford Dictionary of National Biography (ODNB) under 'Knollys [*née* Carey], Katherine, Lady Knollys (*c.* 1523–1569)' are persuasive. Jonathan Hughes argues that Mary's son, Henry Carey (b. 4 March 1526), was not the king's, despite rumours to the contrary circulating by the mid-1530s. See his ODNB article on 'Stafford [*née* Boleyn; *other married name* Carey], Mary (*c.* 1499–1543)'.

11 The starting point for understanding the controversy over Henry VIII's divorce is Virginia Murphy's introduction to Edward Surtz and Virginia Murphy (eds), *The Divorce Tracts of Henry VIII* (Angers, 1988). See also Virginia Murphy, 'The literature and propaganda of Henry VIII's first divorce', in D. MacCulloch (ed.), *The Reign of Henry VIII* (Basingstoke, 1995), pp. 135–58.

12 Although the term 'divorce' was as commonly used then as now to denote what Henry sought, in strict law what he sought was an 'annulment' – that is, a judgement that the apparent matrimonial union was invalid. Henry believed as firmly as any other Catholic at that time that a valid marriage could be dissolved only by the death of one spouse.

13 Three of the best works ever written on More are all by John Guy: *The Public Career of Sir Thomas More* (Brighton, 1986); *Thomas More* (London, 2000); and *A Daughter's Love: Thomas & Margaret More* (London, 2008). See also George M. Logan (ed.), *The Cambridge Companion to Thomas More* (Cambridge, 2011).

14 *A Dyaloge of Syr Thomas More knyghte* (London, 1529. STC 18084);
now best consulted in Thomas More, *A Dialogue Concerning Heresies*, ed.
T. Lawler, G. Marc'hadour and R. C. Marius (2 vols. New Haven, 1981, The
Complete Works of St. Thomas More, 6).

15 The most thorough account of Elizabeth Barton, notwithstanding its flaws,
remains Alan Neame, *The Holy Maid of Kent* (London, 1971). There is
useful further analysis in Diane Watt, *Secretaries of God: Women Prophets in
Late Medieval and Early Modern England* (Cambridge, 1997) and Ethan H.
Shagan, *Popular Politics and the English Reformation* (Cambridge, 2003),
ch. 2. Fisher's see, Rochester, was not far from Canterbury, and both he and
the archbishop had residences in Lambeth.

16 Wolsey to Richard Sampson, 13 February 1525, *State Papers . . . Henry the Eighth*,
11 vols (London, 1830–52), VI, pp. 386–402, especially pp. 391 and 394–7.

17 Sir Robert Wingfield to Cromwell, Calais, 16 February 1535, LP 8.225.

18 For the significance of these councils and consultations in the early 1530s,
see R. Rex, 'Councils, counsel and consensus in Henry VIII's Reformation',
in Jacqueline Rose (ed.), *The Politics of Counsel in England and Scotland,
1286–1707* (London, 2016), pp. 135–50.

19 Gardiner to Protector Somerset, London, 14 October 1547, in *The Letters of
Stephen Gardiner*, ed. J. A. Muller (Cambridge, 1933), pp. 379–400, at p. 390.

20 G. R. Elton, 'King or minister? The man behind the Henrician Reformation',
History 39 (1954), 216–32 and *Reform and Reformation: England 1509–1558*
(London, 1977); J. J. Scarisbrick, *Henry VIII* (London, 1968); G. W. Bernard,
The King's Reformation: Henry VIII and the Remaking of the English Church
(New Haven, 2005).

21 See C. D. C. Armstrong, 'Stephen Gardiner (*c.* 1495x8–1555)', ODNB.

22 This act, presumably because it was provisional, was not included in the
sessional print of 1532.

23 Peter Marshall, 'Thomas Becket, William Warham and the crisis of the Early
Tudor Church', *Journal of Ecclesiastical History* 71 (2020), 293–315.

24 Diarmaid MacCulloch, *Thomas Cranmer: A Life* (New Haven, 1996) is the
definitive biography; see page 72 for Cranmer's marriage. This was Cranmer's
second marriage: it is not quite clear how this serious reader of St Paul
reconciled his promotion with the apostle's instruction that a bishop should be
a man of one wife (1 Tim. 3:2).

25 Thomas Abell, *Invicta Veritas* (Luneburg, 1532. STC 61. USTC 410498) and
*Non esse neque divino, neque naturae jure prohibitum . . . adversus aliquot
academiarum censuras, tumultuaria, ac brevis apologia* (Luneburg, 1532.
USTC 403837) were responses to the *Determinations*; while *Philalethæ
Hyperborei in Anticatoptrum suum quod propediem in lucem dabit, ut patet
proxima pagella, Parasceue* ('Luneburg', 1533. USTC 337916 and 2213662)
took on *The Glasse of the Truthe*.

26 *Articles Devisid by the holle consent of the kynges moste honourable counsayle* (London, 1533. STC 9177). Chapuys to Charles V, London, 10 December 1533, LP 6.1510.

27 R. Rex, 'The execution of the Holy Maid of Kent', *Historical Research* 64 (1991), 216–20.

REFORMATIONS, 1535–1553 3

1 Maurice Chauncy, *Historia aliquot nostri saeculi martyrum* (Cologne, 1550), sig. D2v. See also Chapuys to Charles V, London, 5 May 1535, *Calendar of State Papers Spanish. Vol. V, Part 1, 1534–1535* (London, 1886), pp. 451–4, at p. 453.

2 LP 8.51. See also Chapuys to Charles V, 28 January 1535, LP 8.121, p. 38.

3 R. Rex, 'The religion of Henry VIII', *Historical Journal* 57 (2014), 1–32, at 30–1.

4 LP 8.190 notes these attestations.

5 PRO SP1/94, fols 24r–5r (LP 8.25), Francis Bigod to Cromwell, Jervaulx, 12 July 1535, enclosing Lazenby's signed statement.

6 G. W. Bernard is, as so often, the exception. See his *The King's Reformation* (New Haven, 2005) for Henry VIII as the unmoved mover of the early English Reformation.

7 David Knowles, *The Religious Orders in England* (3 vols. Cambridge, 1950–59), III, pp. 268–90. See also James G. Clark, *The Dissolution of the Monasteries* (New Haven, 2021), pp. 230–63, though this account is unfortunately marred by numerous errors and inaccuracies.

8 John Mirk, *The Festyuall* (London: Wynkyn de Worde, 1508. STC 17971), fols 200r–201v.

9 With the exception of G. W. Bernard, most historians who have scrutinised the evidence have concluded that the charges are not credible. The best account remains E. W. Ives, 'Faction at the court of Henry VIII: the fall of Anne Boleyn', *History* 57 (1972), 169–88. See the debate between Bernard and Ives in *English Historical Review* 106 (1991), 584–610 and 107 (1992), 651–74.

10 Hugh Latimer, *Concio* (London, 1537. STC 15285; in English translation, STC 15286).

11 David Wilkins (ed.), *Concilia Magnae Britanniae et Hiberniae* (4 vols. London, 1737), III, pp. 804–7.

12 Henry VIII to the justices of the peace etc., Westminster, 25 June 1535, PRO SP1/93, fols 135r–137r, at 136v (LP 8.921), reporting his instructions to bishops and clergy (issued on 3 June) to preach the supremacy, and instructing JPs to back this up with public addresses at the Assizes and Quarter Sessions.

13 For the military aspects of the rebellion, see M. L. Bush, *The Pilgrimage of Grace* (Manchester, 1996).

14 Henry VIII to the Duke of Norfolk, 22 February 1537, LP 12.i.479. For Pickering's role in the Pilgrimage, see Susan E. James, 'Against them all to fight: Friar John Pickering and the Pilgrimage of Grace', *Bulletin of the John Rylands Library* 85 (2003), 37–64.

15 R. Rex and C. D. C. Armstrong, 'Henry VIII's ecclesiastical and collegiate foundations', *Historical Research* 75 (2002), 390–407, at 396–7.

16 For Lewes, see D. MacCulloch, *Thomas Cromwell: A Life* (London, 2018), pp. 431–5. Cromwell took the lion's share of the spoils.

17 In the words of the immortal British Prime Minister, the Rt. Hon. Jim Hacker, 'First rule in politics: never believe anything until it's officially denied'. See *Yes Minister*, 'Party Games' (BBC2, 17 December 1984; scripted by Jonathan Lynn and Antony Jay).

18 Charles Wriothesley, *A Chronicle of England during the Reigns of the Tudors*, ed. W. D. Hamilton (London, 1875–77), I, p. 81. For Stokesley's pardon, 3 July 1538, see LP 13.i.1519 (3). Some new recruits may have been admitted to religious houses after this date, but the only evidence produced for this is from the more remote regions of the realm, where this signal might not have been effectively transmitted and received. See Clark, *Dissolution of the Monasteries*, pp. 56–7, though it is not entirely clear when the novices still sometimes found in monasteries and nunneries at their closure had originally been admitted to them.

19 Wriothesley, *Chronicle* I, pp. 74–6 and 86–7. For analysis of iconoclasm under Henry VIII, see Margaret Aston, *England's Iconoclasts. Vol. I. Laws against Images* (Oxford, 1988), pp. 222–46.

20 Hughes and Larkin, *Tudor Royal Proclamations* I, pp. 270–76, especially pp. 275–6.

21 R. McEntegart, *Henry VIII, the League of Schmalkalden and the English Reformation* (Woodbridge, 2002).

22 R. Morison, *A lamentation in whiche is shewed what ruyne and destruction cometh of seditious rebellyon* (London, 1536. STC 18113.3), sig. C3v. See R. Rex, 'The crisis of obedience: God's Word and Henry's Reformation', *Historical Journal* 39 (1996), 863–84, at 883 for Morison, and at 865–7 for Luther's understanding of political obedience.

23 Glyn Redworth, 'A study in the formulation of policy: the genesis and evolution of the Act of Six Articles', *Journal of Ecclesiastical History* 37 (1986), 42–67.

24 Glanmor Williams, *Renewal and Reformation: Wales, c. 1415–1642* (Oxford, 1993), pp. 253–78.

25 S. G. Ellis, *Ireland in the Age of the Tudors, 1447–1603* (London, 1998).

26 On this see Brendan Bradshaw, *The Dissolution of the Religious Orders in Ireland under Henry VIII* (Cambridge, 1974).

27 On Henry's increasingly imperial vision of Britain, see Jessica S. Hower, *Tudor Empire: The Making of Early Modern Britain and the British Atlantic World, 1485–1603* (Basingstoke, 2021), ch. 4. See also Clare Kellar, *Scotland, England, and the Reformation, 1534–1561* (Oxford, 2003) for the complex religious interactions between the two realms as they experienced religious upheavals in the mid-sixteenth century.

28 David Starkey, 'Court and government', in Christopher Coleman and David Starkey (eds), *Revolution Reassessed* (Oxford, 1986), pp. 29–58, at pp. 55–56.

29 See Susan Wabuda, 'Anne Askew', in D. J. Crankshaw and G. W. C. Gross (eds), *Reformation Reputations* (Basingstoke, 2020), pp. 255–90. See also Thomas S. Freeman, 'One survived: the account of Katherine Parr in Foxe's *Book of Martyrs*', in Thomas Betteridge and Suzannah Lipscomb (eds), *Henry VIII and the Court* (Farnham, 2013), pp. 235–54.

30 Gardiner to Ridley, Southwark, 23x28 February 1547, in *The Letters of Stephen Gardiner*, no. 116, pp. 255–63, especially pp. 255–6.

31 A. G. Dickens, 'Robert Parkyn's narrative of the Reformation', *English Historical Review* 62 (1947), 58–83, at 66. For the Injunctions, see Gerald Bray (ed.), *Documents of the English Reformation* (Cambridge, 1994), pp. 247–57. See Eamon Duffy, *The Stripping of the Altars* (New Haven, 1992), pp. 448–64 for analysis of their impact.

32 See *The Letters of Stephen Gardiner*, e.g. nos. 121, to Somerset, Winchester, 6 June 1547, pp. 286–95; 124, to Cranmer, Winchester, July 1547, pp. 299–316; and 126, to the Privy Council, Waltham, August 1547, pp. 361–77. Gardiner's religious conservatism is highlighted in C. D. C. Armstrong's account of him in ODNB.

33 J. Andreas Löwe, *Richard Smyth and the Language of Orthodoxy* (Leiden, 2003), pp. 34–40.

34 MacCulloch, *Thomas Cranmer* is the authoritative but monumental biography. Susan Wabuda, *Thomas Cranmer* (Abingdon, 2017), offers a handier analysis.

35 Andy Wood, *The 1549 Rebellions and the Making of Early Modern England* (Cambridge, 2007) not only emphasises, rightly, that 'socio-economic' grievances are not separable from religious and moral attitudes in sixteenth-century England, but also draws attention to the role of religious conservatism in the East Anglian risings (pp. 60–1 and 177–84).

36 See Diane Willen, 'Lord Russell and the Western Counties, 1539–1555', *Journal of British Studies* 15 (1975), 26–45. Alan Bryson has further observations about this in 'Edward VI's "speciall men": crown and locality in mid-Tudor England', *Historical Research* 82 (216), 229–51.

37 For further reflections on the crisis of 1553, see Dale Hoak, 'The succession crisis of 1553 and Mary's rise to power', in Elizabeth Evenden and Vivienne Westbrook (eds), *Catholic Renewal and Protestant Resistance in Marian England* (Farnham, 2015), pp. 17–42; and Paulina Kewes, 'The 1553 succession crisis reconsidered', *Historical Research* 90 (2017), 465–85.

REFORMATIONS REVERSED, 1553–1568 4

1 Wriothesley, *Chronicle* II, pp. 93–5.

2 Henry Machyn, *The Diary of Henry Machyn*, ed. J. G. Nichols (London, 1848), p. 5.

3 Dickens, 'Robert Parkyn's narrative', 79.

4 Peter Marshall, 'The naming of Protestant England', *Past and Present* 214 (2012), 87–128, especially 100–105. Marshall makes a complex and subtle argument, but the source-base is too weighted towards print.

5 Miles Huggarde, *The Displaying of the Protestantes* (London: Caly, 1556. STC 13557), fol. 5v.

6 1 Mary cc. 1 and 2.

7 C. H. Garrett, *The Marian Exiles* (Cambridge, 1938). But see also Andrew Pettegree, *Marian Protestantism* (Aldershot, 1996), ch. 1 and appendix 2 for the refugees at Emden, mostly not recorded by Garrett.

8 John Foxe, *The Actes and Monumentes* (London, 1570. STC 11223), p. 1580.

9 *The Diary of Henry Machyn*, p. 55.

10 W. H. Frere (ed.), *Visitation Articles and Injunctions of the Period of the Reformation* (3 vols. London, 1910), II, pp. 370–71.

11 See the extensive report sent to Italy by a member of Pole's household shortly afterwards. It is summarised in Thomas F. Mayer (ed.), *The Correspondence of Reginald Pole* (4 vols. Aldershot, 2002–8), II, no. 998, at p. 380.

12 *The Chronicle of Queen Jane*, ed. J. G. Nichols (London, 1850), p. 161.

13 *Chronicle of Queen Jane*, p. 163.

14 'Device for alteration of religion', in H. Gee (ed.), *The Elizabethan Prayer-Book & Ornaments* (London, 1902), pp. 195–202, at p. 196.

15 Duffy, *The Stripping of the Altars*, pp. 526–43. See also Eamon Duffy, 'The conservative voice in the English Reformation', in his *Saints, Sacrilege and Sedition* (London, 2012), pp. 213–32.

16 John Dudley, *The Saying of John, late Duke of Northumberlande upon the Scaffolde* (London, 1553. STC 7283); *An acte against offenders of preachers* (London, 1553. STC 7853); and *An acte against unlawfull an rebellious assemble* (London, 1553. STC 7854).

17 Matthew Sutcliffe, *An Answere unto a Certaine Calumnious Letter* (London, 1595. STC 23451), fol. 45v. For a salutary corrective to romantic misreadings of early English Protestantism as proto-republican or even proto-democratic, see Ryan M. Reeves, *English Evangelicals and Tudor Obedience, c. 1527–1570* (Boston, 2014).

18 Foxe, *Actes and Monumentes*. All the recensions of Foxe's masterpiece are now available at *John Foxe's The Acts and Monuments Online.*

19 E. A. Wrigley and R. S. Schofield, *The Population History of England, 1541–1871: A Reconstruction* (London, 1981), pp. 332–6.

20 J. E. Neale, 'The Elizabethan acts of supremacy and uniformity', *English Historical Review* 65 (1950), 304–32; Norman Jones, *Faith by Statute* (London, 1982). Most recently, see Peter Marshall, *Heretics and Believers* (New Haven, 2017), pp. 419–33.

21 *Proceedings in the Parliaments of Elizabeth I. Vol. I. 1558–1581*, ed. T. E. Hartley (Leicester, 1981), p. 19.

22 Philip Hughes, *The Reformation in England* (3 vols. London, 1952–54), III, pp. 22–3.

23 D. MacCulloch, *Reformation: Europe's House Divided, 1490–1700* (London, 2003), p. 289.

24 John Whitgift, *Answer to the Admonition* (1572), p. 180.

25 Eamon Duffy, *Fires of Faith: Catholic England under Mary Tudor* (New Haven, 2009), pp. 201–203.

26 Brett Usher, *William Cecil and Episcopacy 1559–1577* (London, 2017), pp. 26–32. Usher's monograph offers fascinating insights into the religious attitudes and aims of Cecil himself.

27 David Crankshaw, 'Preparations for the Canterbury Provincial Convocation of 1562–63: a question of attribution', in S. Wabuda and C. Litzenberger (eds), *Belief and Practice in Reformation England* (Aldershot, 1998), pp. 60–93.

28 Patrick Collinson, *The Elizabethan Puritan Movement* (London, 1967), p. 76.

29 Stephen Alford, *The Early Elizabethan Polity: William Cecil and the British Succession Crisis, 1558–1569* (Cambridge, 2002).

30 *Proceedings in the Parliaments of Elizabeth*, pp. 150–1.

31 J. E. Neale, *Queen Elizabeth* (London, 1934), p. 153.

32 The best analysis of the alleged involvement of Mary in the assassination of Darnley is found in John Guy, *My Heart is My Own: The Life of Mary Queen of Scots* (London, 2004). The main outlines of the 'case for the defence' have long been known, but the weight of inherited attitudes to Mary long rendered them suspect.

33 Henry Jefferies, *The Irish Church and the Tudor Reformations* (Dublin, 2010), pp. 246–7.

34 This is a major theme of Stephen Alford, *Burghley: William Cecil at the Court of Elizabeth I* (New Haven, 2008). See for example his discussion of the 'Device for alteration of religion', pp. 91–94.

35 Wallace MacCaffrey, 'Cecil, William, first Baron Burghley, 1520/21–1598' in ODNB. See also Alford, *Burghley*, pp. 154–55, for Cecil's conviction that there was an international Catholic conspiracy against Elizabeth.

THE ELIZABETHAN EXCLUSION CRISIS, 1568–1587 5

The title of this chapter is borrowed from Patrick Collinson, 'The Elizabethan exclusion crisis and the Elizabethan polity', *Proceedings of the British Academy* 84 (1994), 51–91.

1 This account of Mary's arrival is based on sources printed in James Anderson (ed.), *Collections Relating to the History of Mary Queen of Scotland* (4 vols. Edinburgh, 1727–28), IV, part 1, especially pp. 1–7 and 29–33; on sources summarised in *Calendar of State Papers Relating to Scotland and Mary Queen of Scots, Vol. II. 1563–1569* (London, 1900), pp. 408–18; and on John Maxwell, Lord Herries, *Historical Memoirs of the Reign of Mary Queen of Scots*, ed. R. Pitcairn (Edinburgh, 1836), pp. 103–4.

2 Anderson, *Collections Relating to the History of Mary Queen of Scotland* IV, part 1, pp. 24–6 and 34–44.

3 John Leslie, *A Defence of the Honour of the Right Highe, Mightye and Noble Princesse Marie Quene of Scotlande* ([Rheims], 1569. STC 15505). For Plowden's analysis, see British Library MS Harley 849.

4 Earl of Sussex to the Privy Council, York, 17 November 1569, summarised in *Calendar of State Papers, Domestic Series, Elizabeth, Addenda, 1566–1579* (London, 1871), p. 110.

5 K. J. Kesselring, *The Northern Rebellion of 1569* (Basingstoke, 2007), pp. 125–6. Kesselring's is the best account of this rebellion.

6 Henry Skipwith to William Cecil, 16 February 1572, in W. Murdin (ed.), *A Collection of State Papers Relating to Affairs in the Reign of Queen Elizabeth from the Year 1571 to 1596* (London, 1759), pp. 171–2.

7 Sandys to Cecil, Fulham, 5 September 1572, BL Lansdowne MS 15, no. 41, fols 79–80: 'Furthwith to cutte off the Scottishe Q. heade. ipsa est nostri fundi calamitas'.

8 Edward Dering, *A Sermon Preached before the Quenes Maiestie* (London, 1570. STC 6699), sigs. A3r, A4r and B3r. Oddly, he was presented by the queen to a canonry at Salisbury in December 1571, during the brief episcopal vacancy after the death of Bishop Jewel. This is more likely to have reflected the influence of some third party on his behalf than a direct favour from the queen herself.

9 John Field and Thomas Wilcox, *An Admonition to the Parliament* (no place, no date [1572]. STC 10847). See sig. B3v for the quotation.

10 John Whitgift, *A Godlie Sermon Preached before the Queenes Maiestie at Grenwiche* (London, 1574. STC 25431), sigs. B3v–B4v and B7r–v.

11 Humphrey Fenn, *The Last Will and Testament, with the Profession of the Faith of Humphrey Fen* (London, 1641. Wing F676), sigs. A2r–A3v. For these various Puritans, see the relevant entries in ODNB.

12 Susan Doran, *Monarchy and Matrimony: The Courtships of Elizabeth I* (London, 1996), chs. 5 and 6, offers the fullest modern account of the matrimonial manoeuvres with France.

13 *A fourme of common prayer to be used, and so commaunded by aucthoritie of the Queenes Maiestie, and necessarie for the present tyme and state* (London, 1572. STC 16511).

14 John Stubbes, *The Discoverie of a Gaping Gulf* (London, 1579. STC 23400), sig. A3v. See also the proclamation of 27 September 1579 (STC 8114), in Hughes and Larkin, *Tudor Royal Proclamations* II, pp. 445–9. See the discussion by Natalie Mears, 'Counsel, public debate, and queenship: John Stubbs's *The discoverie of a gaping gulf*', *Historical Journal* 44 (2001), 629–50.

15 Stubbs, *Gaping Gulf*, sig. E1r.

16 Cathryn Enis, 'Edward Arden and the Dudley Earls of Warwick and Leicester, c. 1572–1583', *British Catholic History* 33 (2016), 170–210.

17 Juan E. Tazón, *The Life and Times of Thomas Stukeley, c. 1525–1578* (Aldershot, 2003), tells his picaresque story.

18 William Fulke, *A Godly and Learned Sermon, preached . . . the 26 day of Februarie, 1580* (London, 1581), pp. 35, 44 and 45.

19 William Fulke, *A Sermon Preached at Hampton Court, on Sonday being the 12 day of November . . . 1570* (London, 1571. STC 11450), sig. D8v.

20 Nicholas Tyacke, 'The Puritan paradigm of English politics, 1558–1642', *Historical Journal* 53 (2010), 527–50.

21 Thomas Cartwright, *A Brief Apologie* (London, 1596. STC 4706), sig. C1r. Dudley Fenner, in a book to which Cartwright had provided a foreword, had alluded to the existence of this right of magistrates in ancient Sparta – the favourite example of this right among French Protestant pamphleteers.

22 George Gifford, *A Sermon Preached at Pauls Crosse the thirtie day of May 1591* (London, 1591), sigs. B7v–C1r.

23 *Calendar of State Papers, Domestic Series, of the Reign of Elizabeth I: 1581–90* (London, 1865), pp. 208–9.

24 PRO SP12/174 is a bound collection of original copies of the Bond, starting with the copy (fol. 10) signed by the Privy Council, from which these citations are taken.

25 Neil Younger, 'Securing the monarchical republic: the remaking of the Lord Lieutenancies in 1585', *Historical Research* 84 (2011), 249–65.

26 Alford, *Burghley*, pp. 255–6.

27 John Cooper, *The Queen's Agent: Francis Walsingham at the Court of Elizabeth I* (London, 2011), pp. 209–21. See also Alford, *Burghley*, pp. 261–7.

28 Anthony Anderson, *A Sermon profitably preached in the church within her Maiesties honourable Tower, neere the Citie of London* (London, September 1586. STC 571). For the quotations, see the dedication, fol. 4v; and the sermon itself, fols 2v, 15v and 38v.

29 John Reynolds, *A Sermon upon Part of the Eighteenth Psalm* (Oxford, 1586. STC 20621.5), especially sigs. B5r–B6v. That same year, Walsingham agreed with the University of Oxford to pay Reynolds a stipend of £20 a year to lecture publicly against the pre-eminent Catholic theologian of the age, Cardinal Robert Bellarmine.

30 *A True Copie of the Proclamation lately published by the Queenes Maiestie, under the Great Seale of England, for the declaring of the Sentence, lately given against the Queene of Scottes* (London, 1586. STC 8160).

THE WAR WITH SPAIN AND THE SUCCESSION, 1587–1603 6

1 Guy, *My Heart is My Own*, pp. 1–8; and F. R. Chantelauze, *Marie Stuart, son procès et son execution d'après le journal inédit de Bourgoing, son médécin* (Paris, 1876), pp. 577–8.

2 Colin Martin and Geoffrey Parker offer the best account of the campaign and its strategic context in *The Spanish Armada* (London, 1988).

3 John Stow, *The Annales of England* (London, 1605. STC 23337), pp. 1259–61. For some discussion of the thanksgiving service see Steven W. May, 'Queen Elizabeth's performance at Paul's Cross in 1588', in T. Kirby and P. G. Stanwood (eds), *Paul's Cross and the Culture of Persuasion in England, 1520–1640* (Leiden, 2014), pp. 301–13.

4 Stow, *Annales*, p. 1259.

5 *A True Report of the inditement . . . of John Weldon, William Hartley, and Robert Sutton* (London, 1588. STC 25229.3).

6 *Elizabetha Triumphans* (London, 1588. STC 847), p. '23' (last page).

7 Francis Knollys to Cecil, Westminster, 13 June 1584, SP 12/171, fol. 41r.; Cecil to Whitgift, 1 July 1584, SP12/172, fol. 2r–v; summarised at *Calendar of State Papers, Domestic Series, of the Reign of Elizabeth I: 1581–1590*, pp. 181 and 188.

8 See P. Collinson, J. Craig and B. Usher (eds), *Conferences and Combination Lectures in the Elizabethan Church, 1582–1590* (Woodbridge, 2003), especially pp. lxxviii–cxii. For the classes in Northamptonshire, see W. J. Sheils, *The Puritans in the Diocese of Peterborough, 1558–1610* (Northampton, 1979), pp. 51–60.

9 T. Rogers, *The English Creede* (London, 1585. STC 21226.5); and his later anti-Puritan version, *The Faith, Doctrine, and Religion professed and protected in the realme of England* (Cambridge, 1607. STC 21228). For his career see the fine account by John Craig in ODNB.

10 R. Hooker, *The Laws of Ecclesiastical Polity*, Book 4, ch. XIV, section 7. I owe this citation to Torrance Kirby's incomparable expertise on Richard Hooker.

11 Patrick Collinson, *Richard Bancroft and Elizabethan Anti-Puritanism* (Cambridge, 2013).

12 Richard Cosin, *Conspiracie for Pretended Reformation* (London, 1592. STC 5823), pp. 96–102. For an excellent interpretation of this strange episode, see Alexandra Walsham, 'Frantick Hacket: Prophecy, sorcery, insanity, and the Elizabethan Puritan movement', *Historical Journal* 41 (1998), 27–66.

13 Lisa Ferraro Parmelee, *Good Newes from Fraunce: French Anti-League Propaganda in Late Elizabethan England* (Rochester, NY, 1996), pp. 31 and 104–9.

14 H. C. Porter, *Reformation and Reaction in Tudor Cambridge* (Cambridge, 1958), pp. 314–413, tells the story of the predestinarian debates there in Elizabeth's later years.

15 Collinson, *Richard Bancroft and Elizabethan Anti-Puritanism*.

16 C. M. Dent, *Protestant Reformers in Elizabethan Oxford* (Oxford, 1983), pp. 167–80.

17 Paul Hammer, *The Polarisation of Elizabethan Politics: The Political Career of Robert Devereux, 2nd Earl of Essex, 1585–1597* (Cambridge, 1999), offers the most strenuous rehabilitation of Essex. Neil Younger highlights some of his political failings in 'The practice and politics of troop-raising: Robert Devereux, Second Earl of Essex, and the Elizabethan regime', *English Historical Review* 127 (2012), 566–91. Alexandra Gajda has portrayed Essex as an intellectual in politics in *The Earl of Essex and Late Elizabethan Political Culture* (Oxford, 2012), and has shown the breadth of his interests, connections and frame of reference. Yet at best the earl emerges as someone who mistook his own wit for wisdom.

18 The most thorough account of the later wars of Elizabeth's reign is R. B. Wernham, *After the Armada: Elizabethan England and the Struggle for Western Europe* (Oxford, 1984).

19 *Acts of the Privy Council* 25, pp. 278–9 (March 1596).

20 Wrigley and Schofield, *Population History of England*, pp. 332–3.

21 J. R. Seeley, *The Growth of British Policy* (2 vols. Cambridge, 1895), I, p. 179.
22 John Guy, 'Introduction: the 1590s: the second reign of Elizabeth I?', in John Guy (ed.), *The Reign of Elizabeth I: Court and Culture in the Last Decade* (Cambridge, 1995), pp. 1–19.
23 Younger, 'Securing the monarchical republic'.
24 *Proceedings in the Parliaments of Elizabeth I*, p. 151.
25 *The copie of a leter, wryten by a Master of Arte of Cambrige, to his friend . . . about the present state* (Paris, 1584. STC 5742.9), title page, running header, and pp. 6 and 11.

CONCLUSION

1 Cooper, *The Queen's Agent*, p. 42.
2 See Conrad Russell, *Parliaments and English Politics, 1621–1629* (Oxford, 1979), p. 3.

Further Reading

TUDOR POLITICS

Christine Carpenter, *The Wars of the Roses* (Cambridge, 1997), sets the scene on which the Tudors entered the stage. Lucy Wooding, *Tudor England* (New Haven, 2022), is the most recent general account of the century. Steven G. Ellis, *Ireland in the Age of the Tudors, 1447–1603: English Expansion and the End of Gaelic Rule* (London, 1998) reminds readers that the Tudors ruled Ireland as well as England, though nowhere near as effectively. Alec Ryrie, *The Age of Reformation: The Tudor and Stewart Realms, 1485–1603* (London, 2013) and Steven G. Ellis, with Christopher McGinn, *The Making of the British Isles: The State of Britain and Ireland, 1450–1660* (London, 2007) place the English experience in the context of the wider story of these islands. Penry Williams, *The Tudor Regime* (Oxford, 1979) remains a work of rare insight into the functioning of Tudor government, while his *The Later Tudors: England, 1547–1603* (Oxford, 1995) is a superb account of what came after Henry VIII. Anthony Fletcher and Diarmaid MacCulloch, *Tudor Rebellions* (seventh edn, London, 2020) deservedly holds the field for its analysis of the ill-fated challenges to Tudor power or policy. Jennifer Loach, *Parliament under the Tudors* (Oxford, 1991) is a concise but insightful account of the English legislature. Aysha Pollnitz, *Princely Education in Early Modern Britain* (Cambridge, 2015) explores a little-known yet crucial and intriguing element in the political history of the Tudor monarchy. Glenn Richardson and Susan Doran (eds), *Tudor England and its Neighbours* (Basingstoke, 2005) offers new perspectives on Tudor foreign policy, for which the authoritative accounts remain those of R. B. Wernham: *Before the Armada: The Growth of English Foreign Policy, 1485–1588* (London, 1966); *The Making of Elizabethan Foreign Policy, 1558–1603* (Berkeley, 1980); and *After the Armada: Elizabethan England and the Struggle for Western Europe* (Oxford, 1984).

TUDOR RELIGION

Eamon Duffy, *The Stripping of the Altars* (New Haven, 1992; second edn 2005) established a new starting point for the history of the English Reformation, but says little about Protestantism. Felicity Heal, *Reformation in Britain and Ireland* (Oxford, 2003) provides an authoritative overview. Peter Marshall's *Heretics and Believers: A History of the English Reformation* (New Haven, 2017) will be 'the' history of the English Reformation for the foreseeable future. In another increasingly crowded field, Henry Jefferies, *The Irish Church and the Tudor Reformation* (Dublin, 2010) offers a much-needed corrective to previous accounts of a failed Reformation with the religion left out. Alec Ryrie, *Being Protestant in Reformation Britain* (Oxford, 2013) covers everything about British Protestantism except its divisions and fissiparousness. Alexandra Walsham, *Charitable Hatred: Tolerance and Intolerance in England, 1500–1700* (Manchester, 2006) takes the trouble to explain the rationale for religious coercion. Patrick Collinson, *The Elizabethan Puritan Movement* (London, 1967) is a venerable tome that retains its relevance through its magnificent and sympathetic reconstruction of an entire mentality. Specialised monographs and collections of essays abound on aspects of and themes in the Reformation. To name but a few of the most significant, Helen L. Parish, *Clerical Marriage and the English Reformation* (Aldershot, 2000); Peter Marshall and Alec Ryrie (eds), *The Beginnings of English Protestantism* (Cambridge, 2002); Jonathan Gray, *Oaths and the English Reformation* (Cambridge, 2012); and Eyal Poleg, *A Material History of the Bible, England 1200–1553* (Oxford, 2020). There is also a gazetteer of local studies, of variable quality, most of them in the form of articles or chapters. Exemplary book-length studies are Susan Brigden, *London and the Reformation* (Oxford, 1989); Caroline J. Litzenberger, *The English Reformation and the Laity: Gloucestershire, 1540–1580* (Cambridge, 1997); and Matthew Reynolds, *Godly Reformers and their Opponents in Early Modern England: Religion in Norwich, c. 1560–1643* (Woodbridge, 2005).

CHAPTER 1

Henry VII is thoroughly explored by Sean Cunningham, *Henry VII* (London, 2007) and Thomas Penn, *Winter King: Henry VII and the Making of England* (London, 2011). The most enlightening recent work on the politics of his reign is found in Paul Cavill, *The English Parliaments of Henry VII, 1485–1504* (Oxford, 2009) and Steven Gunn, *Henry VII's New Men and the Making of Tudor England* (Oxford, 2016). David Starkey, *Henry: Virtuous Prince* (London, 2008) covers the early life of Henry VIII. Henry's war with France, the main event of his early years, has received no extensive attention since C. G. Cruickshank, *Army Royal:*

Henry VIII's Invasion of France, 1513 (Oxford, 1969). G. W. Bernard, *The Late Medieval English Church: Vitality and Vulnerability before the Break with Rome* (New Haven, 2012) is a patchy but provocative account of English religion before the Reformation. For sharply contrasting views of religious dissent before the Reformation see Anne Hudson, *The Premature Reformation* (Oxford, 1988) and Richard Rex, *The Lollards* (Basingstoke, 2002). On John Fisher, see Maria Dowling, *Fisher of Men: A Life of John Fisher, 1469–1535* (Basingstoke, 1999). For John Colet, see Jonathan Arnold, *Dean John Colet of St Paul's: Humanism and Reform in Early Tudor England* (London, 2007). There is no substantial study of William Warham, Wolsey's predecessor as Chancellor. For Catherine of Aragon, see Julia Fox, *Sister Queens: Katherine of Aragon and Juana, Queen of Castile* (London, 2011). Helen Miller, *Henry VIII and the English Nobility* (Oxford, 1986), explores the new relationship that the king built from the start of his reign, which was later to underpin his abasement of his clergy.

CHAPTER 2

J. J. Scarisbrick, *Henry VIII* (London, 1968) remains the most scholarly single-volume biography, though now showing its age. Susan Doran (ed.), *Henry VIII, Man and Monarch: Exhibition Curated by David Starkey & Andrea Clarke* (London, 2009) marvellously captures and explains artefacts illustrative of his entire reign. Another richly illustrated book, Thomas P. Campbell's *Henry VIII and the Art of Majesty: Tapestries at the Tudor Court* (New Haven, 2007) portrays and interprets the art form that dominated Henry's palaces. On Henry's first great minister, Peter Gwyn's monumental *The King's Cardinal: The Rise and Fall of Thomas Wolsey* (London, 1990) gets bogged down in argument and detail, and is ultimately a disappointment. Glenn Richardson, *Wolsey* (London, 2020), handles the subject more surely. It's worth saying again that three of the best works ever written on Thomas More are all by John Guy: *The Public Career of Sir Thomas More* (Brighton, 1986); *Thomas More* (London, 2000); and *A Daughter's Love: Thomas & Margaret More* (London, 2008). On Henry VIII and Luther, see Richard Rex, *Henry VIII and Martin Luther: The Second Controversy, 1525–1527* (Woodbridge, 2021). H. A. Kelly, *The Matrimonial Trials of Henry VIII* (Stanford, 1976) is still an excellent survey of Henry's various divorces, especially the first. Catherine Fletcher, *Our Man in Rome: Henry VIII and his Italian Ambassador* (London, 2012) tells the fascinating story of Gregorio Casali, the Italian agent who worked tirelessly for the king's first divorce. Studies of Henry's six wives, jointly and severally, abound. The best is David Starkey, *Six Wives: The Queens of Henry VIII* (London, 2003). Anne Boleyn is, as ever, the most argued over. See for example George Bernard, *Anne Boleyn: Fatal Attractions* (New Haven, 2010) and Retha M.

Warnicke, *The Rise and Fall of Anne Boleyn* (Cambridge, 1989). Michelle L. Beer, *Queenship at the Renaissance Courts of Britain: Catherine of Aragon and Margaret Tudor, 1503–1533*, opens a novel perspective on the period.

CHAPTER 3

Diarmaid MacCulloch's twin biographies, *Thomas Cranmer: A Life* (New Haven, 1996) and *Thomas Cromwell: A Life* (London, 2018) are definitive accounts of two of Henry's most important servants as well as imposing contributions to the study of the politics of his reign. Stanford Lehmberg covered most of Henry's parliaments in *The Reformation Parliament, 1529–1536* (Cambridge, 1970) and *The Later Parliaments of Henry VIII, 1536–1547* (Stanford, 1977), but the topic is due a fresh look. G. W. Bernard, *The King's Reformation: Henry VIII and the Remaking of the English Church* (New Haven, 2005) recounts the changes of the 1530s in unparalleled detail and with a sharp argumentative edge. Ethan H. Shagan, *Popular Politics and the English Reformation* (Cambridge, 2003) investigates responses to religious change. Among much else on the Henrician Reformation, see Susan Wabuda, *Preaching During the English Reformation* (Cambridge, 2002) and Alec Ryrie, *The Gospel and Henry VIII: Evangelicals in the Early English Reformation* (Cambridge, 2003). On the Pilgrimage of Grace, see R. W. Hoyle, *The Pilgrimage of Grace and the Politics of the 1530s* (Oxford, 2001) and the many indispensable studies of M. L. Bush, most notably *The Pilgrimage of Grace: A Study of the Rebel Armies of October 1536* (Manchester, 1996). James G. Clark's *The Dissolution of the Monasteries* (New Haven, 2021) fails to do justice to its important subject. Stephen Gunn, *The English People at War in the Age of Henry VIII* (Oxford, 2018) is more about the manner, experience and impact of warfare than about military history in the classical sense, but sheds a good deal of light on Henry's military campaigns, especially the later ones. David Potter, *Henry VIII and Francis I: The Final Conflict, 1540–1547* (Leiden, 2011) teases out the diplomatic and military detail. Neil Murphy, *The Tudor Occupation of Boulogne: Conquest, Colonisation, and Imperial Monarchy, 1544–1550* (Cambridge, 2019), seeks to make sense of Henry VIII's last assault on France.

Stephen Alford, *Edward VI: The Last Boy King* (London, 2014) has now superseded Jennifer Loach, *Edward VI* (New Haven, 1999). The reign of Edward VI has attracted far less attention than that of Mary (see below) in recent decades, although a good deal has been done on the risings and rebellions of 1549, most notably Andy Wood, *The 1549 Rebellions and the Making of Early Modern England* (Cambridge, 2007). David Loades, *John Dudley: Duke of Northumberland, 1504–1553* (Oxford, 1996) covers one of Edward's chief ministers, but a thorough and up-to-date account of the other, Edward Seymour, Duke of Somerset, is wanted.

CHAPTER 4

Anna Whitelock, *Mary Tudor: England's First Queen* (London, 2009) is the best account of the life of Mary I. In recent years a good deal of thought has been given to the distinctive challenges posed and faced by female monarchy: for a start, see Anna Whitelock and Anna Hunt (eds), *Tudor Queenship: The Reigns of Mary and Elizabeth* (Basingstoke, 2010). See also John Edwards, *Mary I: England's Catholic Queen* (New Haven, 2011) and Sarah Duncan, *Mary I: Gender, Power, and Ceremony in the Reign of England's First Queen* (New York, 2012). Natalie Mears, *Queenship and Political Discourse in the Elizabethan Realms* (Cambridge, 2005) explores this theme through Elizabeth's reign. Over the last twenty years, the reign of Mary has been rescued from centuries of misunderstanding by a host of detailed studies. Among the most important are Elizabeth Evenden and Vivienne Westbrook (eds), *Catholic Renewal and Protestant Resistance in Marian England* (Farnham, 2015); Susan Doran and Thomas S. Freeman (eds), *Mary Tudor: Old and New Perspectives* (Basingstoke, 2011); Eamon Duffy, *Fires of Faith: Catholic England under Mary Tudor* (New Haven, 2009); and Eamon Duffy and David Loades (eds), *The Church of Mary Tudor* (Aldershot, 2006). Thomas F. Mayer, *Reginald Pole: Prince & Prophet* (Cambridge, 2000) is the most thorough biography of Mary's cardinal, but struggles at times with the sophistication of its own argument. John Edwards, *Archbishop Pole* (Farnham, 2014) is best on his work under Mary. For the direct effect and wider repercussions of epidemic disease in this reign and at other times, see Paul Slack, *The Impact of Plague in Tudor and Stuart England* (London, 1985).

Norman Jones, *The Birth of the Elizabethan Age: England in the 1560s* (Oxford, 1993) helpfully revises the classic account of Elizabeth's early years offered by Wallace MacCaffrey, *The Making of the Elizabethan Regime: Elizabethan Politics, 1558–1571* (Princeton, 1971). Stephen Alford, *The Early Elizabethan Polity: William Cecil and the British Succession Crisis, 1558–1569* (Cambridge, 1998) places that story in a broader context. Thomas Gresham is now better understood than ever thanks to John Guy, *Gresham's Law: The Life and World of Queen Elizabeth I's Banker* (London, 2019), Susan Doran and Norman Jones (eds), *The Elizabethan World* (London, 2011), offers an encyclopaedic overview of the entire reign. Susan Doran, *Monarchy and Matrimony: The Courtships of Elizabeth I* (London, 1996), recounts the frustrations of a stream of European princely suitors for the hand of the later sixteenth century's most powerful woman.

CHAPTER 5

On Mary Queen of Scots, Elizabeth's most threatening rival, see John Guy, *My Heart is My Own: The Life of Mary Queen of Scots* (London, 2004). The modern case for the prosecution is found in Jenny Wormald, *Mary Queen of Scots: A Study in Failure* (London, 1988). The Elizabethan case against Elizabeth is analysed with characteristic flair by Peter Lake, *Bad Queen Bess? Libels, Secret Histories, and the Politics of Publicity in the Reign of Queen Elizabeth I* (London, 2016). Anna Whitelock, *Elizabeth's Bedfellows: An Intimate History of the Queen's Court* (London, 2014) and Susan Doran, *Elizabeth I and her Circle* (Oxford, 2015), provide intriguing insights into Elizabeth's relationship with the English elite. Natalie Mears, *Queenship and Political Discourse in the Elizabethan Realms* (Cambridge, 2005) is a fine introduction to a considerable literature on the special issues raised by female rule in a deeply patriarchal political culture. Krista Kesselring, *The Northern Rebellion of 1569* (Basingstoke, 2010), supersedes previous work on that topic. Aislinn Muller, *The Excommunication of Elizabeth I: Faith, Politics and Resistance in Post-Reformation England, 1570–1603* (Leiden, 2020) unpacks the consequences of Pius V's bull *Regnans in Excelsis*. On the experience of Catholic life in this era, see Michael Questier, *Catholics and Treason: Martyrology, Memory, and Politics in the Post-Reformation* (Oxford, 2022). Gerard Kilroy, *Edmund Campion: A Scholarly Life* (London, 2015) has at last given its subject a thorough modern biography. Thomas M. McCoog, *The Society of Jesus in Ireland, Scotland, and England 1541–1588* (Leiden, 1996) sets Campion's mission in its wider context. Patrick Collinson, *The Elizabethan Puritan Movement* (London, 1967) remains the starting point for understanding the religious tensions within the Elizabethan Church of England. There is no adequate modern study of Thomas Cartwright. Simon Adams, *Leicester and the Court: Essays on Elizabethan Politics* (Manchester, 2002) partly fills the need for a modern study of Robert Dudley. Joanne Paul, *The House of Dudley: A New History of Tudor England* (London, 2022), explores the tangled links between Dudley and his forebears and their sovereigns. Stephen Alford's *Burghley* (New Haven, 2008) answers the need for a modern study of Elizabeth's chief minister. Norman Jones, *Governing by Virtue: Lord Burghley and the Management of Elizabethan England* (Oxford, 2015) explores his governance in practice. On the English approach to rule in Ireland, see Rory Rapple, *Martial Power and Elizabethan Political Culture: Military Men in England and Ireland, 1558–1594* (Cambridge, 2009).

CHAPTER 6

John Guy, *Elizabeth: The Forgotten Years* (London, 2016) explicitly addresses the final period of her reign, but in effect offers a complete biography. The best account of the Spanish Armada used to be Colin Martin and Geoffrey Parker, *The Spanish Armada* (London, 1988). However, it has now been superseded by Colin Martin and Geoffrey Parker, *Armada: the Spanish Enterprise and England's Deliverance in 1588* (New Haven, 2022). Neil Younger, *War and Politics in the Elizabethan Counties* (Manchester, 2013) shows how the emerging English State coped with the unprecedented stresses of the war with Spain in the 1590s. For the war in Ireland, see James O'Neill, *The Nine Years' War, 1593–1603: O'Neill, Mountjoy, and the Military Revolution* (Dublin, 2017) and Hiram Morgan, *Tyrone's Rebellion: the Outbreak of the Nine Years' War in Tudor Ireland* (Woodbridge, 1993). On the Earl of Essex, see Paul J. Hammer, *The Polarisation of Elizabethan Politics: The Political Career of Robert Devereux, 2nd Earl of Essex, 1585–1597* (Cambridge, 1999); Alexandra Gajda, *The Earl of Essex and Late Elizabethan Political Culture* (Oxford, 2012); and Janet Dickinson, *Court Politics and the Earl of Essex, 1589–1601* (London, 2012). Polly Ha, *English Presbyterianism, 1590–1640* (Stanford, 2010) takes on the story of a central strand within Puritanism. *The Martin Marprelate Tracts: A Modernized and Annotated Edition*, ed. Joseph L. Black (Cambridge, 2008), makes these inflammatory pamphlets accessible to modern readers. Patrick Collinson, *Richard Bancroft and Elizabethan Anti-Puritanism* (Cambridge, 2013) casts new light on Whitgift's right-hand man. Whitgift himself awaits a full modern reappraisal. There is an immense literature on Richard Hooker, to which the best introduction is W. J. Torrance Kirby (ed.), *A Companion to Richard Hooker* (Leiden, 2008). Neil Younger, *Religion and Politics in Elizabethan England: The Life of Sir Christopher Hatton* (Manchester, 2022) explores the impact of one of the key lay figures in Elizabethan England's turn away from Puritanism. Peter Lake and Michael Questier unpick the quarrel that fractured England's Catholics in the 1590s in their monograph *All Hail to the Archpriest: Confessional Conflict, Toleration, and the Politics of Publicity in Post-Reformation England* (Oxford, 2019). Susan Doran and Paulina Kewes bring together a team of scholars to address the issue Elizabeth always sought to dodge in their edited volume *Doubtful and Dangerous: The Question of Succession in Late Elizabethan England* (Manchester, 2016).

Index

Anne (Boleyn), Queen 43, 46, 47,
    52, 56, 57, 67
Anne (of Cleves), Queen 75–6
Armadas, Spanish, against England
    153, 155–7, 170
Arthur, Prince of Wales 9, 25–6
assassination and attempted
    assassination 7, 125–6,
    141–2, 145–6, 148–9, 167,
    169
Association, Bond of 146–7

Bancroft, Richard, Bishop of
    London 161, 162, 164, 165
Barnes, Robert, friar and Protestant
    40–1, 76
Barton, Elizabeth, the 'Holy Maid
    of Kent' 47–8, 55, 58, 60, 61
Beaufort, Lady Margaret, the
    'King's Mother' 11–12, 20
Bible, English 41, 73, 76
Bigot, Francis, Sir 65, 69–70
Boulogne 79, 88
Bosworth Field (1485) 8, 11
Brandon, Charles, Duke of Suffolk
    28, 32, 36, 46, 47, 59

Cadiz, English raids on 155, 170
Calais 22, 29, 31, 41, 79, 106, 115,
    118

Cambridge, University of 41–2,
    52, 110, 114, 118, 130, 131,
    160, 163, 164
Campion, Edmund 139–41
Canterbury 18, 47–8, 105
Cartwright, Thomas 104, 131–3,
    137, 144
Catherine (of Aragon), Queen
    25–6, 27, 31, 36, 43–4, 47,
    52, 57
Catherine (Howard), Queen 76–7
Catherine (Parr), Queen 77, 79, 86
Catholics, repression of 139–40,
    145–6, 158–9, 165
Cecil, Robert, Earl of Salisbury
    169
Cecil, William, Lord Burghley 102,
    107, 108, 112, 114, 120–2,
    129, 137, 147–8
censorship 41, 83, 103–4
Charles V, Holy Roman Emperor
    41, 44–5, 56, 61, 75, 78–9,
    96, 99
Church, power of 14–15, 16, 33,
    46, 50, 53–4, 60
Clement VII, Pope 45, 50
Colet, John, Dean of St Paul's 28,
    36, 37
Common Prayer, Books of 84–5,
    87, 89, 95, 109, 117

Convocations of the Church of
England 33, 35, 51, 52, 53,
56, 57, 61, 67, 109, 112–13
coronations 8, 27, 57, 95, 108
Cranmer, Thomas, Archbishop of
Canterbury 50, 56, 64, 73,
81, 83–4, 105
Cromwell, Thomas, Earl of Essex
49, 51–2, 54, 64, 65, 67, 73,
74, 76, 106

Devereux, Robert, Earl of Essex
166–7, 168, 169–70, 171–2,
179
Drake, Francis, Sir, pirate and naval
commander 145, 155
Dudley, Edmund 23, 26
Dudley, Guildford 90
Dudley, John, Duke of
Northumberland 86, 87,
88–9, 90–1, 93, 103
Dudley, Robert, Earl of Leicester
111, 115, 127, 132, 135,
142, 156–7, 166

Edward VI 67, 78
accession 80
court 80
education 87
illness and death 90
piety 87
Elizabeth I 57, 86
accession 107
court 124, 127, 130, 166, 169
excommunication 128–9, 135,
139, 150, 158
finances 118, 176–8
and marriage 111, 112, 115–16,
135, 136–7
piety 109–10, 113
as 'Virgin Queen' 138
war with or in France 115, 136,
167–8, 169

war with Scotland 114–15
war or conflict with Spain (*see
also* Armadas, Spanish) 119,
121–2, 144–5, 147, 148,
157, 166, 167, 168, 171, 174
Elizabeth of York, wife of Henry
VII 8, 25
enclosures of common land 38
epidemics 91, 106, 117, 171–2
Erasmus, Desiderius, of Rotterdam
26, 37, 38–9
executions for heresy 18, 29, 76,
79, 104–5
executions for treason 24, 62–3,
65, 67, 70, 76, 77, 80, 86,
89, 98, 103, 128, 139–40,
145, 153, 158, 162, 163, 171

Fisher, John, Bishop of Rochester
44, 47, 48, 50, 55, 57, 60,
65, 68
Flodden Field (1513) 31
Foxe, John, author of 'Book of
Martyrs' 105
France 36, 45, 52, 56, 75, 129, 144
Francis I, King of France 36, 41, 42
Francis II, King of France 114

Gardiner, Stephen, Bishop of
Winchester 51, 52, 53, 64,
75, 76, 80, 81, 87, 89, 93, 96
gentry, power and influence of 14,
21, 38, 182, 183
Grafton, Richard, London citizen
and printer 73, 85, 102, 103
Greenwich, royal palace 17, 27, 61
Gregory XIII, Pope 142, 157
Grey, Lady Jane, claimant to the
throne 91, 103
Grindal, Edmund, Archbishop of
Canterbury 133–4
Guise family, French nobility 114,
115, 145, 167–8, 171

Hacket, William, self-appointed
    Messiah 162–3
Hall, Edward, *The Union of the
    Two Noble and Illustrate
    Houses* 1, 28
Hampton Court 49, 120–1
Henry VI 7, 18
Henry VII
    death 26
    finances 23, 26
    invades France 23–4
    piety 17–18, 26
Henry VIII
    accession 26
    *Assertion of the Seven
        Sacraments* (1521) 40, 53
    children 28, 37, 43, 50, 56, 57,
        64, 67, 142
    court 27–8, 37, 38, 39–40, 41,
        46, 75, 79–80
    death 80
    divorces 43–4, 47, 50, 51, 54,
        56–7
    excommunication 72, 75
    finances 28, 30–1, 42, 54,
        60, 65
    marriages 27, 56, 67
    piety 28–9, 43, 76
    war with France 29, 30–2,
        41–42, 78–9
    war with Scotland 31, 78
Howard, Charles, Baron Howard
    of Effingham 156
Howard, Henry, Earl of Surrey
    79–80
Howard, Thomas, 2nd Duke of
    Norfolk 14, 21, 31, 32, 36,
    43
Howard, Thomas, 3rd Duke of
    Norfolk 42, 46, 47, 59, 64,
    70, 76, 79–80, 88, 91, 93
Howard, Thomas, 4th Duke of
    Norfolk 125, 127, 129

Hunne, Richard, mysterious death
    of 32–3

iconoclasm 72, 81
injunctions, ecclesiastical 68, 72–3,
    81, 98, 110
Innocent VIII, Pope 7–8, 9
Ireland 21, 41, 77, 117, 142, 169,
    170–1, 182

James IV, King of Scotland 31
James V, King of Scotland 78
Jane (Seymour), Queen
Jervaulx Abbey 65, 66, 70
jousting 27, 166
Julius II, Pope 29, 31

Latimer, Hugh, Bishop of
    Worcester 67
Lazenby, George, Cistercian monk
    65
Leo X, Pope 31, 37
Lewes (Sussex), Cluniac Priory 71
lieutenancy, county 88, 146–7,
    175–6
Lollardy 18, 33
London 32, 35, 45, 61, 86, 93,
    95–6, 97, 114, 118, 151,
    162, 172, 177
    Paul's Cross (preaching venue)
        41, 57, 58, 72, 76, 83, 95–6,
        101, 116, 130, 144, 157–8,
        188 n.5
    St Paul's Cathedral 7, 94, 128,
        157–8
    Tower of 7, 13, 14, 20, 25, 58,
        63, 64, 80, 87, 88, 93, 112,
        137, 150
    Treaty of (1518) 37
    Tyburn 61, 63, 65, 158
Louis XII, King of France 32
Luther, Martin 39, 40–1, 43, 46, 60
Lutheranism 49, 56, 73, 74

Mary I 37, 61, 177
  accession 91
  death 106
  marriage 96, 99, 105–6
  piety 87
  pregnancy (psychosomatic) 100,
    105
Mary (Stewart), Queen of France
    and Scotland 78, 82, 91, 112,
    114–17, 123–7, 129–30,
    141, 144, 145–6, 148–9,
    150–1, 153–4
Mary Tudor, Queen of France and
    Duchess of Suffolk 32, 46
Mass (Catholic rite) 26, 35, 73,
    81–2, 83, 87, 89, 94–5, 96, 99,
    108, 110, 116, 128, 140, 147
monasteries, dissolution of 65–6,
    68, 70–2
More, Thomas 26, 37, 39, 46, 53,
    55, 65, 68

Nowell, Alexander, Dean of St
    Paul's 112–13, 157

O'Neill, Hugh, Earl of Tyrone 169,
    170–1
O'Neill, Shane, Earl of Tyrone 117
Oxford, University of 39–40, 83,
    110, 114, 130, 150, 164

Paris 167–8
  Massacre at (1572) 129, 136
Parker, Matthew, Archbishop of
    Canterbury 110–11, 113
Parkyn, Robert, Yorkshire priest
    81, 94
Parliament 15–16, 21, 23–4, 28,
    30, 35, 42, 45–6, 49, 50,
    53–4, 55, 56, 59, 60, 61–2,
    75, 76, 77, 79, 82, 89, 95,
    97, 101, 108, 111, 112,
    115–16, 135, 143, 150, 183

Paul III, Pope 72, 75
Paul IV, Pope 106, 142
Percy family, Earls of
    Northumberland 13, 27, 124
peerage 20–1
Philip II, King of Spain 96–7, 99,
    100, 101, 121, 139, 145,
    171, 174
pilgrimage 17, 18, 68
Pole, Reginald, Cardinal
    Archbishop of Canterbury
    74, 99–100, 106
poor relief 172–4
Pontefract Castle 69–70
praemunire, legal offence of 32, 46,
    50–1, 55, 60, 71
Presbyterianism 113, 131, 159–60,
    163
print and politics 9–10, 40, 47–8,
    54–5, 57–8, 83, 85–6, 103,
    125–6, 129, 150–1, 178–9
Privy Council 48–9, 58, 76, 80, 81,
    84, 87, 88, 111, 112, 136,
    146, 151, 168, 172, 174–5,
    182
Puritanism 113–14, 130, 132–5,
    143–4, 159–62, 164

rebellions 11, 42, 85–6, 87, 97, 117
  Cornwall and West Country
    24–5
  Ireland 13, 77, 142
  of Northern Earls 127–8
  Pilgrimage of Grace 68–70, 72
religion and politics 5–6, 17–19,
    28–9, 32–3, 35–6, 46–8,
    52–4, 59–60, 69, 75, 77–8,
    83, 87, 94, 97, 101–2, 104,
    108–9, 114–15, 128–9,
    143–4, 146–7, 162–3, 165
  see also under supremacy, royal.
Russell, John, Lord Russell 86, 87,
    88

Schmalkaldic League 74–5
Scotland 24, 77–8, 82, 114–15, 119, 125
Seymour, Edward, Lord Protector, Duke of Somerset 78, 80–2, 85, 86, 88–9
Seymour, Thomas, Lord Sudeley 86
Shakespeare, William 1, 9
Simnel, Lambert, pretender 11–13
Smyth, Richard, Dr, Oxford theologian 83, 139
Spain 29, 96, 97, 119, 136
  see also under Elizabeth I, war with Spain.
Stafford, Edward, Duke of Buckingham 27, 43
Stokesley, John, Bishop of London 71
Stubbs, John 136–7
succession, royal 1–2, 4–5, 8, 60–1, 90, 111, 112, 125–7, 179–80
supremacy, royal 51, 61–2, 64, 108–9, 144, 159

taxation 13, 16, 23, 30–1, 42, 51, 54, 65, 68, 79, 85, 176–7, 178
theology 44, 67, 73–5, 81, 87, 89, 94, 121, 160, 161, 163–4
Thomas of Canterbury (Thomas Becket), saint 8, 17, 55, 68, 72
torture 98, 128, 140, 145, 149, 169

treason 24, 43, 97–8, 104, 128–9, 141, 145, 163, 171
Tunstall, Cuthbert, Bishop of Durham 47, 59, 60, 84, 110
Tyndale, William 41, 46, 48, 73
Tyrrell, Anthony 141, 158

Wales 22, 77
Walsingham 17
Walsingham, Sir Francis 129, 135, 136, 141, 147, 148–50, 183
Warbeck, Perkin, pretender 24–5
Warham, William, Archbishop of Canterbury 16, 42, 48, 52, 55–6, 59
Westminster Abbey 18–19, 35, 180
Whitehall Palace (aka York Place) 35, 49, 61, 101
Whitgift, John, Archbishop of Canterbury 110, 131, 133, 159–64
Windsor Castle 18, 45, 52, 86
Wolsey, Thomas, Cardinal Archbishop of York 16, 29–30, 32, 35–8, 42, 43, 45, 49, 50, 52, 59
Wriothesley, Thomas, Lord Chancellor, Earl of Southampton 80, 87, 88

York 13, 124, 125
York Place, *see* Whitehall